Class Conflict and Economic Development in Chile, 1958-1973

Class Conflict and Economic Development in Chile, 1958-1973

BARBARA STALLINGS

STANFORD UNIVERSITY PRESS

Stanford, California 1978

Stanford University Press
Stanford, California
© 1978 by the Board of Trustees of the
Leland Stanford Junior University
Printed in the United States of America
ISBN 0-8047-0978-5
LC 77-89181

Published with the assistance of the
Andrew W. Mellon Foundation

To my parents
in hopes that this book
will help them better understand
what the Unidad Popular
experience was all about

and

to the memory of
Charles Horman and Frank Teruggi
who understood very well

CHILE IS a small country of only some ten million people. It is not vitally important either economically or strategically. Yet in political and symbolic terms, the Chile of the 1970's has had a tremendous impact in all corners of the world. From Lagos to Lima, from Paris to San Francisco, the three years of the Unidad Popular brought hope to all who were interested in the possibility of a peaceful transition to socialism. As a result, it also brought hope to those concerned with the question of development in the Third World. Precisely because so many pinned such great hopes on the UP government, the outrage at the brutal coup that ended it, and reversed the process of change it had initiated, was both vehement and predictable. Less predictable, perhaps, was the fact that this initial outrage would turn into an international movement of solidarity against Allende's successors, a movement that is still strong after four and a half years of military dictatorship.

For those of us who lived in Chile during the 1971–73 period, the emotions generated by those years were particularly intense. For one thing, most of us recognized even then that we were participating in an experience that would mark our generation and have ramifications spilling far beyond the narrow boundaries of Chile. In addition, those years marked a personal turning point for many of us in terms of political awareness and intellectual development. In part, this was because the crisis of Chilean society laid bare the fundamental nature of political-economic relationships, so that one had to take notice of things that might have been passed over under more normal circumstances. I remember, for example, writing to a friend in California, that "I never completely understood what Marx meant when he talked about class struggle until I found it here in the streets." Like many others, I have tried to channel this heightened awareness into book form to try to explain what happened in the UP period and why it was so important.

Still, scores of books have been published about Chile since the coup, and so it seems to me useful to explain briefly how this one differs. First, it contains some material in categories where data had not previously been available—notably, information on income distribution, on the class basis of voting patterns, on the views and actions of the Chilean industrialists. In addition, it analyzes a considerable amount of the statistical material on Chile over the 15-year period 1958–73.

More important, however, my approach to the study of the UP differs from other studies in three significant respects. First, I have examined the Allende period against the background of the two preceding administrations, since it is impossible to understand the Allende period without understanding the relationship among all three governments. Second, I have used an explicitly comparative framework to complement a historical analysis of the 1958–73 period. This framework takes advantage of the fact that these 15 years come as close as possible in the real world to providing "laboratory conditions" in which to study the effects of three governments with very different class bases and development ideologies. Finally, I have attempted to integrate political analysis with economic analysis by focusing on three sets of factors that bridge those two spheres: social classes, the state, and the foreign sector.

Such an approach, in its emphasis on historical analysis, in its combining of economic and political factors, and in its focus on social classes, the state, and foreign capital, clearly owes a great deal to Marxist theory. At the same time, I have put more emphasis on short-term analysis and government policy than is found in most Marxist works, and in this respect the approach owes much to Keynesian theory as well.

I started this project some six years ago, and many debts are accumulated in such a period of time. My research work in Chile was financed by the Social Science Research Council, and I later received a grant from the Center for Research in International Studies at Stanford University. Several other institutions also provided me with valuable services of many kinds, not the least of which were the friendship and support of the people working there. I wish particularly to acknowledge the help of the School of Sociology of the Latin American Faculty of Social Science (FLACSO) in Santiago, the Center for Planning Studies (CEPLAN) of the Catholic University in Santiago, the Economics Graduate Program (Escolatina) of the University of Chile in Santiago, the Center for Research in Public Administration (CIAP) of the Di Tella Institute in Buenos Aires, and the Center for Latin American Studies at Stanford. Those who know something about the social sciences in Latin America will recognize that the first four institutions either no longer exist or have drastically changed form or location because of political repression in Chile and Argentina.

In terms of data gathering, a number of people were especially helpful. Arturo León of FLACSO gave me access to the FLACSO/PREALC data bank on employment and personal income distribution in Santiago. Helio Varela, former director of the income distribution division of the National Planning Office (ODEPLAN), provided me with unpublished data and his estimates on functional income distribution. Eduardo Hamuy allowed me to use unpublished data from his political surveys in Santiago. Marcelo Cavarozzi of CIAP (now CEDES) gave me access to his notes on the minutes of the meetings of the National Industrial Society's (SOFOFA) board of directors for the period 1959–68, and I was then able to use the SOFOFA archives to acquire comparable information for 1969–73. In addition, Claudio Ramos and Matoia Cerda helped gather some of the data used in Chapter Three.

Finally, I am indebted to many people for commenting on drafts of various chapters or for general discussions that helped me clarify my ideas (or both). Barry Ames, Sergio Bitar, Oscar Muñoz, Jack Spence, John Strasma, and Peter Winn read and commented on the entire manuscript. Robert Bates, Jens Christiansen, Cheryl Payer, Robert Williams, and the members of several seminars in the Economics Faculty at Cambridge University commented on a previous version of the first chapter. David Abernethy, Richard Feinberg, Ricardo Ffrench-Davis, Albert Fishlow, Carlos Portales, Nano Rosenberg, Bill Smith, and Phil Stone helped with the book's earlier incarnation as a Ph.D. dissertation. J. G. Bell, Betty Spurr, and Barbara Mnookin of the Stanford University Press were both helpful and patient in the lengthy process of going from dissertation to book. Richard Fagen—

both as dissertation adviser and as friend—faithfully read every version from the first draft of the dissertation proposal to the final draft of the last chapter of the book. His continuous advice was invaluable. But most important of all is my debt to the many Chileans, not all of whom can be named here, who assisted me either directly by providing information or indirectly by helping me to know and understand their country.

B.B.S.

New York City
March 1978

CONTENTS

Contents

ABBREVIATIONS

ASMAR Navy Metal Works (Astilleros Marítimas)
CAP Pacific Steel Company (Compañía de Acero del Pacífico)
CEPAL See ECLA
CORFO State Development Corporation (Corporación de Fomento de la Producción)
CPC Confederation of Production and Commerce (Confederación de Producción y Comercio)
CPI Consumer Price Index
CUT National Workers' Confederation (Central Unica de Trabajadores)
ECLA U.N. Economic Commission for Latin America (CEPAL, Comisión Económica para América Latina)
ENAP National Oil Company (Empresa Nacional de Petroleo)
ENDESA National Electricity Company (Empresa Nacional de Electricidad)
FAMAE Army Metal Works (Fábrica de Municiones y Armamentos del Ejército)
FASSA Sulfuric Acid Company (Fábrica de Acido Sulfúrico)
FRAP Popular Action Front (Frente de Acción Popular)
GDP Gross domestic product (*producto geográfico bruto*)
IANSA National Sugar Company (Industria Azucarera Nacional)
IEP Institute of Economics, University of Chile (Instituto de Economía y Planificación)
INE National Institute of Statistics (Instituto Nacional de Estadísticas)

ISS Wage and Salary Index (Indice de Sueldos y Salarios)

ITT International Telephone and Telegraph Company

MAPU-OC Popular Action Movement—Workers and Peasants (Movimiento de Acción Popular Unitaria—Obrero y Campesino)

MIR Movement of the Revolutionary Left (Movimiento de la Izquierda Revolucionaria)

ODEPLAN National Planning Office (Oficina de Planificación Nacional)

PC Communist Party (Partido Comunista)

PCU Conservative Party (Partido Conservador Unificado)

PDC Christian Democratic Party (Partido Democrata Cristiano)

PL Liberal Party (Partido Liberal)

PN National Party (Partido Nacional)

PR Radical Party (Partido Radical)

PS Socialist Party (Partido Socialista)

SABA Wagner-Stein electronics factory

SMA minimum agricultural wage (*salario mínimo agrario*)

SMI minimum industrial wage (*salario mínimo industrial*)

SNA National Agricultural Society (Sociedad Nacional de Agricultura)

SOFOFA National Industrial Society (Sociedad de Fomento Fabril)

SV minimum salary (*sueldo vital*)

UP Popular Unity (Unidad Popular)

Class Conflict and
Economic Development
in Chile, 1958-1973

CHAPTER ONE

Toward a Political Economy
of Development

THE PROBLEMS OF economic development in the Third World have confounded policy makers and social scientists alike, ever since the revival of interest in the subject in the postwar period. One source of trouble has been the failure to agree on what economic development means. Is it to be defined merely as an increase in per capita income, or is it a broader concept that involves distributive aspects and/or structural change? To fall back on the growth definition leaves the dilemma of how to attain this goal. Conventional economists have been able to offer some help. Their advice has enabled many Third World countries to grow rapidly for short periods, and, under some very special circumstances, this growth has continued over many years. Even in these cases of apparent success, however, there is serious disagreement over the causal mechanisms involved, and once a broader definition of development is accepted, the problems increase geometrically.

The premise underlying this study is that the main reason for the continued failure to understand the economic development process lies in the lack of a political economy of development; that is, there has not been an adequate grasp of the relationship between the political and economic factors that affect development. It now seems clear, on the basis of experiences by various types of regimes in Latin America and other Third World countries, that economic development is not purely a technical matter. If they embody major changes in the socioeconomic system, the best-conceived development plans, put together by the most competent technicians, inevitably run into political obstacles to their implementation that leave them useless pieces of paper. Some of these obstacles come from sources that conventional political scientists know a good deal about—the refusal of a legislative body to approve a plan, the failure of a bureaucracy to implement it. In addition, however, there are structural problems growing out of the domestic class structure, as well as out of the international context in which Third World countries are embedded, that can thwart development attempts even if the proposed changes are put into practice. The most obvious examples of such problems in Latin America have been the so-called "reformist" regimes of Eduardo Frei in Chile, Fernando Belaúnde in Peru, and João Goulart in Brazil, among others.

A concern with the relationship between politics and economics is certainly not unique to this book. The economics profession began as the study of political economy, and such an interdisciplinary focus remained until the neoclassical "revolution" in the 1870's. In the post–World War II period, as interest has returned to questions of growth and structural change which characterized the early study of economics, attention has again focused on the relationship between politics and economics, especially in relation to the Third World. Finally, in the past five years, this trend has culminated in an absolute explosion of books that purport to deal with political economy. The problem then becomes what is meant by political economy and how does one go about studying it.[1]

The approach taken in this book centers on three sets of factors that function as "bridges" between the economic and political spheres: social classes, the state, and the foreign sector. Social classes have their roots in the economic sphere in different groups' relationship to the production process. But these groups, defined in economic terms, then act in the political as well as the economic sphere in the form of class organizations (e.g. unions) and political parties. The state, although a preeminently political institution, nevertheless has great influence on how the economy functions through its power over such areas as wages, prices, credit, foreign trade, and even ownership of the means of production. Finally, the foreign sector participates in both political and economic spheres through its influence in the production process, on the one hand, and on political groups and governments, on the other.

The main thesis of the book concerns the relationship between these three sets of factors. In simplest terms, it is posited that there

2

is a direct relationship between the class alliance which controls the state apparatus; the resulting economic policies which are implemented; and the outcomes, which are discussed here in terms of economic growth and income distribution. In other words, the development outcomes will depend primarily on the nature of the class alliance which controls the state apparatus. The rest of this chapter will develop this framework in more detail, and the rest of the book will use the framework to analyze the Chilean case during the period 1958–73.

ELEMENTS OF A POLITICAL ECONOMY FRAMEWORK

Like the concept of political economy itself, social classes, the state, and the foreign sector have been used in a variety of ways in the development literature of Marxist and non-Marxist traditions. These different conceptualizations will be briefly reviewed, and then a more precise definition will be given of the use each will have in this study.

Social Classes

In strictly neoclassical analysis of Third World countries, whether in international trade theory or with specific reference to the domestic economy, social classes do not enter at all, since the basic unit of analysis is the individual. These individuals, in fact, are completely independent and do not have any interaction with each other except through the market. This is the condition necessary in order to be able to combine individual preferences into an aggregate demand schedule for the entire economy. The lack of realism of the independence assumption is admitted by neoclassical economists themselves, and it constitutes a major obstacle to producing a more "realistic" version of the neoclassical model.[2]

In other types of development literature, however, social classes have played an important role, although the meaning of the term has varied. The most common use has been the consideration of classes as consisting of income strata, e.g. the wealthiest 10 percent as the "upper class," the next 30 percent as the "middle class," and the remaining 60 percent as the "lower class." A slightly more sophisticated version is the use of class as "socioeconomic status," which combines income with educational achievement and occupational prestige. Often this type of analysis is purely descriptive and has no theoretical content whatsoever. At other times, however, these categories are embedded in functional analysis, which attrib-

3

utes to social classes (or the "stratification system") a crucial theoretical task. That is, differential rewards and status are necessary in order to allocate roles in society and to motivate people to work.[3]

More often, functionalists speak of classes in terms of occupational groups. Lenski, for example, lists the following classes as characteristic of industrial society: the entrepreneurial class, the class of party functionaries, the managerial class, the military class, the professional class, the clerical class, the sales class, the working class, the farming class, the unemployed and slave-labor classes. There can obviously be as many classes as the particular observer feels like identifying; there is no criterion for what constitutes a class.[4] This variety of functional analysis may have surface similarities to Marxist class analysis in some of the categories used (e.g. urban workers and proletariat, entrepreneurs and bourgeoisie). In reality, however, the two are very different—in the nature of the classes themselves and in the relationships between them. Traditional functional analysis stressed the harmony and equilibrium between classes. Now conflict theory has been superimposed, but conflict is seen as being manageable and as having a functional and integrative role to play. The Marxist view of conflict as involving fundamental irreconcilable contradictions between classes is alien to functional analysis.

In political terms, both variants of functional analysis—the income strata approach as well as the occupational category approach —give emphasis to the so-called middle class. The middle class is defined as individuals who have in common a certain level of income and perhaps educational attainment and/or who occupy certain roles including owners of small business establishments, professionals, and workers in certain administrative-type jobs. These are the groups who are said to be harbingers of democracy as well as modernization in the Third World.[5]

This study uses "class" in the Marxist sense because it is believed to provide the most accurate conceptualization of political/economic groups in capitalist society. The basis for dividing society into antagonistic classes in the Marxist framework is ownership of the means of production; that is, there is one class that owns capital (the bourgeoisie) and one that owns nothing but its own labor power (the proletariat), which it must sell to the bourgeoisie in order to earn a livelihood. Both these classes can be subdivided into class fractions; such divisions can be based on various types of criteria. Probably the most important is the monopoly/nonmonopoly dis-

tinction. This distinction does not necessarily refer to literal monopoly power but merely distinguishes large firms with modern
technology that have at least oligopoly control of their sectors from
those firms that are smaller, with less advanced technology, and
that account for only a small percentage of business in their sectors.
A second, and closely related though not identical, distinction is the
division into large, medium, and small firms. A third focuses on
economic sector—industrial, financial, commercial, or agricultural.
All three types of divisions exist in both the bourgeoisie and the
proletariat. Within the proletariat, however, there is also another
crucial distinction: the division between blue-collar workers (those
who physically participate in production) and white-collar workers
(those who handle the organizational and technical operations associated with production).

In any existing capitalist society (which Marx calls a *social formation*, as opposed to a *mode of production*, which is a theoretical
construct), there are other classes in addition to the bourgeoisie and
the proletariat. For example, there is the petty bourgeoisie, a class
that owns its own means of production but works on a small scale
and does not hire paid labor (although unpaid family members are
often used). This class originated in the competitive phase of capitalism, but still exists in the monopoly phase. In a dynamic capitalist society, however, it tends to be absorbed into the wage-earning
class with the process of monopolization, i.e. the free professionals
go to work for large firms and receive salaries, small neighborhood
stores disappear to be replaced by supermarkets, small farmers mi-
grate to the cities or become employees on large mechanized farms,
and so on. The same can be said about precapitalist classes such as
sharecroppers and tenants.

It should not be assumed from these brief comments that all
Marxists are in agreement with respect to the application of class
analysis. There are at least two areas of serious debate. The first
concerns disagreement over which categories of wage earners should
be considered part of the working class. The alternatives run from
the narrowest definition of only manual workers producing physical
commodities for private capitalists to the broadest definition, which
includes all wage earners. The latter version is followed in this
study, with a distinction being drawn between manual (blue-collar)
and nonmanual (white-collar) workers.* The most prominent Marx-

---

* An elaboration of the above discussion can be found in Erik Olin Wright, *Classes,
Crisis, and the State* (London, 1978), chapter one. Wright makes a strong case for

ist to argue for a narrow definition of the working class is Nicos Poulantzas, who then goes on to propose a greatly expanded petty bourgeoisie that would include both "traditional" and "modern" sectors. The traditional sector would consist of the petty bourgeoisie as defined above, i.e. small shopkeepers, workers in cottage industry, small farmers; the modern sector would include white-collar workers, professionals, and service workers.[6]

The Poulantzas approach leads into the second area where Marxists disagree about class analysis. This concerns whether class position should be defined exclusively according to economic criteria or whether political and ideological factors should also be brought in. Poulantzas argues for the latter, but the analysis here follows the dominant Marxist trend, which sticks to the economic definition.[7] This is not to say that subjective criteria are not important, but they are incorporated in another way. Structural position in the production process forms the basis of class analysis; the resulting categories represent the ultimate possible division between the small minority that owns the means of production and the mass that owns only its own labor power. But, if these structural categories are to become historical actors, the members of each class must first realize their class status and identify with it. Then they must organize to pursue their short- and long-term interests. If they do not do so, this means certain ideological factors are present that prevent them from acting on these interests. This is Marx's well-known distinction between a "class of itself" and a "class for itself." *

The ideological factors refer to those attempts by the bourgeoisie

---

the inclusion of service workers ("nonproductive labor") in the working class. He also sets out a much more sophisticated framework for conceptualizing class relations, focusing on "contradictory locations within class relations." Thus he points to managers as being in a contradictory position between bourgeoisie and proletariat, small employers between bourgeoisie and petty bourgeoisie, and semiautonomous wage earners between petty bourgeoisie and proletariat. The Wright scheme has many advantages on the conceptual/theoretical level, but is impossible to implement with the data available for Chile. In this study, small employers are included in the bourgeoisie, semiautonomous employees in the petty bourgeoisie, and managers in the proletariat. The biggest problem remains that of the class analysis of state employees—bureaucrats, the military, and other employees of state services. Wright argues for dividing state employees into bourgeoisie, petty bourgeoisie, and proletariat, according to their power in the policy-making process. Again, this procedure cannot be followed with the Chilean data, and state employees are included as members of the working class.

* The term "class consciousness" is often used—incorrectly—in this context. That is, class consciousness does not refer to the subjective identification of an individual, but rather is defined as "the *possible* conscious representation of the interests of a

to prevent the workers from becoming a "class for itself," i.e. uniting to oppose the capitalists' interests. One important tool used in this context has been the attempt to form a "class" in between the bourgeoisie and the workers: the so-called middle class. Thus, the white-collar workers are told they are not really workers but members of the middle class, together with elements of the petty bourgeoisie. Sometimes the small and medium bourgeoisie are also included. Since this group is so heterogeneous, it has no definable interests of its own. Rather, objectively speaking, it serves to divide the working class and provide a buffer between the bourgeoisie and the workers.

A final topic concerns the way in which classes interact. Obviously there are many small-scale conflicts both within and between classes. These range from intrabourgeois disputes over credit to wage bargaining between the bourgeoisie and proletariat. These conflicts take place in three arenas: economic, political, and ideological. The outcomes of this type of conflict determine the developments within the capitalist mode of production. However, there is also a higher level of conflict possible which involves the organization of the proletariat to capture control of the state apparatus and move toward a socialist mode of production. For the purpose of engaging in various types of class struggle, classes organize themselves into class associations (e.g. labor unions) and political parties.

The State

The second element that is suggested as necessary for a political economy framework is the state. As was the case with social classes, neoclassical economics and international trade theory make no provision for a positive role for the state in the economic sphere. Economic operations are thought to be best regulated by automatic market forces, and state intervention will only make the market less effective. At most the state will be assigned the task of removing impediments to the functioning of market mechanisms and perhaps acting when questions of externalities are involved.[8] Although some economists have indeed wanted the state to stay out of the development process, in general this view has been seen as unrealistic. Even economists who would favor laissez-faire in the United

---

class within a given mode of production" (emphasis added). "Class psychology" is the term that refers to an individual's perceptions. See Theotonio dos Santos, *Concepto de clases sociales* (Santiago, 1973), p. 50.

States or Western Europe admit the need for the state to take a positive role in Latin America and elsewhere in the Third World.*

One of the earliest and most influential calls for positive state action in Latin America was put forth by the U.N. Economic Commission for Latin America (ECLA). ECLA economists identified development with industrialization, and, because they saw the conditions in Latin America as being quite different from those of the advanced countries at a similar level of development, they did not believe that industrialization could come about via laissez-faire policies. Rather, the state would have to undertake a number of tasks that the private sector had fulfilled in earlier capitalist societies, such as investment in certain basic industries, regulation of wages and prices, and control of foreign trade. Perhaps even more important was ECLA's call for Latin American governments to undertake economic planning in their countries. This planning was not to be of the socialist variety, however, but something similar to what is now known as indicative planning.[9]

Most U.S. and European economists also advocate state intervention in the development process. Thus, almost all textbooks on economic development devote a large amount of space to development *policies*. The difference then arises as to what should be the main aim of these policies. On the one hand, there are those who argue that the government should concentrate on improving the market system—creating markets (e.g. for capital) where they do not exist and facilitating access to markets where they do exist (e.g. through investment in transportation and communications).[10] On the other hand, there are economists who advocate that the state should supplement or even replace the market. The latter groups all talk about planning in some form, but this varies between minimal calls for shadow prices and project evaluation to arguments for full-scale planning models.[11]

Both ECLA and the Western economists just mentioned tend to ignore the relationships between the state and the social class structure. That is, the state tends to be seen as an autonomous or-

* This fact is well illustrated in the first edition of Higgins' textbook on economic development when he says: "In accordance with our promise to make this book 'as much of a textbook as possible,' we feel obligated to mention that there are economists—even some with knowledge of underdeveloped countries—who still seem to think that economic development can be achieved by a policy of nineteenth century laissez-faire." He then goes on to cite as an example the work of P. T. Bauer and B. S. Yamey. See Benjamin Higgins, *Economic Development* (New York, 1959), p. 441.

gan, above the class struggle. This may take the form of a neutral state that listens to all "interest groups," combining their views into a "national interest," or it may take the form of a technocratic group (civil or military) that makes its own decisions quite apart from the rest of society. Marxist analysis of the state immediately calls such views into question. The traditional Marxist view, in fact, regards the state as a direct reflection of the interests of the dominant class ("the executive committee for managing the common affairs of the whole bourgeoisie").*

Recent Marxist theory, however, is much more sophisticated, analyzing the state with a focus on the concept of "relative autonomy."[12] This concept, although important, is hard to specify; it generally refers to the fact that the state is capable of transcending the immediate interests of any one fraction of the bourgeoisie in order to serve the long-term interests of the class as a whole. The main long-term interest of the bourgeoisie, of course, is the maintenance of the capitalist mode of production and its protection against various threats. Some of the ways in which Marxist theorists see the state as carrying out this protective function include dividing the working class; avoiding anticapitalist policies; synthesizing the diverse interests of the different fractions of the capitalist class; assisting in the accumulation process; maintaining peace and harmony in the society, using repression when necessary; and maintaining the legitimacy of the capitalist system by disguising its class nature and portraying the state as representing the interests of the nation as a whole. This last function serves to explain such apparently anticapitalist policies as minimum wage legislation, restrictions on the length of the working day, and regulations on working conditions.†

---

* The quotation is from the Communist Manifesto. Marx also had another view of the state that is best exemplified in his historical writings on France. See, for example, *The Eighteenth Brumaire of Louis Bonaparte* (New York, 1963), where an analysis of the Bonapartist state is presented. The state was one of the many topics that Marx intended to deal with on a more systematic basis, but for which he never found time.

† The new Marxist analysis of the state has dealt primarily with the advanced countries, although some beginnings have been made with respect to Latin America. Most of the latter have focused on one particular *form* of state—the so-called bureaucratic-authoritarian state. This type of state is based on an alliance of three groups: the state bureaucrats (military officials and civilian technocrats), certain dynamic elements of the national bourgeoisie, and the international bourgeoisie. Its main tasks are to control the working class and other dominated classes and to assist in the establishment of a new accumulation process in which foreign capital and the international market play a more important role than they did in the import-substi-

In this study, the view of the state is nearer to the traditional Marxist model than it is to the more recent versions. That is, the emphasis is on the connections between the state and the class structure rather than on the relative autonomy of the state, although the latter is certainly not denied. The state is defined as the institutions that make up the public sector. This is to be distinguished from the terms regime or administration or government, which refer to the specific group that controls the executive branch at any particular time. The state can also assume various *forms*, such as the oligarchical state, the liberal democratic state, the populist state, and the bureaucratic-authoritarian state. Depending, then, on the form of state and the particular situation, the state consists of some or all of the following: the executive and the associated ministries and bureaucracy, the legislature, the courts, the armed forces, the police, and any additional public institutions that may be present. This means that, where the state is very strong, it may also include sectors that are private in most nations—e.g. newspapers, industries, transportation and communications facilities—and any organizations controlled by the government, such as trade unions or political parties.*

Because of the influence the state can exert over the economy, in-

---

tution stage. In this formulation, the state has a definite class content, though the dominant class rules indirectly through the military and civilian technicians. The indirect role obviously creates the potential for the exercise of relative autonomy. The most important work on the bureaucratic-authoritarian state has been done by Guillermo O'Donnell. See especially his article "Reflections on the Patterns of Change in the Bureaucratic-Authoritarian State," *Latin American Research Review*, 13, No. 1 (1978): 3–38, and his forthcoming book on Argentina. For a discussion that differentiates the concept of the bureaucratic-authoritarian state from the superficially similar corporatist model, see Guillermo O'Donnell, *Acerca del "corporativismo" y la cuestión del estado* (Centro de Estudios de Estado y Sociedad, Buenos Aires, 1975).

*Some Marxists use a much broader definition of the state, as can be seen in Althusser's work (following Gramsci). Althusser says there are two aspects of the state: the repressive apparatus, which is more or less equivalent to what is being defined as the state in this study; and the ideological apparatus, which includes the church, schools, family, legal system, political parties, trade unions, communications media, the arts, and sports. With this kind of definition, however, the concept of the state loses all of its meaning and becomes indistinguishable from society itself. See Louis Althusser, "Ideology and Ideological State Apparatuses," in Althusser, *Lenin and Philosophy* (London, 1971), pp. 121–77. Yet another Marxist definition of the state focuses on the highest level of abstraction: the state as a relationship of domination. The term "regime" then refers to the particular form of state, and "government" refers to the group of people in control.

tense political struggle takes place among different class alliances over control of the state apparatus. In the particular case considered in this book, the struggle took place principally through elections. However, military coups, social revolutions, or other means could also be used. Although the institutions composing the state can operate in different ways, depending on the goals of the group that controls them, this process is subject to certain limitations. First, the manner in which the institutions are structured and the rules laid down for their operation give them certain biases toward the class(es) that originally designed them. Thus, for example, the system of checks and balances between autonomous branches of the state apparatus, which many Latin American governments adopted from the United States constitution, greatly impedes any efforts to control the economy through the executive branch. Second, the state apparatus is also biased in a certain direction by the people already occupying positions in it and who cannot (according to the rules) be removed. Primary examples here would be bureaucrats and military officers.

In spite of these very real limitations, however, two points should be kept in mind. First is the fact that in most Latin American countries, like the United States itself, the executive branch has become "first among equals." Especially in the economic policy arena, many decisions can be taken by the executive branch alone. Second, as long as the same class controls the various branches—as is usually the case—differences in policy are often easy to compromise. This is even true when different fractions of a class control different branches. Thus, the executive can, under normal conditions, find some compromise that will enable his program to be implemented, although in modified form. Real problems arise, to be sure, when different classes control different branches. However, under any other circumstances, it is hypothesized that a class *can* use the executive branch to carry out significant parts of its economic policies.*

* These paragraphs are not meant to be an entry in the debate over whether it is possible to use the capitalist state apparatus to spearhead a transformation from capitalism to socialism. The policy goals that are the main subject of this book are the more limited ones of economic growth and the distribution of income. It was precisely when Allende tried to combine these more traditional goals with structural transformations that the problems with the state structure became apparent. For attaining more limited goals, however, the capitalist state apparatus may be more amenable.

The Foreign Sector

The third element postulated as necessary for a framework to study political economy is the foreign sector. That is, in order to understand economic development, it is necessary to understand the international context in which a Third World economy is embedded. Development is not a process that takes place in a nation in isolation, but rather a process that is conditioned and limited by what is happening in the rest of the world. This proposition, unlike that on the necessity for considering social classes and the state, has been accepted in all types of development literature; the main differences in opinion have arisen over whether foreign influence has been positive or negative in terms of economic development.

International trade theory, by very definition, incorporates the role of international forces in its analysis. The basic argument derives from the theory of comparative advantage, whereby each nation will develop to its fullest potential by exporting those products for which it is best endowed and importing the rest. Free trade is seen as a positive stimulus to development and welfare, and any interference with free trade—such as tariffs to protect industry—will only lead to inefficient use of resources, and all countries will be worse off. (The one exception is the optimal tariff argument.) In a recent extension, advocacy of free international mobility of capital through multinational corporations has been added to the argument for free mobility of goods.[13]

By the late 1940's, Raúl Prebisch and his colleagues in ECLA were challenging international trade doctrine, claiming that it was a deterrent rather than an aid to development. The critique was based on a refutation of two basic assumptions of neoclassical theory: first, that productivity increases in the developed countries would be spread to the underdeveloped regions and, second, that demand for primary products exported by the peripheral nations would increase as fast as that for industrial goods exported by the center. ECLA economists claimed that neither of these processes was occurring; rather, the center was growing richer while the periphery grew poorer. The primary mechanism was said to be unequal terms of trade.[14] In other words, ECLA saw *existing* international relations as an impediment to development in the Third World, but it did not see these harmful effects as inevitable; rather, it believed they could be reversed by simple policy changes in the advanced countries. In fact, ECLA encouraged increased capital flows from advanced countries in order to aid in the import-substitution industrialization program that it prescribed as the remedy for the terms-of-trade problem. Thus, in this sense, ECLA joined with liberal economists in the United States and Western Europe who saw lack of capital (and perhaps technology embodied in this capital) as the main impediment to development. Both groups saw foreign aid and foreign investment as solutions to the capital shortage.[15]

The so-called Dependency School, which emerged in the late 1960's, was partially a critique of the ECLA position. The dependency theorists saw the development of the advanced capitalist countries and the underdevelopment of the Third World as two sides of the same coin; the existence of the former required the existence of the latter. Some members of this school concentrated on the international linkages between dependent and advanced countries (international trade, foreign aid, foreign investment), while others put more emphasis on the internal aspects (support for the local bourgeoisie, implantation of consumption norms among middle-income groups). They all converged, however, in seeing the negative effects of the relationship between advanced and Third World countries as deriving from the nature of the capitalist system itself, not merely from problems of mistaken policy. On the other hand, dependency theorists also tended to change the terms of the debate by changing the definition of development.[16] Development was no longer to be synonymous with the characteristics of advanced capitalism, but would focus on national sovereignty, the integration of the national economy and society, and production and distribution systems geared to satisfy the basic needs of the entire population rather than a small minority. If development were to be defined in this way, then there was an inevitable contradiction between the advanced countries and the Third World.*

Some versions of dependency theory converge on Marxist theories of imperialism,† which form the basis of the foreign sector used

---

* Whether development by a capitalist definition is incompatible with dependency is a more controversial matter. For an argument that the two are *not* contradictory, see Fernando Henrique Cardoso, "Imperialism and Dependency in Latin America," in Frank Bonilla and Robert Girling, eds., *Structures of Dependency* (Stanford, Calif., 1973), esp. pp. 15–16.

† The term imperialism is used in two somewhat different ways in Marxist literature. Lenin's definition was of imperialism as a certain *stage* of capitalist development, defined by a set of characteristics among which was the expansion abroad of capital (as opposed to commodities through trade). Elsewhere the term is used to mean the economic, political, and military expansion of advanced countries into the Third World. The two are not incompatible.

in this book. Although the emphasis varies, Marxists agree that expansion abroad occurs as a result of certain needs of capitalism in the advanced countries. Some focus on the need for markets; others discuss the need to find raw materials and cheap labor; still others stress the need to find an outlet for investing surpluses generated at home. Often the common element between these analyses is the need to combat the tendency toward a falling rate of profit in advanced capitalist countries. Governments of the imperialist powers will then be called upon to provide support for the expansion of private capital. In the nineteenth century, this took the form of colonialism; in the twentieth century more subtle forms of neo-colonialism have been substituted. Although it is not denied that, in certain cases, expansion may have directly political roots (e.g. a government beginning a foreign war to divert attention from difficulties at home), Marxists agree that the dominant motivation is economic.[17]

In the postwar period, the organization of the capitalist system became more complex, with the establishment of multilateral economic agencies such as the International Monetary Fund (IMF), the World Bank, and the Inter-American Development Bank (IDB). All have the function of shoring up the system. On the one hand, they provide a tool for regulating the activities of governments that threaten to cause trouble, either through design or incompetence. On the other, they increase the flexibility of response to potential crises that appear in individual countries or the system as a whole.

In sum, there are three types of institutions that constitute what is here being called the foreign sector: multinational corporations, foreign governments, and multilateral agencies. There are obviously strong ties between the three (insofar as the governments referred to are Western governments). On the superficial level, the connections can be seen through the movement of personnel from one institution to another. Perhaps the most prominent example is the case of Robert McNamara, who went from the post of president of the Ford Motor Company to U.S. Secretary of Defense to president of the World Bank. Such mobility is not uncommon, but neither is it the crucial factor unifying the views and actions of the different component institutions of the foreign sector. Rather, it is the capitalist structure itself with its supporting ideology that provides the main link.

The relationship between the U.S. government and the multinational corporations has been well documented; in recent books, this analysis has been extended to include the international agencies as well.[18] The interaction became quite transparent, for example, in the case of Chile under Allende, when then President Nixon said specifically that the U.S. government would withhold its own aid, as well as its support for aid from international agencies, from any government that expropriated the property of U.S. citizens without prompt and just compensation.[19] On the other hand, it would be a serious mistake to see these interconnections only in terms of conspiracy theory. Conspiracies there may have been (and in the Chilean case there is much evidence to support such a conclusion),[20] but the fact remains that the three types of institutions—each acting separately and following its own logic—would probably arrive at the same policies. Although there are some who, looking toward the future, see potential contradictions between the interests of the multinational corporations and their home governments,[21] these breaches have not yet come to dominate policies.

Although originating from outside the Third World, the foreign sector operates from within as well as from without. Multinational corporations with subsidiaries in the Third World, for example, become almost domestic actors. They are part of the domestic production process as well as participants in domestic politics. The relationship becomes even closer when multinationals go into partnership with local capital or join forces with local political groups. The external relationships are more obvious, though not necessarily more important. These include the provision or withholding of investment funds, foreign aid, trade credits, and key imported inputs.

While analysis of imperialism provides an idea of why such intervention by the foreign sector takes place and what actors will be involved, dependency analysis is useful in indicating the mechanisms through which imperialist actors are able to influence Third World countries. That is, it is because a Third World country has become dependent on the advanced capitalist world—for loans, for investment funds, for technology, for raw materials, for capital equipment, for spare parts (or, in the case of certain African countries after independence, for personnel to run the state apparatus itself)—that the imperialist actors can, by cutting off the flow of these elements, cause not only severe economic damage but serious political problems as well. Thus, in most cases, foreign sector intervention can be limited to the use of economic leverage. It is only in special circumstances that overt force is used, although the provision of military aid—as well as the activities of the CIA and related organizations—should probably be seen as a more sophisticated and more indirect version of sending in the marines.*

RELATIONSHIPS BETWEEN THE ELEMENTS

The presence of all three elements—social classes, the state, and the foreign sector—is necessary for any framework for studying the political economy of development. The relative importance of the three and the specific nature of their interrelationship, however, vary according to the historical development of each individual country. The framework presented below should be seen only as one possible pattern that these relationships might assume, based on the Chilean experience. Before this framework is inspected, however, a more precise definition must be given of what is meant by economic development.

It should be made clear from the beginning that any conceptualization of economic development involves value judgments. The idea of development implies development toward something, i.e. toward some situation that is considered superior to the present one. With respect to the definition of development as growth, value judgments enter in about the kind of capital that will be accumulated and the sectors of the economy that will be emphasized. A broader definition of development involves a wider range of choices, perhaps including political, social, and cultural as well as economic factors. Some of the trade-offs inherent in a broader definition, of course, may threaten the higher growth rates themselves.

The approach taken here focuses on two of the most important aspects of economic development—growth and equity. It includes growth because, in Latin America, there is still a serious shortage of even the most basic items related to quality of life: food, clothing, housing, health care, education, and so on. Even if all the wealth that currently exists were divided evenly among the population, shortages would still impose a serious constraint, although the

---

* The emphasis in this study is on the foreign sector as a conscious actor, "helping" or "hindering" the political-economic process in Third World countries, depending on the perceived interests of the multinationals, the foreign governments, and the multilateral agencies. It must be emphasized, however, that this is not the only way in which the foreign sector affects Third World countries. The capitalist world provides the *context* in which Third World countries are inserted, and so the operation of this system affects them by definition. Thus, for example, a recession in the advanced countries will affect international prices as well as the amount of exports the Third World can sell. Of course, even the latter types of variables can be manipulated (quotas, tariffs, price manipulations), but Third World countries will be affected even without the conscious effort of the advanced countries.

Cuban experience has shown that it is possible to go a long way toward the goal of a better standard of living for all, even in the face of a shortage economy. The Cubans themselves, however, are obviously interested in the rapid growth of their economy.

On the other hand, experience has shown that growth alone will not lead to greater equity, which is also an essential goal of development. Therefore, a measure of equity is included: the distribution of income both between and within social classes. Distribution of monetary income obviously leaves much to be desired as a measure of distribution in general, for it leaves out all collective consumption items, which become important in a mixed economy. Going back to the Cubans again, it is clear that they were much more concerned with providing collective consumption items such as schools, health clinics, day care centers, and transportation than in raising salaries. In addition, they were also more interested in making cheap or free such individual consumption goods as housing and basic household items than in increasing monetary incomes. Nevertheless, it is obvious that if monetary income distribution in Cuba today were compared with prerevolutionary Cuba, the current distribution would be far more equal. Thus, the assumption is that income distribution measures can serve as a stand-in for other measures that are more difficult to work with in an economic analysis, measures that indicate a government's intentions and/or policies with respect to the subject of equity in general. This assumption is particularly valid in cases, like the Chilean, where income distribution constitutes the basis of the more general redistributive efforts.

The simplest version of the framework for explaining economic development, i.e. the growth and distribution patterns, is shown in diagram form in Figure 1.1. (The arrows indicate only those relationships that are important for the purposes of this study; they are obviously not the only ones.) The framework is a combination of elements from the economic base and the superstructure. It begins on the former level with property relations, which divide the society into classes according to those who own means of production and those who do not. In Chile, like all major Latin American countries, the principal classes were the industrial bourgeoisie and the workers. The monopoly fractions of both classes were closely tied to foreign capital, which gave them many advantages over the non-monopoly sectors. Thus, the bourgeoisie connected to foreign capital had access to the latest technology, international financial markets, and so forth. The workers in these firms usually got higher

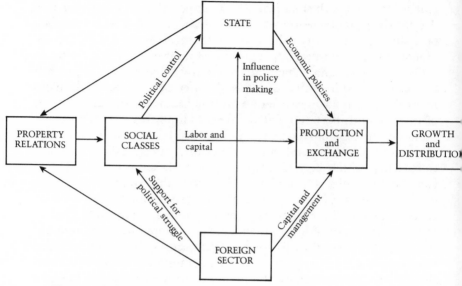

Fig. 1.1. A political economy framework for explaining economic growth and income distribution.

wages and more fringe benefits. This put both groups in a stronger position, both economically and politically, than the rest of their respective classes.

The classes organize themselves into class associations and/or political parties in order to further their various interests. In Chile during the period being considered, both of these forms of organization were important, with the class nature of the political parties being very clear. The industrial bourgeoisie were represented by the National Industrial Society, the National Party, and the Christian Democrats, and the workers by the National Workers' Confederation, the Communist Party, and the Socialist Party. By the 1958 election, the parties had consolidated themselves into three large electoral blocs; these represented the traditional bourgeoisie, the modern industrial bourgeoisie and certain petty bourgeois and white-collar sectors, and the rest of the white-collar and blue-collar workers. Each bloc espoused a development ideology, consisting of its views on the role of the state in the economy, the role of foreign capital, and the relationship between investment and consumption.

The framework then moves to the superstructural level, where the various political (class) forces vie for control of the state. In the

Chilean case, unlike most others in Latin America, this battle took place within an electoral framework; that is, the electoral manifestation of the class struggle was primary. Control of the state apparatus, and especially the executive branch, was of major importance in Chile because the state had become so extensively involved in the operation of the economy. In this sense, the distinction between base and superstructure becomes somewhat clouded. In the process of these electoral battles for control of the state apparatus, the foreign sector played an important role. Foreign corporations, foreign government agencies, and non-Chilean political parties and religious organizations offered various kinds of financial and technical assistance. Obviously this support went to those candidates who were seen best to represent the interests of the foreign actors.

Once a given class alliance won control of the state, it then proposed a series of economic policies that, if carried out, would implement its development ideology and benefit the dominant members of the alliance itself. The policies dealt with such areas as wages, prices, taxes, employment, fiscal expenditures, money and credit, foreign investment, and property relations. Some of these policies were successfully carried out; others failed because of political pressures from groups whose interests were affected. Behind-the-scenes pressure was exerted by groups whose political representatives were in power (the Industrial Society during the Alessandri and Frei regimes and the Workers' Confederation during the Allende government). For those groups on the outside, techniques for influencing the policy-making process included strikes, public demonstrations, or congressional pressures. Foreign interests also made their voices heard, especially through the provision or withholding of money and other forms of material assistance. Thus, foreign corporations used investment funds and imports as sources of pressure, while governmental and international agencies maneuvered through the use of long-term developmental loans and balance-of-payments assistance.

Once policy decisions were made, there were still opportunities to sabotage the policies at the implementation stage, either through actions of the government bureaucracy or through direct actions of the participants. For example, after a decision was made at the national level on a recommended wage increase, strikes in individual factories could win larger increases for the workers involved. Or goods could be sold for prices above those that were officially sanctioned. Congress could also obstruct the fiscal operations of the government by refusing to finance certain budget items. And, ultimately, of course, various opposition forces could unite to over-throw a government that was seen as opposing their interests.

These policies, however important, did not directly produce the growth and distribution outcomes. Rather, the policies influenced the operation of the production and exchange processes, which then led to the outcomes. For instance, a policy on wages was made operative through workers producing certain goods and being paid for these services. Or a policy on prices was implemented during the exchange process, when the goods, once produced, were sold. The combined effect of the wage and price policies then resulted in a preliminary step toward producing the overall structure of in-come distribution between and within the bourgeois and working classes. The same was true for growth outcomes. A government policy on investment, for example, influenced what the private sector (national and foreign) invested, but this investment affected growth only by operating through the production process.

It must be admitted from the beginning that the framework pre-sented here is extremely simplistic. It ignores, or glosses over, many of the subtleties and complexities that would be both interesting to explore and important in their theoretical and practical implica-tions. One of the most important omissions is the failure to ade-quately consider the autonomous aspects of behavior by the bureau-crats in the state apparatus; the view of the state contained in this framework concentrates on the state as instrument of the class in control of the executive branch. Another omission is the failure to specifically formulate a multisector framework; in the analysis of Chile that follows, attention is focused almost entirely on the in-dustrial sector, even through agriculture contributed heavily to the problems of economic development. A full model would have to in-corporate intersectoral relationships. A third problem is the sim-plistic nature of the class structure employed, focusing only on the bourgeoisie, petty bourgeoisie, white-collar workers, and blue-collar workers. There are important divisions within each class that are not adequately dealt with. A particular problem is state employees, including the military, who play such an important role in the po-litical-economic process in Third World countries. Finally, the framework ignores the effects of feedback. To give only the most obvious example, the growth and distribution outcomes would cer-tainly have repercussions at various points in the process—on the class structure itself, on the options open to those controlling the state, on foreign sector participation, and so on.

Nevertheless, in spite of these and other problems, the framework also has important strengths. First, on the theoretical level, it goes beyond saying that both politics and economics are important and shows some ways in which the two might interact. Second, on the empirical level, it seems to reflect reality as indicated by its ability to "explain" the pattern of growth and distribution that actually occurred in Chile during this period.[22] Whether it would work as well for other periods of Chilean history or for other countries must be determined through individual case studies.

UTILIZING THE FRAMEWORK

Although the framework that has been presented is not a theory of economic development, some general propositions can be derived from it. (1) Social classes will combine into alliances to promote their respective interests. (2) Different class alliances will have different development ideologies. (3) There will be a struggle between the alliances to capture control of the state. (4) Once in control of the state, an alliance will attempt to implement its development ideology through a series of economic policies reflecting that ideology. (5) These economic policies will lead to different outcomes in terms of growth and distribution, i.e. economic development.

The best way to illustrate these propositions was through a comparative analysis of a sample of regimes representing different sets of class interests. There were two obvious possibilities in the Latin American context. One was to choose several countries where different classes or class fractions controlled the government—probably post–1964 Brazil, Frei's Chile, and post–1959 Cuba. The overwhelming differences between the three in terms of size, history, and sociopolitical structure, however, indicated that such a comparative analysis would be difficult in the extreme. The alternative was to find one country where regimes with different class bases of support had held power at various times. Chile stood out as the most likely possibility in this sense, with a comparison of the conservative bourgeois regime of Jorge Alessandri (1958–64), the reformist regime of Eduardo Frei (1964–70), and the radical regime of Salvador Allende (1970–73). The latter alternative was chosen, but many methodological problems nevertheless remained.

One of the main problems of a study of this type is to choose the proper subject of analysis—restricted enough to avoid extreme superficiality but still broad enough to capture the basic relationships involved. The decision was made to focus on one sector of the

21

economy, more or less as a case study, although there is a good deal of information on the macro level as well. The industrial sector was selected, since, in a capitalist mode of production, industry is the most important sector. It is the largest (in Chile, industry produces almost 30 percent of the GDP and employs almost 20 percent of the work force) and the most dynamic of the major sectors, such that its growth or stagnation greatly influences trends in other parts of the economy. In addition, it is the conflict between the industrial bourgeoisie and the proletariat that dominates the other types of class relations in a capitalist society.

In spite of, or because of, its dominant role, industry is not "typical" of other sectors of the economy. In any case, since there is no such thing as a typical sector, all that can be done is to indicate the ways in which industry differs from other sectors. In terms of growth in the postwar period, industry was more dynamic than the rest of the economy, with output increasing at an average rate of 8.5 percent per year compared with 4.8 percent for the economy as a whole. With respect to income distribution, wages and salaries were generally higher in industry than the average. At the same time, however, the capitalist class in industry was also better off than its counterparts in other sectors. Percentage of income to capital in the mid–1960's was 60 percent in industry and only 50 percent in the economy as a whole. The combination of both workers and capitalists being in above-average economic conditions was due, of course, to high productivity in industry. Finally, in terms of political organization, the industrial workers were better organized than other sectors, while the large capitalists were about average, and the petty bourgeoisie were less well organized than many of their counterparts outside industry.[23]

In terms of the comparative analysis, there were a number of data-oriented problems. First was the problem of "controlling" the variables that were not specifically considered in the study. It is obvious that no real-life situation will ever be a laboratory such that it can be said with a high degree of precision what caused what. In a rigorous scientific sense, then, no true comparisons could be made. The interesting aspect of the Chilean experience during the 1958–73 period, however, and the justification for attempting such a comparison were that it came nearer to an experimental situation than any other in recent history; therefore, it seemed logical to take advantage of the opportunity to study some important phenomena and not be paralyzed by lack of precision.

Second was the problem of homogeneity of data. When making longitudinal comparisons, it obviously becomes extremely important to find data with the same base and assumptions. In terms of growth data, this problem was minimized by new time series calculated by the National Planning Office (ODEPLAN) for the 1960–72 period. The main problem, then, became finding comparable statistics for the 1958–59 biennium and 1973. Functional income distribution statistics also came from the new ODEPLAN series. Data for personal distribution of income and unemployment were taken from the quarterly surveys of the Institute of Economics of the University of Chile, which had used a similar sample and methodology since the survey began in 1956. A further difficulty with homogeneity was caused by the chronic inflation problem in Chile, which averaged over 25 percent per year during the 1959–70 period. In 1972, the annual average rate was 78 percent, and during the first eight months of 1973, it was 235 percent. Thus, finding an appropriate index for deflating statistics was important. The index that was finally chosen was the annual average consumer price index (CPI), with the base year of 1965, calculated by the National Institute of Statistics. This was the most commonly used index in Chile and usually the most appropriate for the data in this study. When another index or base year was used, this is noted in the tables.*

Third was the problem that the Allende administration figures were for only three years, compared with six years for the other two. This was closely related to the difficulty that even six-year periods are very short for trying to examine the effects of development models; many of the consequences can be seen only in a much longer-term framework. There was no solution to this problem; all that can be done is to keep it in mind. A final problem was more relevant to the historical than the comparative analysis and concerned the relation between the three strategies. That is, in what sense did the Alessandri period make the Frei model possible, and how did the Frei years facilitate the Allende model? There are some quite obvious answers to these questions, especially in the economic sphere. For example, without the reserves accumulated at the end of the Frei period and the idle capacity that existed, the Allende

---

* Perhaps the best indexes were those developed by Ricardo Ffrench-Davis, based on corrections of the official figures. The Ffrench-Davis indexes, however, were available only through 1970 and generally did not differ greatly from the index used here. See Ricardo Ffrench-Davis, *Políticas económicas en Chile, 1952–70* (Santiago, 1973), pp. 237–49.

23

regime could not have followed the reactivation policy that was chosen. More difficult to analyze, however, are the political interrelations. These will be dealt with in the historical chapters.

The discussion on Chile proceeds in the following manner. Chapter Two presents background information on the historical development and socioeconomic structure of the country. Chapter Three introduces the three development models, with data on both the class base of each regime and its developmental ideology. Chapters Four to Six are historical chapters; they try to show both how each model came into being and how each changed in the process of implementation. Chapters Seven and Eight examine the economic policies of the three regimes; Chapter Seven focuses on the policy differences among regimes, while Chapter Eight studies the similarities. Chapter Nine presents the developmental outcomes of the policies: the growth and distribution patterns. Finally, Chapter Ten tries to draw some political and economic "lessons" from the Chilean case which might be relevant for other countries.

CHAPTER TWO

Historical Development and Structural Characteristics

$\mathbf{B}$EFORE ANALYZING the 1958–73 period, it is necessary to present some background information on the economic, social, and political structure of Chile and on how these structures developed historically. The brief historical analysis of the post-independence period focuses on changes in the economy and on the emergence of the various social classes and political groups. Then more detailed information is given on the three main elements of the framework outlined in Chapter One—social classes, the state, and the foreign sector—as they had evolved by the 1958–73 period.

HISTORICAL DEVELOPMENT, 1830–1958

Desarrollo hacia afuera (1830–1920)

Economic development in nineteenth-century Latin America has been characterized as outward-oriented (*desarrollo hacia afuera*), since these economies basically functioned by exporting agricultural or mineral products to Western Europe and the United States and importing industrial consumer goods in exchange. Chile was one of the most successful examples of this type of economy. The country was fortunate in that post-independence feuds were quickly settled, in contrast with the situation in the rest of Latin America, and a period of exceptional stability followed under the authoritarian rule of Diego Portales.

This stability opened the way for what has been described as the greatest economic boom in Chilean history. Wheat produced in

25

Chile's central valley was shipped to Australia and California, and Chilean copper was dispatched to markets in Europe. The domestic economy thrived as tariff-protected industries were founded, and major infrastructure projects were undertaken by the state. By the early 1860's, however, partially in response to the growing influence of free trade–oriented England, the state began to withdraw from its strong role in the economy. The fledgling industries found going much harder as tariffs were lowered, but some of them managed to survive in spite of competition from imports.[1]

Freed of many of its domestic economic obligations, the Chilean government turned its attention northward toward Peru and Bolivia. In 1879, the three countries went to war, and Chile's victorious forces won control of the nitrate fields in what are now the provinces of Antofagasta and Tarapacá. The enormous revenues generated by the newly won mineral wealth had an important impact on the economic, social, and political development of the country, as will be seen below; nitrate soon overshadowed both agriculture and industry as it came to dominate the economy. By the 1930's, however, this wealth had disappeared as quickly as it had come, as a result of the development of a synthetic substitute for nitrate.[2]

The export orientation of the economy in this period obviously meant that Chile was firmly inserted in the international capitalist system. The rise and fall of prices on the international market had major repercussions in Chile. In addition, however, foreign capital was already beginning to burrow its way into the domestic economy itself, as British-based merchant firms began to invest in Chile. Their main interest was in international trade, but they also invested in mining, agriculture, and industry when opportunities arose. By 1849, there were 50 of these merchant firms operating in the country.[3] A qualitative leap came in the aftermath of the War of the Pacific. The nitrate fields, for which Chile had fought so hard, were turned over almost immediately to British investors. The fact that the main export sector was then foreign-owned created a situation quite different from that in neighboring Argentina or Brazil, where nationals owned the cattle and coffee industries, respectively. It meant that the Chilean state came to control very large sums of money—the taxes paid by the nitrate companies—and so was in a position to decide how to distribute these revenues. Thus, in spite of the reigning liberal philosophy, the state was forced into a key role in the economy.

The nineteenth century also witnessed the formation of the political and social organizations that characterize modern Chile. The agrarian oligarchy, which was represented by the Portales regime, was joined by commercial, financial, and industrial fractions of the bourgeoisie as the productive structure developed and diversified. By the latter part of the century, these groups had organized themselves into associations to promote their various economic interests—the National Agricultural Society (SNA), the Central Chamber of Commerce (CCC), and the National Industrial Society (SOFOFA). The domestic mine owners also formed the National Mining Society (SNM).[4]

At the same time, the bourgeoisie was organizing itself in more directly political ways. Three political parties were formed in the nineteenth century, differentiated mainly by religion and ideology since their economic views were quite similar. The earliest party-like groups were the *pelucones* and the *pipiolos*, which indirectly evolved into the Conservative and Liberal parties by the 1860's. The pelucones, Portales' main supporters, were above all a party of order; stability was their main concern. They were closely associated with the Catholic Church and the agricultural sector. The pipiolos were more influenced by European ideas of individual freedom; they were against a state-sponsored religion and were more prominent in urban than rural areas. The third party was the Radical Party, which later came to represent the petty bourgeoisie and state bureaucrats but in its early stages was also strictly a bourgeois party since only the bourgeoisie participated in politics at this time.[5]

Another effect of the Chilean nitrate boom was the formation of the first proletariat in Latin America. Because the mines were located in isolated parts of the north, it was necessary to import large numbers of workers from the south. Thus there were thousands of workers in remote areas, working under arduous conditions which led to the rapid formation of class consciousness. In 1890, the first general strike broke out among the nitrate workers of Tarapacá; they demanded monthly payment; payment in money, not tokens; the freedom to buy in places other than the company store; and the end to a series of abuses by their employers. Although President Balmaceda recommended an examination of their petitions, the Army moved in, killing large numbers of workers and wounding others.

The union movement also had its origins in the nitrate area in the form of the *mancomunales* or brotherhoods. The first one was formed in Iquique in 1901, and three years later it had several thousand members. All of the important strikes in the north—concentrated during the 1905–7 period—were led by these groups. They also had a crucial role in training leaders, and spreading ideas and organization, often through a lively press, and in preparing the way for future union development. The latter dates from 1917, when the mancomunales joined with the Railway Workers' Federation to form the Workers' Federation of Chile (FOCh), which was the first national labor federation in the country's history. The FOCh aims were quite militant, demanding the abolition of the capitalist system and proposing that industry be run by the unions. It is estimated that, just after World War I, the FOCh had close to 60,000 members, although, by 1922, the number had dropped to half that because of unemployment and repression.[6]

In 1887, the first nonbourgeois party—the Democratic Party—was formed by a group of young Radicals who broke with their party. The party was essentially social democratic rather than socialist and proposed the formation of a Ministry of Labor, social security, accident insurance, unionization, and so forth. None of these proposals were accepted, and the party eventually turned toward the Right. It was not until 1912 that the first real socialist party was formed—the Socialist Workers' Party (POS)—as a breakoff from the Democratic Party. The POS had some petty bourgeois members, but its main base was workers. As one of its founders explained, the POS was not originally a Marxist party; it only became so later. Nevertheless, the members had a strong sense of the injustice of society and a high level of class consciousness.[7]

Transition (1920–38)

The period 1920–38 was one of transition in Chile—with all the chaos that transitions usually produce. After an economic boom in the 1920's, Chile was hit harder by the Great Depression than any other country in the hemisphere. The crash was led by the mining sector, the output of which fell by 70 percent in three years; it spread rapidly to other sectors of the economy, however, such that total output fell by 46 percent between 1929 and 1932.[8]

In socioeconomic terms, the 1920–38 period saw the virtual completion of the present organizational set-up. The 1920 presidential election is often hailed as marking the entry of the "middle sectors" into political power. That is, the candidate of the Liberal Alliance, Arturo Alessandri, appealed for the votes of the petty bourgeoisie and the workers on the basis of a platform of social reform.[9] Alessandri won a narrow victory, but his reforms were not implemented. This, together with the obvious corruption of the Congress, eventually led to one of the few breakdowns of the bourgeois democratic system in Chilean history. Periods of military rule, alternating with short-lived civilian governments, marked the years 1924–32, including the 12-day rule of the so-called Socialist Republic under Colonel Marmaduke Grove. A number of key reforms were enacted by decree—a university reform was approved, the President was given the right to concede and cancel mining property rights, the state was authorized to take over industries that were not producing, and so on—and some of this legislation stayed on the books and was later used by the Unidad Popular (UP). By 1932, the party system had regrouped, and Arturo Alessandri was reelected President; this time, however, he was quite clearly representing the old oligarchy and the new bourgeoisie.

The first important organizational change in this period was the decision of the POS in 1920 to change its name to the Communist Party and to seek membership in the Third International. From the beginning, the Communists relied primarily on miners and blue-collar workers in industry as a membership base, and were characterized by a strong sense of discipline and hierarchy and a close adhesion to the Moscow line. They also tended to be so cautious that even the Third International was critical.[10] It was precisely these characteristics that led to the formation of a second Marxist party in Chile.

In 1933, the remnants of the Socialist Republic coalition joined with others who left the Communist Party to form the new Socialist Party. The Socialists were a more diverse party than the Communists, with significant sectors of white-collar workers and professionals as well as blue-collar workers. They claimed to be an authentically Chilean party, a reaction against the pro-Moscow line of the Communists. The result was a much less cohesive ideology than the Communists' and a tendency toward personalism. Two main factions existed almost from the beginning—the Social Democrats and the Trotskyists. The other main feature that distinguished the Socialists from the Communists was the former's lack of discipline and organization, which were major characteristics of the Communists.[11]

The other party that emerged in this period was the predecessor of the Christian Democrats—the National Falange. The Falange, essentially a group of intellectuals of bourgeois and petty bourgeois backgrounds, began as the youth section of the Conservative Party. The Falange deplored both the laissez-faire practices of the Conservative Party and the class struggle advocated by the Marxists. Their alternative was a vague concept known as communitarianism, which involved cooperation between classes for the common good.[12]

In addition to the new political parties, another organizational development during this period saw the formation of the Confederation of Production and Commerce in 1934. Formed because the bourgeoisie saw themselves as being threatened by the post-Depression militancy, the CPC was a coordinating association of the four bourgeois sectoral organizations—SOFOFA, SNA, SNM, and CCC —and was supposed "to insure that national legislation proceeds in accordance with the just interests of commerce and production."

Desarrollo hacia adentro (1938–52)

The first real turning point in the twentieth century was the election of the Popular Front government in 1938. The Popular Front was a coalition of the Communist, Socialist, and Radical parties; the Radicals had the major voice in the coalition, and the presidential candidate was from their ranks.[13] When the Radical candidate, Pedro Aguirre Cerda, won the election, the Chilean bourgeoisie lost their direct control of the presidency, since by this time the Radical Party had become more of a petty bourgeois than a bourgeois party. This is not to say that the industrial bourgeoisie were not the principal beneficiaries of the policies of the Popular Front and the series of Radical governments that followed it; they definitely were. The nature of the political process, however, changed significantly. Persons of nonbourgeois background came to occupy many important government posts, and it was necessary for the industrialists to work through them—convincing them that "policies good for the bourgeoisie were also good for the country." The Popular Front government lasted only a few years and was succeeded by other Radical governments which grew more conservative over the years.

It was during this period that the big push toward industrialization began in Chile. This was similar to events in other major Latin American countries, and the process was later labeled inward-oriented development (*desarrollo hacia adentro*) in contrast to the previous export-led economic strategies. The mid-1930's had already seen a type of spontaneous industrial spurt, brought about by the unavailability of imports due to the lack of foreign exchange during the Depression. This spurt was strengthened when SOFOFA convinced the government to double the tariff walls to 50 percent. The inauguration of the Popular Front government, however, changed the situation drastically as the government began to directly promote industrialization through a number of policies. Perhaps the most important of these was the establishment of the State Development Corporation (CORFO) in 1939. There was an ambiguous relationship between CORFO and the industrialists. On the one hand, they wanted its assistance; on the other, they feared its competition and interference. The dominant attitude, though, seemed to be to participate and take advantage of the new institution. Several prominent industrialists, for instance, became officials of CORFO, though it would probably be a mistake to assume that CORFO was directly controlled by the industrialists.[14]

CORFO's main activity was the founding, often in association with the private sector, of many of Chile's most important industrial firms. Techniques for creating mixed companies varied; sometimes the government would buy shares in existing firms, while at other times it would join with industrialists to form new corporations. Those corporations with CORFO participation gained significant benefits, since the latter generally provided capital far beyond the proportion represented by its ownership share in a firm. CORFO's other main activity was providing loans to the private sector. Sometimes these loans were in local currency, but of greater importance were the dollar loans that CORFO obtained or guaranteed for the private sector. In fact, this was the main reason for SOFOFA's interest in CORFO. As soon as the new institution was established, SOFOFA advocated the contraction of large foreign loans; CORFO agreed, and the main source of such funds became the U.S. Export-Import Bank. This did provide a source of funds, but at the same time such loans gave the United States a new tool to use against any type of leftist action on the part of the Popular Front government. Plans to nationalize several companies were canceled on account of such pressure. In addition, such loans also had a series of restrictions. Projects had to be approved in advance, and materials often had to be purchased in the United States.[15] There have also been suggestions that the first set of Export-Import loans was tied to the 1942 agreement whereby the Chilean government guaranteed a stable price of 12 cents per pound for copper sold to the United States during World War II.[16]

At about the same time, private U.S. capitalists began to take a more active role in the industrialization process; various techniques were used to obtain investment opportunities. One was the use of technology and patents. Second was the condition placed on U.S. loans such that U.S. private companies be allowed to invest in the projects. Third was the formation of subsidiaries of foreign corporations, sometimes in cooperation with local firms and sometimes alone.

The industrialization process obviously had a profound impact on the class structure in Chile. One such effect was the growth and strengthening of the industrial bourgeoisie, which was composed of two main groups—recent immigrants from well-off backgrounds in Europe, and large agriculturalists, merchants, or bankers who moved into industry. These individuals, sometimes in connection with foreign capital or CORFO, started large industries from the beginning. There were very few examples of small or medium firms becoming large.[17] The consequences of this type of industrialization will be discussed below. As a corollary of the rapid industrialization process, there was a corresponding increase in the industrial proletariat. Whereas, formerly, union activities had mainly involved mining, railroad, and port workers, the industrial work force now became the key sector. The bourgeoisie had originally been worried that the Popular Front government would strongly support the working class. As the Radical governments became more conservative, however, the government began intervening in labor disputes on the side of capital. It also permitted industrialists to undertake such antilabor measures as strikebreaking, massive political dismissals, and direct attacks on the unions and leftist parties. In May 1948, the Communist Party was declared illegal through the "Law for the Defense of Democracy," and all known members of the Party were fired from their jobs and removed from the voting rolls. The result of these actions was the temporary demobilization of the workers and a decline in real wages, especially of the blue-collar workers.

"What Is to Be Done?" (1952–58)

The weakness of the Left, the charges of corruption against the Radicals after their 14-year rule, and problems between the Radicals and the Right meant that four parties ran candidates in the 1952 presidential election. They were all beaten out, however, by former dictator Carlos Ibáñez, who ran as an independent, denouncing the party system. The political problems that led to the voters' abandonment of the party system had their counterpart in the economic sphere. By the beginning of the decade of the 1950's, the import substitution process was beginning to exhaust itself, and, as a consequence, industry became much less dynamic. During the 1952–58 period, the sector grew at only 2.4 percent per year in contrast to the 9 percent average annual growth during the previous decade.[18] Goods that required small amounts of capital, relatively low-level technology, and small markets were now being produced domestically rather than being imported. In order to move ahead in import substitution into more sophisticated goods, more capital, more advanced technology, and larger markets were necessary. These factors were not available, and thus the growth rate in industry began to fall.

The fall was exacerbated by the inflation problems of the Ibáñez period. In 1950 and 1951, the annual rates were 17 and 23 percent, respectively. In 1953 and 1954, however, these rates leaped to 56 and 71 percent. Faced with the political and economic necessity of doing something to slow inflation (the highest in Chilean history up to that point), Ibáñez finally called in a private team of U.S. consultants known as the Klein-Saks Mission. The Klein-Saks recommendations were straight from orthodox economics, based on the idea that inflation results from excess demand. Therefore, the recommendations centered on cutting this demand by cutting the fiscal budget and bank credit, eliminating subsidies on basic consumer goods and services, and giving wage increases that were less than the increase in the cost of living. The Mission also recommended tax reforms that would have struck the wealthier sectors, but the right-wing Congress adopted only those measures that were in their own self-interest. The key was the cut in wages. The effect of these measures was to further increase the industrial recession. Demand and inflation fell, but the industrial growth rate fell too. In addition, the income distribution of the country took a sharp regressive turn.[19]

The initial indecision of the Ibáñez government and the later attempts to implement the Klein-Saks recommendations (which no one, either the industrialists or the workers, approved of) apparently convinced Chilean voters that the solution of Chile's problems was not to be found in a leader "above politics." In any case, there was a gradual return to the old-style politics and the class organizations. There was also a tendency toward consolidation of forces during this period. The scattered factions of the labor movement came together in 1953 to form a new labor confederation, the Central Unica de Trabajadores (CUT). Other unifying tendencies saw the two Socialist parties regroup themselves in 1956 and, a year later, join with the still illegal Communist Party, to form the Popular Action Front (Frente de Acción Popular—FRAP). In 1958, the Communists were relegalized in one of Ibáñez's last moves as president. And, finally, the old Falange joined with the Social Christian wing of the Conservative Party to form the Christian Democratic Party in 1957.

The ultimate effect of these unifying trends meant that the 1958 presidential election saw rather sharply defined alternatives. The FRAP nominated Salvador Allende as its candidate, and the Liberals and Conservatives ran industrialist Jorge Alessandri (theoretically an independent). The two centrist forces—the new Christian Democratic Party and the old Radical Party—also ran candidates. Thus, after almost a decade of stumbling around, looking for a political force to replace the Radicals and an economic model to replace import substitution, the 1958 election provided right, center, and left alternatives. Each had its own answer to the question of what was to be done, and these answers were tried in turn during the 15 years that followed.

The rest of the chapter will provide a more detailed analysis of the social classes, foreign sector, and the state, which have been described developing over time in this historical account.

CLASS STRUCTURE AND ORGANIZATION

An analysis of the class structure must include at least four topics: (1) the class structure and contradictions between classes and fractions; (2) the problem of objective vs. subjective class identification; (3) the class organizations; and (4) the relationship between classes and political parties.

The easiest way to begin an analysis of the class structure in Chile is to present a breakdown of the total labor force by occupational position and economic sector; the 1970 census estimates of these data are presented in Table 2.1. The table shows a work force of 2.6 million, of which 3.2 percent was classified as bourgeoisie (employers), 19.5 percent as petty bourgeoisie (self-employed), 28.7 percent as white-collar workers, and 42.6 percent as blue-collar workers (including 7 percent domestics); 6.0 percent were of undeclared occupational category.[20]

The bourgeoisie were the dominant class in Chile's capitalist society; they owned the means of production and hired labor with

TABLE 2.1

Work Force by Economic Sector and Occupational Category, 1970

(Thousands)

Sector	Employer	Self-employed	White-collar workers	Blue-collar workers	Undeclared	Total
Agriculture	18.5	153.3	26.8	314.6	7.4	520.6
Mining	0.9	4.8	17.4	50.5	1.4	75.0
Industry	14.7	64.5	99.3	221.7	13.8	414.0
Electricity, water, gas	0.3	0.4	11.8	8.3	0.4	21.2
Construction	3.1	11.7	21.0	109.0	3.4	148.2
Commerce	22.4	127.8	87.0	54.4	7.7	299.3
Transportation, communications	5.0	26.7	80.7	38.1	4.6	155.1
Finance	1.8	6.3	31.0	1.8	1.0	41.9
Services	10.0	88.6	315.3	236.4	15.6	665.9
Other	4.2	17.3	44.8	57.7	99.2	223.2
TOTAL	80.9	501.4	735.1	1,092.5	154.5	2,564.4

SOURCE: Instituto Nacional de Estadisticas, *IV censo nacional de población y III de vivienda* (1971), p. 42, cuadro 17.

which to produce surplus value. There were approximately 80,000 members of this class, and they, in turn, could be subdivided according to the amount of capital they owned. In industry, for example, large firms (over 200 workers) represented only 3.2 percent of the total number of firms; medium firms (20–200 workers) 25.4 percent; and small firms (under 20 workers) 71.4 percent.[21]

The first important point about the Chilean bourgeoisie is that the agrarian, financial, and industrial fractions were not separate antagonistic groups, but were closely interrelated through both personal and business ties. Many industrial firms, in fact, were founded by the agrarian obligarchy, and the banks were generally owned by industrial-agrarian-financial groups. Data for the mid-1960's show that 42 percent of bankers and 31 percent of corporation executives either owned large estates themselves or had close relatives who did so.[22]

A second point about the Chilean bourgeoisie concerns the high degree of concentration within each sector of the economy. According to the 1965 agricultural census, less than 0.3 percent of all landholdings occupied approximately 55 percent of the land and averaged 23,000 hectares apiece. At the opposite extreme were those 50 percent of the plots that occupied only 0.7 percent of the land and averaged 1.7 hectares per plot.[23] A similar, though slightly less

35

dramatic, situation existed with respect to industry. In 1968–69, 27 percent of the industrial corporations possessed 80 percent of the assets, while the remaining 73 percent controlled only 20 percent.[24] The main effect of this concentration was to divide the economy into monopoly and nonmonopoly sectors.* The monopolies, however, did not exist only within sectors, but there were strong between-sector linkages through what have been called the major "financial groups" in the country.[25] These groups of persons and families owned or controlled large numbers of financial, industrial, agricultural, and commercial enterprises. As an idea of the reach of such groups, the important Edwards group was known to control 12 financial enterprises in addition to the Banco Edwards, 12 major industrial firms, and two major publishing chains, one of which published three of the ten daily newspapers in Santiago as well as various newspapers in the provinces.[26] The Edwards family also had large landholdings in both rural and urban areas as well as investments outside Chile.

The third characteristic of the bourgeoisie was a growing association between the monopoly sector and foreign capital, concentrated mainly in the more modern industries—consumer durables, paper, and chemicals. The foreign connections, of course, further strengthened the monopoly sector with respect to the other firms, since these connections provided increased access to capital and technology. And, finally, there were important connections between the bourgeoisie and the state. The Chilean bourgeoisie were not the risk-taking, innovating entrepreneurs that Schumpeter and others talked about. They did not save and invest large portions of their profits, but rather had managed to shape the state apparatus so that the state took the risks while they pocketed the profits. These connections between the bourgeoisie, foreign capital, and the state will be spelled out in more detail in later sections of this chapter.

Thus, the main contradictions within the bourgeoisie did not involve the different economic sectors but the monopoly and nonmonopoly groups *within* each sector. To take the industrial bourgeoisie as an example, the monopolies had a wide variety of advantages over the small and medium bourgeoisie. Not only did they have access to foreign technology and credit, but they also had superior access to national credit. These factors meant that the gap

---

* It should be remembered that monopoly here is not being used in its literal sense, but rather to indicate those large firms with oligopoly control of their sectors.

between the monopoly and nonmonopoly firms in terms of relative capital-intensiveness tended to increase. This set of contradictions, in turn, generated another set. The capital-intensive monopoly firms were much more willing and able to give large wage increases to their employees—both because their workers were more productive (given the higher ratio of capital to worker) and because the wage bill represented a small portion of total costs. But, since the large firms tended to be pacesetters in wage negotiations, this meant that demands also increased in the nonmonopoly sector, where the owners were less able to grant them. The result was a continuous trickle of small and medium firms going bankrupt or being incorporated into the vertical organizations of the larger firms. On the other hand, it is important to note that many of the contradictions between the two sectors of the bourgeoisie were not played out directly but through the state as intermediary. This is not an unimportant distinction because the potential opposition within the bourgeoisie thus remained latent.

The petty bourgeoisie consisted of those individuals who owned their own means of production but who hired no workers although unpaid family members often worked in such shops. Their total membership was about 500,000, and they were spread across all economic sectors. The largest groups were in agriculture (owners or renters of small plots of land) and commerce (small shopkeepers or street vendors); other members of the petty bourgeoisie owned artisan industries or such equipment as a truck or a bus. The petty bourgeoisie was also the category that served as a cover-up for much of the disguised unemployment so prevalent in Chile. In an advanced industrial country, these sectors would be in the process of merging with the proletariat. In an underdeveloped, dependent country like Chile, however, the opposite happens—unemployed members of the proletariat tend to become part of the lowest stratum of the petty bourgeoisie (e.g. street vendors) because the industrial sector is not capable of generating enough employment to absorb the growing labor supply.

The proletariat was composed of about 1,828,000 persons in 1970: 1,093,000 blue-collar workers and 735,000 white-collar workers. The divisions within the bourgeoisie, between monopoly and nonmonopoly sectors, were also reflected in the working class. That is, the workers in the monopoly sector had different characteristics than those employed by small and medium-sized firms. The former tended to be more skilled, better organized, and therefore better paid. The overall effect was that the monopoly workers got large wage increases, which then led to price increases; the workers in small and medium firms were not always able to keep up with the resulting inflation rates. Thus, the immediate economic interests of the two sectors might be contradictory.

A second type of structural division within the working class was the legal distinction between white-collar workers (*empleados*) and blue-collar workers (*obreros*). White-collar workers generally received higher salaries (though a blue-collar worker in the monopoly sector might earn more than a white-collar worker in a small firm). The more important differences, however, were in terms of fringe benefits and status. Family allowances and social security benefits were higher for white-collar workers; in addition, they often worked different hours, ate in better cafeterias, had access to company recreation facilities, and so on. These divisions were reinforced by separate unions for the two subclasses.

The preceding discussion of class structure and contradictions was based on "objective" class criteria—the location of an individual with respect to the production process. Although this is the most adequate way of defining class status, it is also necessary to consider "subjective" class identification in order to account for certain actions taken by individuals or groups. The main focus of the subjective identification problem in Chile concerned the "middle class." Within the Marxist framework, as explained in Chapter One, there is no such thing as the middle class; rather, it is an ideological creation of the bourgeoisie in order to divide the working class. The Chilean "middle class" was rather vaguely defined to include white-collar workers, certain petty bourgeois elements such as professionals, and small employers. This heterogeneous collection essentially represented an income stratum and a set of aspirations— toward a bourgeois life-style.

The middle-class myth is important because it has served important political functions. These groups, organized through the Radical Party, served as the basis of the series of Radical governments between 1938 and 1952. They also formed the main mass base for the Frei government. Because of their lack of coherence, however, all of these governments ended either by destroying themselves through vacillation or by serving the interests of the bourgeoisie. It was also on the basis of the so-called middle-class interests that the bourgeoisie were able to fashion the anti-Allende coalition. The white-collar workers and petty bourgeoisie were wooed precisely on this basis.*

The class organizations were extremely important in determining the abilities of the different classes and groups to act effectively. Historically, both the bourgeoisie and the blue-collar workers had been organized in Chile; the petty bourgeoisie and the white-collar workers followed in later periods. The large (and, to some extent, the small and medium) bourgeoisie were organized into five sectoral associations called *gremios*.[27] By the 1960's, the most important of the bourgeois gremios was the National Industrial Society (SOFOFA), which had an annual budget of around $200,000, a staff of 40 (15 professionals, five *técnicos*, and 20 clerical workers), and a membership of 2,200. This membership represented only 6.5 percent of all industrialists in the country but comprised 80 percent of private industrial capacity.[28] The purposes of the organization were essentially threefold: to provide technical services for its members, to regulate the sector internally, and to represent the interests of the industrialists in government decision making.

The organization of the petty bourgeoisie was of much more recent origin. The three most important petty bourgeois gremios were the Truck Owners' Confederation (founded in 1955), the Confederation of Retail Commerce and Small Industry (1965), and the Association of Medium and Small Industries (1953). The latter two organizations had a history of uneasy relations with the large bourgeois gremios, which wanted to be the only organizational representatives in their sectors. In addition, there were the organizations of the professionals, which were called colleges (*colegios*). During the Allende years, the various professional colleges began to unite into confederations to defend their interests, which they saw being threatened.

The other development among the bourgeois associations during the 1970–73 period was the formation of coordinating organizations of the various gremios themselves. The first was the National Front of the Private Sector (FRENAP), formed in the latter half of 1971. Later, during the October 1972 owners' strike, the Gremial Defense Command was founded under the leadership of León Vilarín, presi-

---

*The term middle class (*clase media*)—or more often a term similar to middle sectors (*capas medias*)—was continually used in newspapers, magazines, and other communications channels as well as by political leaders in Chile.

dent of the Truck Owners' Confederation. In November, the group was made permanent, again under Vilarín's direction, and its name was changed to the Gremial Action Movement.

The main labor organization in Chile was the National Workers' Confederation (CUT). The CUT had a history of divisions and reconciliations, but by the late 1960's, it united most of the organized workers in the country.[29] There are varying opinions on what percentage of the work force was organized in this period, but the most reliable estimate is probably around 30 percent.[30] In absolute numbers, organized workers exceeded 700,000 out of a work force of 2.6 million in the late 1960's. The level of unionization, however, varied greatly between sectors of the economy, ranging from 14 percent in agriculture to 40 percent in industry to over 60 percent in mining. There was also significant variation *within* sectors such that the larger the firm, the more likely it was to be unionized. In industry, for example, if the entire labor force is used as the base for calculating, the unionization level was only slightly over 30 percent; if firms with ten or more workers constituted the base, then the level of unionization rose to 60 percent; using firms with 25 or more workers (the legal minimum for a union), the rate increased further to 70 percent.* All of these figures, of course, were higher by the Allende years. Estimates are that, by 1973, almost all workers who could legally be organized were members of unions.[31]

Chilean unions were always closely connected with the Communist and Socialist parties; and the two were often bitter rivals for domination of the labor movement, a situation tending to weaken the unions. Because of the general orientation of the two parties, the unions concentrated on economic demands and ignored the question of political power even though they claimed to support socialist principles. Their major incursions into the political field prior to the Allende period were in the form of supporting certain candidates in elections—though even this was not done formally for fear of alienating the minority groups of Christian Democratic and Radical Party workers.[32]

Like the bourgeoisie, the workers also saw the need to form new

---

* It should be noted for all of the calculations on percentage of workers in unions that the denominator of the fraction is the *total work force* (i.e. including employers, self-employed, and unpaid family workers), and the numerator includes only blue- and white-collar union members. Since employers and self-employed unions are *not* included as union members (this was precisely one of Alan Angell's criticisms of the CUT figures; see his *Politics and the Labor Movement in Chile* [London, 1972], pp. 45–46), it would seem that they should be excluded from the work force as well for

organizations, as the intensifying class struggle outgrew the bounds of the bureaucratic framework of the CUT. It was not until mid-1972, however, that a new form of industrial organization—the *cordones industriales*, geographically based groups of factories—was initiated. The cordones then joined with other local-level groups such as neighborhood councils, mothers' centers, student associations, and peasant unions, to form *comandos comunales*. Both the cordones and comandos had immediate practical tasks, especially during crisis periods, but, in addition, they were seen as the basic units for a possible alternative governmental structure.[33]

The final topic to be discussed in this section is the relationship between classes and political parties. More than in any other country in Latin America, the Chilean political parties were divided along class lines. During the period studied here, there were six major parties functioning in Chile. On the right were the Liberal and Conservative parties, which fused in 1965 to form the National Party (PN); in the center were the Radical (PR) and Christian Democratic (PDC) parties; and on the left were the Socialist (PS) and Communist (PC) parties.

The Conservative and Liberal parties both represented the interests of the bourgeoisie but were differentiated by economic sector. That is, the Conservative Party was closely associated with the agrarian oligarchy, whereas the Liberals primarily represented the urban bourgeoisie—the financiers and the industrialists. For electoral purposes, of course, these bourgeois parties had to seek followers among other classes; such support came primarily from tenants and agricultural workers in the countryside and the petty bourgeoisie and unorganized workers in the cities.[34] The support for the Liberals and Conservatives declined significantly after the 1920's; the only times they won presidential elections or came close in recent times was when their candidate was Jorge Alessandri, who appealed to independent voters on the basis of his well-known family name and his paternalistic image.

The Radical Party had its main support among urban middle-income groups, especially those working in the bureaucracy. It also had a strong following among the petty bourgeoisie and the intellectuals in the large cities and in the smaller towns.[35] Its domination of these groups—sometimes known as the *capas medias*—was un-

---

these calculations. When we look at union membership as a percentage of blue- and white-collar workers, Angell's figure increases from 30 percent to over 40 percent; it would be much higher if only those who could legally join unions were included.

disputed until the Christian Democrats became a major electoral force in the late 1950's; at this time, some of the Radical constituency switched its allegiance.

Although they had certain characteristics in common, the PR and the PDC were very different kinds of parties. In the first place, the PDC was clearly associated with the most modern sectors of the economy; for example, its share of the capas medias was concentrated in the largest, most technologically advanced industries and in large chain stores, etc.[36] Second, the PDC was the only real multiclass party in Chile. It drew its support from different classes in approximately the same percentage that each class represented in the population as a whole, and all classes had a voice in the party. This is not to say, however, that all had equal weight. It seems clear that, in the final analysis, the bourgeois sectors were the dominant force in the party (see discussion in Chapter Three). Those sectors of the bourgeoisie represented in the PDC, as opposed to the PN, were essentially the modern industrialists—those in consumer durables and in certain intermediate industries, such as chemicals and plastics.

The main strength of the Communist Party was among blue-collar workers in the mining area in the north and in the large industries in the major cities; it had very little following in the rural areas until the agrarian reform began. In this sense, the PC, like the PDC, was essentially a modern-sector party.[37] The Socialists had a more diverse base of support. Although strong among the blue-collar proletariat in large industry, the PS was also important in smaller industry both in cities and towns. In addition, the PS had a stronger following than the PC among white-collar workers and even among certain professionals sectors.[38]

THE FOREIGN SECTOR

The foreign sector played two roles in Chile. On the one hand, it acted almost as a domestic participant in the political and economic process; the best example of this type of activity was the foreign corporations with investments in Chile. On the other hand, the foreign corporations and other private institutions, foreign governments, and multilateral organizations constituted the international context into which Chile—as a dependent capitalist country—was inserted. The activities of the capitalist countries affected Chile whether intentionally or not. For example, a recession in the United States and Western Europe lowered the price of copper as well as the amount of copper that Chile could sell. In addition, however, governments and corporations could deliberately place limits on the actions of the Chilean government. Their leverage existed because Chile's need for foreign exchange was usually beyond what could be provided by fluctuating copper revenues; thus the government was continually searching for sources of loans and foreign investment. The results of this dependency will be made clear in later chapters; here the purposes will be to examine the basic parameters of Chile's insertion in the international capitalist system.

Exports were the most important source of foreign exchange, and copper accounted for about 80 percent of exports by value. During the early 1960's, almost 40 percent of all exports went to one country alone—the United States—and about 40 percent of imports also came from the same source.[39] These facts alone provided the basis of Chilean dependency. In addition, however, until 1965, the U.S.-based Anaconda and Kennecott corporations owned 100 percent of the stock in the large mines.[40] Under Frei, programs of "chileanization" and "pacted nationalization" were enacted whereby the Chilean government became part owner of the mines. The corporations agreed to increase investment (and thus production) while selling the Chilean government majority ownership in some of the mines. However, the prices were above book value, the terms were short, and the companies invested none of their own money in the expansion process but rather obtained Chilean and international financing. Furthermore, the companies retained control of administration and sales. The only advantage to the Chileans was a larger share in the profits while control of the mines remained, as always, in the hands of the foreign corporations.[41] In addition to copper, iron ore and nitrate were also important export products in Chile. Up until 1970, almost all of the former was owned by Bethlehem Steel; the latter was dominated by the Anglo-Lautaro Company (all foreign capital) until 1968, when the state bought 37.5 percent interest.

Although the vast majority of foreign investment in Chile was in mining, during the 1960's (and especially during the Frei years), foreign capital began to move into industry. For example, while U.S. mining investment in Chile increased only from $517 million to $586 million between 1960 and 1968, investment in manufacturing increased from $22 million to $68 million.[42] Considering the entire set of industrial corporations, 25.5 percent had some foreign participation, and this 25.5 percent represented 59.9 percent of the capital of the corporations.[43] That is, foreign participation was concentrated

TABLE 2.2

Distribution of Capital in Industrial Corporations, 1969

Sector	Number of corporations	Capital (Million E°)	Percent national	Percent foreign	Percent state
Basic consumer goods:					
Food	141	788	59.7%	9.0%	31.3%
Beverages	30	226	73.3	24.6	2.1
Tobacco	1	80	41.4	58.6	—
Textiles	142	498	90.1	9.9	—
Clothing, shoes	70	116	80.3	18.7	1.0
Furniture	8	2	93.3	6.7	—
Printing	36	47	84.5	15.2	0.3
Diverse	39	45	80.3	18.9	0.8
Intermediate goods:					
Wood	24	46	94.3%	2.0%	3.7%
Paper	9	306	59.5	16.4	24.1
Leather	19	32	97.8	2.2	—
Rubber	9	118	54.9	45.1	—
Chemicals	115	349	52.5	38.3	9.2
Oil	5	62	98.4	0.6	1.0
Nonmetallic minerals	37	348	44.0	13.6	42.4
Basic metals	37	915	81.6	18.4	—
Durable consumer and capital goods:					
Metal products	81	199	81.6%	18.4%	—
Nonelectrical machinery	18	62	85.3	14.7	—
Electrical equipment	44	227	38.8	59.9	1.3%
Transportation equipment	37	66	45.5	43.8	10.7

SOURCE: Luis Pacheco, "La inversión extranjera y las corporaciones internacionales en el desarrollo industrial chileno," in Oscar Muñoz, ed., Proceso a la industrialización chilena (Santiago, 1972), p. 115.

in the largest industrial firms. It was also concentrated in the fastest growing industrial sectors—paper, chemicals, rubber, electrical equipment, metal products, transportation equipment, etc. The third characteristic of foreign investment in industry was that it was concentrated in those corporations that had monopoly or oligopoly control in their sectors.[44] Table 2.2 gives an idea of the sectoral distribution of foreign investment within the industrial sector.

Foreign capital was also important in the commercial and financial sectors. It is estimated that, during the 1960's, about half of all wholesale commerce in Chile was conducted through foreign firms; chief among them were three British (Weir Scott, Duncan Fox, and Williamson Balfour) and three U.S. firms (W. R. Grace, Wessel

Duval, and Agencias Graham).[45] In the banking sector, in 1970, five foreign banks represented 10 percent of the capital in the private banking sector and accounted for 18 percent of *escudo* loans and 12 percent of loans in foreign currency. These banks were the First National City Bank, Bank of America, Banco Francés e Italiano, Banco de Londres y América del Sur, and Banco do Brasil.[46] It should also be added that foreign companies controlled the telephone system (ITT) as well as most of the distribution of electricity in the country, although the bulk of the electricity was generated by ENDESA, a Chilean government corporation.

Although it is obvious that foreign control of such important parts of the economy would displace much of the decision power to the dominant nation (the United States), it is often thought that there is a compensating side of the situation whereby the dependent country gains additional capital. This was not the case with Chile (nor is it the case with most other Third World nations); the profit repatriation and depreciation that accompanied direct foreign investment implied a large net *outflow* of funds. During the decade of the 1960's, direct investment totaled $900 million, compared with $839 million in profits and $873 million in depreciation, producing a net outflow of $812 million.*

Another type of link between Chile and the international capitalist system concerned bilateral and multilateral loans. This source had provided a net inflow in Chile during the 1960's (unlike the situation in some other Latin American countries), but it had also created a huge foreign debt. This debt increased from $598 million in 1960 to around $2,300 million in 1970,[47] which gave Chile the second highest per capita foreign debt in the world and meant that an ever-increasing percentage of export earnings had to be spent on debt service. By 1969, 20 percent of export earnings was spent on profits and interest alone in addition to amortization payments. Furthermore, over half of this debt was owed to a single country— the United States.[48] For the period 1971–76, payments of $1,400 million of interest and amortization payments were due, of which $566 million had to be paid during 1971–72 because of the renegotiation of the debt in 1965 by the Christian Democrats.[49] The only

---

*These estimates ignore the contribution of foreign investment in generating foreign exchange through exports and saving it through import substitution. Such a calculation is impossible to make, however, for lack of knowledge of what portion of the investments made by foreigners would have otherwise been undertaken by domestic capital. Figures come from Sergio Ramos, *Chile: ¿una economía en transición?* (Santiago, 1972), p. 57.

practical way of repaying this amount, of course, was to borrow more money, thus increasing the debt and service and continuing the vicious cycle.

A final link centered on technology. The increasing foreign penetration in the Chilean economy, especially in the industrial sector, produced an increased use of foreign technology. Thus payments for patents, royalties, and other such items increased from slightly over $7 million in 1962 to $16.5 million in 1968.[50] Sometimes this technology enabled Chile to produce new goods that could not otherwise have been produced for lack of know-how. A CORFO study of a group of Chilean firms with foreign participation, however, showed that technology payments were often just a disguised way of transferring profits. Only in 45.1 percent of the cases was a patented production process transferred, in spite of the fact that the foreign firm is seen as an important source of technological transfer.[51]

THE ROLE OF THE STATE

The Chilean state has traditionally had an exceptionally strong role in the economy, as was seen in the historical analysis at the beginning of the chapter.[52] One very important aspect of its economic role involved ownership of the means of production. By the late 1960's, the state owned 100 percent of the stock in the National Oil Company (ENAP), the National Electricity Company (ENDESA), the National Sugar Company (IANSA), the Army and Navy metal works (FAMAE and ASMAR, respectively), the telecommunications industry (Empresa Nacional de Telecomunicaciones—ENTEL), and so on. It was also partial owner of many other crucial industries, including the large copper mines, the petrochemical complex, and the Pacific Steel Company (CAP).[53]

In addition, the state set minimum wages and salaries as well as prices on various essential consumer goods. Through the Banco del Estado, the state had direct control over about half of all credit going to the private sector. The state controlled exports and imports. It invested heavily in infrastructure and basic services and employed large numbers of people in the burgeoning state bureaucracy. These last two functions meant that the public sector budget came to constitute an ever larger share of national income. Thus, by the late 1960's, the state controlled over 40 percent of the total GDP; by 1970, the figure was 47 percent.[54] Table 2.3 shows estimates of the impact of the public sector expenditures on various aspects of the economy.

46

TABLE 2.3

Impact of the Public Sector on the Economy, 1970

(Millions of 1970 escudos)

Category	Total economy (1)	Induced by public sector (2)	(2) ÷ (1)
Value added	91,528	42,713	46.7%
Employment*a*	2,998	1,218	40.6
Surplus	41,012	17,997	43.9
Foreign trade:*b*			
Exports	1,307	507	38.8%
Imports	1,320	449	34.0
Balance of payments	160	230	143.8
Family consumption:*c*			
Agricultural	4,448	1,662	37.4%
Industrial	38,502	14,735	38.3
Other	15,132	5,967	39.4

SOURCE: Sergio Ramos, *Chile, ¿una economía en transición?* (Santiago, 1972), p. 78.

a Thousands of persons.

b Millions of dollars.

c Only consumption of national origin.

Another index of the strong role of the state was the percentage of gross domestic investment in fixed capital supplied by the state. By the late 1960's, this figure was over 70 percent. In 1969, it reached 75 percent, with 50 percent channeled through direct investment and 25 percent of indirect investment.[55] It must be pointed out, however, that this investment was not spread evenly over the economy but concentrated in a few sectors, principally those that provided some kind of service. These sectors (electricity, gas, and water; transportation; education; health; and housing) were those that had the highest capital-output ratios and longest periods of maturation; they also had the lowest rates of profit. In other words, those sectors that had the highest profit rates and the lowest maturation periods were left for the private sector, while the state provided the supplementary services to make private investment more profitable.

As has been implied in the above discussion, although the state was very powerful, its strength did not make it an autonomous organ above the class structure. Quite the contrary, the Chilean state had been molded by the bourgeoisie to fit their own purposes. The state was bourgeois in two senses. First, it was structured in such a way that the Executive could not use the state to control the economy; at most he could regulate it. This was accomplished through a complex set of checks and balances. There was a strong Congress with total power over taxation and some control over the military among other crucial areas; an independent Judiciary; and an additional check—the Comptroller—an institution with power to rule on the legality of certain executive actions. The Chilean President had only limited power of appointment over the Judiciary and the Comptroller, and congressional elections were timed so as never to coincide with presidential elections. Thus a newly elected President might have to deal with a previous Congress for up to two and a half years. In addition, the military, although formally under control of the Executive branch, in reality maintained a large amount of autonomy.

The second sense in which the Chilean state was bourgeois was in its direct service to the capitalist class. Many examples can be given. First was the system of wage and price controls. Whenever a wage increase was decreed, the bourgeoisie were always allowed to pass this increase on in the form of higher prices;[56] often price increases exceeded wage increases. Second was the tremendous number of tax exemptions given to the bourgeoisie to induce them to invest.[57] The largest exemptions were given to foreign capital, to the point that the national bourgeoisie complained of not being able to compete. In comparison with other classes in Chile, however, the bourgeoisie were privileged in the tax system.

Perhaps the most notorious example of the state being at the service of the bourgeoisie was seen in certain actions of CORFO. In the years between 1938 and 1954, CORFO founded many of the most important industrial corporations in Chile: RCA (communications), Pesquera Iquique (fishing), MADEMSA (household appliances), Electromat (electronics), Siam di Tella (household appliances), INSA (rubber products), Laboratorio Chile (chemicals), Farmoquímica del Pacífico (chemicals), SOCHIF (fertilizers), Cerro Blanco (cement), MADECO (copper products), CAP (steel), El Melón (cement), IMPREGNA (National Forestry Corporation), ENAP (oil), IANSA (sugar), and FASSA (sulfuric acid), among others. Of these 17, ten were among the 50 largest companies in Chile. CORFO put up the initial capital and took the risks involved in establishing a new enterprise. Once the companies were functioning well and profit margins were established, however, the majority were sold to the private sector. Thus, by the mid-1960's, CORFO retained majority ownership only in SOCHIF, IMPREGNA, ENAP, IANSA, and FASSA.[58] With respect to the terms on which the companies were sold, there is some evidence that they went for less than book value;

they were also often bought with money borrowed from the state itself.[59] Those firms that never became profitable were retained by the state.

ECONOMIC PERFORMANCE

The combined effects of a dependent capitalist economy, a highly organized class system, and a strong state at the service of the bourgeoisie were to produce a number of chronic problems and deformations in the operation of the Chilean economy. Perhaps the most obvious problem was stagnation. In the postwar period, GDP had grown at an annual rate of around 2 percent per capita.[60] Although industry had been much more dynamic, agricultural output had not even kept up with population growth. Additional difficulties were created, since the economy grew, not at a steady, slow rate, but rather in starts and stops as business cycles resulted from internal inflation, foreign exchange crises, and Keynesian economic policies. It should also be pointed out that, although industry was growing fairly rapidly during the postwar years, this growth was concentrated in basic consumer goods and later in consumer durables.

Closely related to the low rate of growth was the problem of unemployment. Statistics go back to the mid-1950's and show an average unemployment rate of 6.5 percent for the period 1956–70 in Greater Santiago; in other areas—for example, the industrial region of Concepción-Talcahuano and the mining area of Lota-Coronel—the rates were much higher. These figures, however, refer only to open unemployment. If disguised unemployment is included, the rates rise to 18 percent (Santiago), 26 percent (Concepción-Talcahuano), and 33 percent (Lota-Coronel).[61] Disguised unemployment existed primarily in the service sector, which was abnormally large in Chile, since the productive sectors (agriculture, mining, and industry) could not provide work for all who wanted it. For example, between 1940 and 1970, occupation in industry rose only from 17 percent of the work force to 20 percent; agriculture declined from 37 to 23 percent; and mining declined from 6 to 3.5 percent. Meanwhile, services (including commerce) increased from 32 to 40 percent of the work force.[62]

A third problem concerned the unequal structure of distribution. A 1960 survey found the following situation with respect to distribution of income: the upper 5 percent of the population had 25 percent of total income; the middle 45 percent had 59 percent; and the bottom 50 percent of the population had only 16 percent of national income.[63] As indicated above, similar inequalities existed with respect to distribution of wealth and property, i.e. high levels of concentration of ownership in industry, agriculture, commerce, and the financial sector. The distribution structure, of course, was closely related to the level and pattern of growth through the demand structure.

The final problem that characterized the Chilean economy was related to all three problems already discussed. This was inflation, which began in the late nineteenth century and averaged almost 30 percent per year between 1940 and 1970.[64] The effects of this chronic inflation were varied. On the one hand, industrialists claimed that it was the main reason for their failure to save and invest;[65] whether this was true or not is hard to say, but the inflation probably shared some of the responsibility for the stagnant economy. Inflation was definitely related to unemployment in the postwar period, since Keynesian economic policies—focusing on a trade-off between inflation and unemployment—were used by all types of regimes in Chile. As will be explained later, in the Chilean case this trade-off was mediated through the public sector budget. Finally, the relation between inflation and income distribution was quite direct; in inflationary periods, the workers—especially the least organized sectors—lost out in their share of national income to the bourgeoisie, especially the large bourgeoisie. It should be pointed out here that it was because of the chronic inflation in Chile that the annual wage readjustment (*reajuste*), which is referred to often throughout this study, assumed such major political and economic importance.

In summary, then, the Chilean economy was characterized by low and fluctuating growth in output and employment, high rates of inflation, and a highly skewed distribution structure. In dynamic terms, the economy was characterized by serious and frequent business cycles. These conditions provide the background for the analysis in the chapters that follow.

CHAPTER THREE

The Development Models

THIS CHAPTER begins the analysis of the 1958–73 period in Chile and the comparison of the three regimes of Jorge Alessandri (1958–64), Eduardo Frei (1964–70), and Salvador Allende (1970–73). First, a comparison will be made of the class alliances that supported each of the three regimes. Then their development ideologies will be examined, with the hypothesis that the ideologies will be an expression of the interests of the dominant classes in each alliance. The two components together—the alliance and the development ideology—constitute what will be called a development model.

ALLIANCES

An alliance is a coalition of social classes, class fractions, and social groups, within which there is a definite hierarchical structure. Following Poulantzas,[1] it is possible to distinguish between four levels of power within an alliance: the *hegemonic class* fraction, which dominates the alliance and gives it its main orientation; the *power bloc*, which is composed of the rest of the dominant classes under the leadership of the hegemonic member; the *allied classes* or fractions, which share in the objective benefits controlled by the alliance though not the power; and the *supporting classes*, whose allegiance is based on ideological illusions.* In organizational

---

* In the discussion of the ideological basis of the allegiance of the supporting classes in the Poulantzas scheme, it should be noted that "ideology" is being used in a very different sense than in the term "development ideology." In the former

terms, alliances are usually put together by political parties, which themselves have definite class compositions. That is, a political party primarily represents one class or fraction (the hegemonic member), and this hegemonic member, in turn, seeks support from others—some as allied classes and others as supporting classes—in order to capture control of the state apparatus.[2]

How is it possible to identify the class nature of an alliance and especially its dominant member? From an empirical point of view, there are four major possibilities. First, it is possible to examine the groups that participate in a given alliance; in the Chilean case, this can be done through analyzing the voting base of the different parties and coalitions. In general, this method is more useful in identifying the allied and supporting classes than the hegemonic member. In particular, it should never be assumed that the class or fraction that makes up the largest percentage of the voting base is necessarily the dominant member of the alliance. A second possibility is to see who benefits most from the policies carried out by an alliance when it is in power. There is obviously a strong interrelationship between these two methods, since the assumption exists that the principal members of the alliance (that is, the hegemonic member, the rest of the power bloc, and the allied classes) will be the main beneficiaries of these policies. Hegemony assures that the dominant member of the coalition will receive major benefits, and if the allied classes do not also share in these benefits, it can be assumed that the alliance will not last. The supporting classes, on the other hand, need receive no objective benefits in return for their support.

A third empirical way of identifying the class nature of an alliance is to look at the formal channels for exerting power or influence on the government that are open to the representatives of the different classes. For example, depending on the class nature of a government, either the bourgeoisie or the workers might be incorporated into certain government advisory or even policy-making boards. A final

---

usage, ideology refers to a type of false consciousness whereby a series of beliefs is used to convince classes or groups that their interests lie in supporting a certain alliance when this is not "objectively" the case, i.e. they receive no material benefits from doing so. In the latter use of the term, ideology is seen as a series of expressed goals that are "true" in the sense that the regimes are hypothesized to want to carry them out. These intentions are different from what actually happens, however, because of the interference of certain structural factors; therefore the term ideology is used to distinguish expressed goals from actual implementation.

method focuses on informal channels of influence. Almost all political observers, including those studying the Chilean situation,[3] agree that informal channels are far more important than formal contacts. Although no direct data are available on informal communication, it is possible to present some indirect information based on the social class background of high government officials. The assumption here is not the often-used mechanical one, which directly correlates class background with policy output, but a more flexible one—that a minister is more likely to come into contact with, and respond to, persons with class backgrounds similar to his own.*

For the Chilean case, evidence of all four types will be examined to try to arrive at some conclusions about the class nature of the three alliances governing during the 1958–73 period. These were, of course, the rightist alliance directed by the National Party, the centrist alliance directed by the Christian Democratic Party, and the leftist alliance directed by the Communist and Socialist parties. This classification leaves out one major political party—the Radicals—and the minor parties. The Radicals are left out because they have traditionally switched alliances; sometimes the Party moved as a whole, and at other times it divided, with different factions supporting different alliances. The Radicals will thus be dealt with on an ad hoc basis over the period, depending on where their support lay at any given time.

Voting Base

The type of voting analysis that will be used involves survey information on party and candidate preference, which is then correlated with information on social class.† The analysis is based on

---

*The hypothesis that people tend to associate with others of their same class (usually defined with respect to occupation) is a generally accepted one in sociology. For one empirical study of the subject in an American urban setting (likely to be much more fluid in terms of social mobility than the Chilean situation) and a review of the literature, see Edward O. Laumann, *Prestige and Association in an Urban Community* (Indianapolis, 1966).

†Another type of voting analysis, which is more common in the Chilean case, involves "ecological analysis." Provinces or *comunas* are classified according to the occupational mix found in each, and these are then grouped and correlated with votes for different parties. In addition to methodological problems (the so-called ecological fallacy), this type of analysis provides very little information on the class nature of voting. For example, it can be shown that agricultural provinces in the 1960's tended to be highly correlated with votes for the PN and PR. This analysis, however, cannot determine which classes *within* the agricultural provinces voted for which parties:

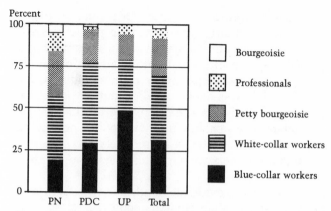

Fig. 3.1. Class composition of political alliances, August 1970. Source: Table A.2.

previously unpublished data collected by Eduardo Hamuy, the major political pollster in Chile. Hamuy conducted surveys before every election since the mid-1950's as well as in nonelectoral periods. His results were generally accurate, although they had the disadvantage of being limited to the major urban areas of the country. The data discussed below, for example, deal only with the Greater Santiago area, which means that the agrarian sector is not included. The samples were drawn on a random basis and consisted of approximately 1,000 people. Figures 3.1 and 3.2, however, eliminate nonworking women as well as those who were undecided about their candidate or party preference. The data in the figures come from the survey conducted in August 1970, i.e., the month before the 1970 presidential election.* In Table A.2, survey results for August 1958, 1964, and 1970 are presented, as well as those for June 1972.

In Figure 3.1, the aim is to analyze the class composition of each

---

it can be *assumed* that PN votes came from the landowners and certain workers whom they controlled, and that PR votes came from the petty bourgeoisie in the small towns, but this cannot be ascertained from the data. Examples of this type of analysis include Enzo Faletto and Eduardo Ruíz, "Conflicto político y estructura social," in Aníbal Pinto et al., *Chile hoy* (Mexico, 1970), pp. 213–54; Robert Ayres, "Unidad Popular and the Chilean Electoral Process," *Studies in Comparative International Development*, 8 (1973); and Maurice Zeitlin and James Petras, "The Working Class Vote in Chile: Christian Democracy versus Marxism," *British Journal of Sociology*, No. 21, 1970.

* The actual voting returns for Greater Santiago were Alessandri, 38.6 percent, Allende, 34.9 percent, and Tomic, 26.5 percent. Thus the UP was slightly underrepresented in the Hamuy results.

54

alliance and to compare this with the composition of the entire sample population. It is evident that the rightist alliance received disproportionately strong support from the bourgeoisie and professionals and less than its share from blue-collar workers. The other class that gave strong support to the Right was the petty bourgeoisie, although this support was less marked than the behavior of the bourgeoisie and blue-collar workers with respect to the rightist alliance. The centrist alliance, by contrast, received support from the different classes in about the same proportion they represented in the population as a whole (evidence supporting the previously expressed view that the Christian Democrats were the only real multiclass party in Chile). The one class grouping that gave the PDC higher than proportional support was the white-collar workers. The leftist alliance received half of its votes from the blue-collar workers, although this class represented only about 30 percent of the sample population, and correspondingly lower support from other groups.

Turning now to Figure 3.2, we see that similar results emerge. Comparing the total percentages of votes received by each alliance (as predicted by the survey) with the way the different classes distributed their votes, it can be seen again that the rightist alliance received disproportionate support from the bourgeoisie, the professionals, and, on a lesser scale, the petty bourgeoisie. The centrist

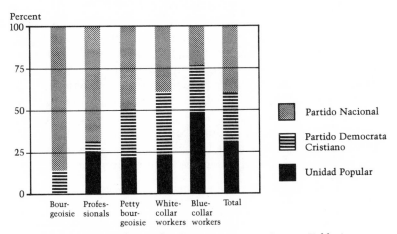

Fig. 3.2. Party preference by class, August 1970. Source: Table A.2.

55

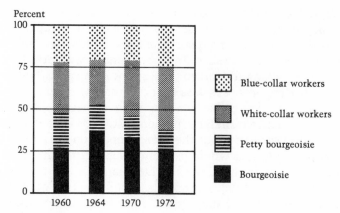

Fig. 3.3. Distribution of income between classes, 1960–72. The class terms bourgeoisie, petty bourgeoisie, white-collar workers, and blue-collar workers correspond to the Chilean National Income Accounting terms of *empleadores, trabajadores por cuenta propia, empleados,* and *obreros.* Source: ODEPLAN, *Cuentas de producción y distribución del ingreso, 1960–71,* and unpublished calculations by Helio Varela, former director of the Income Distribution Division of ODEPLAN.

alliance received exceptionally high support from the white-collar workers. With respect to the leftist alliance, the importance of the blue-collar workers is again confirmed.*

Material Benefits

In examination of the benefits received by different classes, primary emphasis will be on trends in income distribution during the periods when each of the three alliances was in power. Figure 3.3 shows the share of national income going to each of the four classes during the 1960–64 period (rightist alliance in power), 1965–70 (centrist alliance), and 1971–72 (leftist alliance). Here it can be seen that the policies of the rightist alliance give the major share of benefits (in terms of monetary income) to the bourgeoisie. This class increased its share of the national income from 27 to 36 percent while the other classes declined proportionally. From inspection of the bourgeoisie to see which sectors were gaining most, it appears

---

*As can be seen in Table A.2, the 1970 results were generally similar to those for 1958 and 1972. The essentially two-way race in 1964, with an absolute majority going to Eduardo Frei, somewhat skewed the pattern for that year. The main anomaly in the 1970 data is the extremely low percentage of professionals' votes going to the PDC, i.e. only 1 percent of the alliance consisted of professionals. The normal figure, based on the other surveys, was about 11 percent.

that the big gainers were industry (both the modern and the traditional sectors) and commerce. The mining (copper and iron) and agrarian bourgeoisies also gained, though to a lesser extent.[4]

The centrist alliance gave major benefits to the working class—especially the white-collar workers. The bourgeoisie, however, did not lose all that much, and, as can be seen in Figure 3.3, their share of the national income in 1970 was still substantially above the 1960 level. In addition, from inspection of the different sectors of the bourgeoisie, it is clear that not all were losing—the copper mining, financial, and modern sector of the industrial bourgeoisie all gained during the 1964–70 period.[5]

Under the leftist alliance, the workers were again the gainers; this time the blue-collar workers gained slightly more than the white-collar workers. All sectors of the bourgeoisie lost, with the biggest losers being the mining, industrial, and agricultural sectors. Construction and commerce were the most favored sectors of the bourgeoisie—more or less maintaining their shares of the national income.[6] As will be explained in greater detail later, nonmonetary benefits (e.g. health care, school lunches, distribution systems) accruing to the blue-collar workers under the leftist alliance significantly augmented monetary gains.

Formal Channels of Influence

According to a study made during the Alessandri period,[7] the bourgeoisie had built-in and legitimized access to the state through membership on advisory committees and voting membership on important policy-making boards. All four major bourgeois associations (SOFOFA, SNA, CCC, and SNM) were voting members in two main types of government bodies. First, all were on the boards of several key financial policy institutions such as the Central Bank (monetary policy), the State Bank (credit and subsidies), and CORFO (government investment). Second, each group voted on the boards of specialized government committees concerned with its particular sector. Table 3.1 shows the representation on the major economic policy-making boards during the 1958–64 period. In addition, during the Alessandri period, the bourgeois associations often actually drafted legislation relevant to their particular areas; sometimes this was at the suggestion of the President or a Minister, but often it was on their own initiative. According to one expert, "The specialized nature of much economic legislation and the recognized ability

57

TABLE 3.1

Voting Representation on Major Economic Policy-Making Boards, 1958–64

Government representatives[a]		Class association representatives		Semiautonomous agency representatives	
Position	Number	Position	Number	Position	Number
Central Bank:					
President	2	SOFOFA-SNA	1		
Senate	2	Central Chamber of			
Chamber	2	of Commerce	1		
		Private banks	3		
		Labor	1		
		Private shareholders	1		
TOTAL	6		7		0
State Bank:					
President	5	SOFOFA	1	Central Bank	1
		SNA	1	State Bank	1
		Central Chamber of		CORFO	1
		Commerce	1		
		National Mining			
		Society	1		
		Retail merchants	1		
		Salaried employees	1		
		Labor	1		
TOTAL	5		7		3
CORFO:					
President	3	SOFOFA	1	Central Bank	1
Senate	2	SNA	1	Agrarian Colonization	
Chamber	2	National Mining		Bank	1
		Society	1	Others	8
		Central Chamber of			
		Commerce	1		
		Institute of Engineers	1		
		Labor	1		
TOTAL	7		6		10

SOURCE: Constantine Menges, "Public Policy and Organized Business in Chile: A Preliminary Analysis," *Journal of International Affairs*, 20, No. 2 (1966): 351.

[a] During the 1958–64 period, the congressional representatives were eliminated. In the Central Bank, the change gave the President four representatives out of 11.

of the business associations to prepare complex studies and draft bills, along with the basic perception of the legitimacy of participation by economic groups, seems to have meant that many ministers have welcomed such 'technical assistance' in spite of their political views."[8] In 1962, for example, SOFOFA took the initiative in trying to form an Industrial Development Bank by drafting a bill that was submitted by the President to Congress in nearly unaltered form. The 1962 tax reform legislation was drafted by the following committee: 15 lawyers from public agencies; 15 lawyers from the

SOFOFA, SNA, CCC, and SNM; two engineers, and two accountants.[9]

Since the same formal structures were maintained through the Frei and Allende periods, it is necessary to see how these two governments dealt with the situation. The Central Bank will be taken as an example, since it was on that board where the government position was most precarious. The Frei government reacted to the situation by submitting a bill to Congress that would reduce the number of representatives on the board that were allotted to the private banks. The bill was defeated, however, which meant that some of the Frei monetary reforms could not be implemented. Allende, on the other hand, by buying out the private banks, automatically increased the government representation.

Frei also set up an additional channel of formal communication between the government and the bourgeoisie. He appointed one of his most trusted aides, Raúl Devés, to head a liaison committee between the government and the private sector. It was said that many bills were submitted to this committee before being sent to Congress. The bourgeois representation, however, was never formalized because then labor would have had to be given representation also.[10] Allende, on the other hand, in line with the very different alliance that he represented, brought the CUT into formal participation on all the major policy-making boards. The 1971 triennial report of the CUT listed seven major boards and committees where the CUT was given formal representation. Allende also set up a National Development Council that was a tripartite advisory group of government, labor, and business representatives. By 1972, however, the bourgeois representatives were eliminated from the council.

Informal Channels of Influence

As mentioned above, the analysis of informal channels of influence is based on the social background characteristics of the highest government officials during the three regimes. Looking at the three from this perspective, we see some commonalities, but significant differences as well. The commonalities center on the fact that the majority of the ministers in all three administrations were university-trained professionals. The way in which they put their training to work, however, varied greatly.

The rightist alliance that governed Chile from 1958 to 1964 was, in many ways, a throwback to the pre-Popular Front period. That is, the bourgeoisie actually held important positions in the government rather than ruling through representatives of other classes, as had been the tendency between 1938 and 1958.[11] The most obvious example was the President himself. Prior to becoming President of the Republic, Jorge Alessandri Rodríguez had spent 16 years as president of the Confederation of Production and Commerce, the top organization of the Chilean bourgeoisie. He was also a long-time director of the National Industrial Society (SOFOFA) and president of one of the largest industries in Chile (the Compañía Manufacturera de Papeles y Cartones), as well as being director of numerous industrial and financial corporations. Of the 37 ministers appointed by Alessandri, every one was a professional. Twelve, however, were also owners of large farms, and 21 were owners, managers, or directors of industrial, financial, or commercial corporations. At least 17 were members of the most prestigious social clubs in Chile. The main exceptions to this pattern were the Radical Party ministers who entered the cabinet after August 1961.

The prominent personalities of the Frei government were somewhat different, although many were also from prestigious bourgeois families. Of Frei's ministers, 24 were professionals; half also had past or present connections with industrial (or construction) firms and four with agriculture. Of the others, several had worked for international organizations, several were university professors, and others had worked in state corporations. Many were among the original founders of the Christian Democratic Party.

During the Allende regime, slightly over half of the ministers (31 of 55) were again professionals. Two new groups, however, were represented that had not appeared previously; one group was workers and/or labor leaders (11 ministers) and the other was the military (ten ministers). The Ministry of Labor was continuously headed by a worker, and the Ministries of Interior, Finance, Education, Agriculture, Housing, and Public Works were also manned by workers at various periods under the UP. The rest of the 55 ministers who served during the 1970–73 period included university professors, técnicos (several having spent many years with international organizations), and public functionaries. Twelve seem to have devoted the majority of their time to politics, while only two had close connections with the bourgeoisie. Table 3.2 summarizes these characteristics of the ministers.

After a look at the nature of the three alliances, it now remains

TABLE 3.2
Social Background Characteristics of Cabinet
Members, 1958–73

Background	1958–64	1964–70	1970–73
Ministers[a]	37	28	55
Professionals	37	24	31
Politicians	8	5	12
Workers or labor leaders	0	0	11
Military	0	1	10
Connections with industry	21	14	2
Connections with agriculture	12	4	0
Social club members	17	6	2

SOURCE: Calculated from information gathered from Chilean biographical dictionaries, newspapers, and other sources by my assistants, Claudio Ramos and Matoia Cerda.

NOTE: Posts include Ministers of Interior, Foreign Relations, Defense, Finance, Economics, Justice, Public Works, Agriculture, Public Lands, Labor, Health, Mining, Housing, and Education, and the heads of the Central Bank and the Development Corporation.

[a] Numbers represent individuals rather than positions; that is, if one person held three different posts, he would be counted only once. A Minister can also fall into more than one category.

to synthesize the various types of data and to give a brief summary of the results. The rightist alliance seems relatively easy to characterize. The hegemonic member was the industrial-financial fraction of the bourgeoisie, with the agrarian bourgeoisie participating as part of the power bloc. From a look at the benefits received by the different classes under the government of the rightist alliance, it would appear that there were no allied classes but only supporting classes. That is, the bourgeoisie (and especially the industrial bourgeoisie) maintained all the benefits for themselves while the petty bourgeoisie, as well as those workers who voted for Alessandri, seem to have received no objective rewards for their support. It was probably for this reason that the support for the alliance fell off so sharply; the rightist alliance provided no tangible benefits for those who had thought they were allies. At the same time, the new centrist alliance managed to persuade large numbers of people from all classes that it could do a better job than the Right in distributing benefits (and therefore co-opting potential opposition) while maintaining the basic framework of the capitalist system.

The centrist alliance itself is somewhat harder to understand because it had at least two identifiable wings. On the one hand, there was the wing led by the modern industrial fraction of the bourgeoisie (and the construction sector); on the other, there was a group headed by elements of the petty bourgeois intelligentsia.* During the 1965–66 period, these two groups worked together, united through a strategy of modernization. In contrast to the rightist alliance, there were real allies in the centrist alliance. The allied classes were all those who would benefit from the modernization process: the landless peasants and farm workers who would be brought into the market economy through redistribution of land and increases in the minimum agricultural salary as well as the increased payments of agricultural salaries in money rather than in kind; the white-collar workers in the modern sector of the economy who would be brought into the market for durable consumer goods including automobiles; even the shantytown dwellers who would be given increased access to housing and education. All of these groups did gain; but the Frei government had made the mistake of promising more than it could provide, and, as a consequence, many former allies became dissatisfied and broke from the alliance. During 1966 and especially 1967, the two wings of the alliance began to distinguish themselves, the petty bourgeoisie urging a speedup of the government's reform program and the bourgeoisie demanding that it be slowed down. The relative power of the latter manifested itself as reforms were slowed down or reversed, and more members of the bourgeoisie began to assume positions of power in the government. Thus, the hierarchical nature of the centrist alliance changed over time. Although the modern industrial fraction of the bourgeoisie remained as the hegemonic member throughout, the composition of the power bloc changed. At first there were certain petty bourgeois elements participating, but these were replaced by other fractions of the bourgeoisie after 1967. At the end of the Frei regime, there was another shift as the majority of the bourgeoisie returned to support the rightist alliance, thus enabling the petty bourgeois wing briefly to retake control of the centrist alliance during the 1970 election. This control, however, was soon lost again following the defeat of the PDC candidate.

The leftist alliance also presents some difficulties in trying to analyze it. On the basis of the UP program and pronouncements, the nature of the alliance seems clear. Its hegemonic member was the blue-collar workers; the white-collar workers were in the power

*The term "petty bourgeois intelligentsia" is used to indicate that the fraction within the petty bourgeoisie that predominated in the leadership of the PDC left wing was mainly professionals rather than the industrial-commercial self-employed.

bloc; and the petty bourgeoisie formed an allied class. An examination of the data, however, calls into question the contribution of the petty bourgeoisie. The voting data show that the UP got only 23 percent of the petty bourgeois vote, compared with 49 percent for the PN and 28 percent for the PDC. Another study that tries to ascertain the contribution of the Radical Party (allegedly the representative of the petty bourgeoisie) comes to similar conclusions.* Furthermore, even though many sectors of the petty bourgeoisie did benefit from the policies of the leftist alliance, they were attracted into what was then the combined rightist and centrist alliances as supporting classes, i.e. on the basis of ideology. Some white-collar workers were also won away. The blue-collar workers, on the other hand, became increasingly supportive of the alliance as some who had previously backed the PDC switched allegiance. As can be seen in Table A.3, in mid-1972 the UP won over 80 percent of the blue-collar vote in the CUT elections (compared with only slightly over 50 percent of the white-collar vote). Thus, the idea of a worker–petty bourgeois alliance seems to have been more a statement of a goal on the part of one faction of the UP leadership than an actual reality. In its mass base, the UP alliance was largely working class, and especially blue-collar working class, although policy decisions were made to try to attract wider support.

ECONOMIC DEVELOPMENT IDEOLOGIES

A development ideology is defined as being composed of three parts: (1) an alliance's view of the proper role of the state in the economy (vis-à-vis the private sector), (2) its views on the proper role of foreign capital, and (3) the general goals of the alliance, with special emphasis on the relationship between investment and consumption. These factors will be examined for each alliance when it was in power through looking at election platforms, official government plans, and certain speeches of the President and key economic leaders. The latter are drawn especially from the two official messages presented each year to the Congress: the President's State of the Union message in May, and the report of the Minister of Finance on the budget and the general economic situation in November.

* This study shows that in the *comunas* where the PR was strongest in the 1960's, also most two-thirds showed a decline in the Allende vote between 1964 and 1970. Correlating the vote of the PR in the 1969 congressional election with the 1970 vote for Allende showed a slightly negative result. (See Robert Ayres, "Unidad Popular and the Chilean Electoral Process," *Studies in International Development*, 8 (1973).

63

Clearly, the information obtained from these sources is not seen as a substitute for actual policy analysis. The purpose of presenting this kind of data is to show the *general orientation* of the different regimes with respect to *who* should run the economy and *how* it should be run. The assumption is that the rhetoric contained in the speeches and documents can be accepted as a true reflection of the *intentions* of the different alliances. In actual practice, however, these ideologies came into contradiction with a series of structural constraints imposed by the Chilean economy, which tended to dilute many of the differences that appear on the ideological level. The results of these contradictions will be seen in the discussions in later chapters.

Role of the State

The economic role assigned to the state is one of the key elements with which to characterize an economic system. The rightist alliance, headed by Jorge Alessandri, believed that the strong role played by the Chilean state since the 1930's was one of the main causes of the economic problems from which Chile suffered. This strong state role had merely served to sap the energy of the private sector through high taxes, regulation, price controls, wage controls, and state ownership. Alessandri himself was a long-time advocate of a limited state role. During the 1940's, he was the most outspoken of the hard-liners within SOFOFA, advocating sanctions against private enterprises that sought or accepted funds from CORFO. As Finance Minister in 1947–50, he implemented a strictly laissez-faire policy.[12] Later he and the spokesmen for his regime returned to this theme:

Without any doubt, the inevitable consequences of the pernicious policies followed during so many years have been to lead people to expect the government to solve all their problems when, in reality, they can only be solved by the people themselves. The proper role for the public sector is to guide and stimulate private action by proper policies and to set an example through its own high standards of conduct.[13]

For a long time now, I have been denouncing the erroneous policies followed by the state in intervening in activities that are not its concern and that can be undertaken by the private sector. The result has been that the state has ignored functions that are its exclusive domain. For example, we should not be surprised by the serious crisis of the public works system, since state resources have been diverted to other ends rather than being spent on construction and maintenance of roads, ports, schools, irrigation projects, water purification, etc.[14]

64

We cannot and should not limit government spending on public works; this is the proper domain of the state. Where the government role must be cut is with respect to industrial activities. The state is not efficient as a producer. It should limit its activities to assisting and stimulating the private sector.[15]

The centrist alliance was much more ambiguous on the proper role of the state. On the one hand, it stressed the need for increased state participation in the economy, including participation as owner of the means of production. But, on the other hand, alliance spokesmen also stressed the importance of the private sector. To some extent, this ambiguity reflected the different views of different sectors of the Christian Democratic Party at different times. But, to a large extent, the ambiguity was simply the inescapable dilemma of those seeking a "third way" between capitalism and socialism.

The debate over socialism and capitalism is carried on in Chile amidst a flood of imported categories and phrases. But, in the meantime, reality continues its course. More than 70 percent of the national investment is carried out by the state; and, of the total national expenditures, the state constitutes almost 50 percent.

In these circumstances, to say that Chile has a capitalist system of development is as contrary to the truth as to say that the country has a totalitarian system. We do not propose for the country either a socialist road or a capitalist road, but one that emerges from our national reality and our national being, in which the state predominates as the administrator of the common good.[16]

The public sector has been the motor force of this process of growth, but it cannot be the only instrument of development. If we want a more dynamic economic development, it is fundamental that the system—which, I repeat, is a mixed economy—have a vigorous response from the private sector. It has been shown in modern societies, where the private sector is prosperous and dynamic, that this sector does not control political power and lacks electoral force. This is especially true where there are governments with popular support and orientation, as in the case of Chile.

The government, conscious of these facts and its role of protecting the social interest, has fully recognized the special function that the private sector represents in vast and varied fields where the state cannot replace it. We are prepared—I repeat once again—to continue adopting just and adequate measures to give the private sector necessary stability and guarantees and to stimulate its action.[17]

The closest the centrist alliance came to an operational definition of state and private spheres was to set three limits on private action:

The state might reserve for itself certain large industries or national services because of the power they represent, their necessary contribution to the economic progress of the country, and/or the indirect benefits they produce.

In certain cases, the state might decide to associate itself with private industry in those activities that, because of the size of the market or the large volume of resources they incorporate, have monopoly character.

The state will maintain a direct control (*tuición*) over the decisions of the private sector with regard to the economic integration of Latin America.[18]

Probably the most basic characteristic of the policy of the leftist alliance was the increased role to be played by the state in the economy. One of the primary instruments of state control was to be the Social Area (state-owned firms), which was to dominate the economy.

The importance of the public sector is traditional in our country. Approximately 40 percent of expenditure is public. More than 70 percent of investment is of public origin. Our government intends to make the public sector quantitatively more important still, but also qualitatively different. The public sector was created by the national bourgeoisie and has been used by the monopolies to rescue themselves from their financial difficulties, obtain economic support, and consolidate the system. What has characterized our public sector up until now is its subsidiary nature with respect to the private sector. All this will change.

The establishment of the Social Area does not mean the creation of state capitalism but rather the true beginning of socialism. The Social Area will be run jointly by the workers and representatives of the state, the latter being the link between the individual firms and the rest of the national economy. They will not be inefficient bureaucratic enterprises but highly productive units which will lead the development of the country and provide a new dimension to labor relations.

We must fortify the Social Area, making full use of state power in credit, fiscal, monetary policy, etc. But at the same time, we must help the small and medium industrial, commercial and agricultural proprietors who, during many years, have been exploited by the monopolists. Our economic policy guarantees them equal treatment. . . . The small and medium industries will have an active role in the construction of the new economy. Inserted in an apparatus more rationally organized and oriented to produce for the majority of Chileans, they will value the support of the Social Area. The limits of the private, mixed, and social areas will be established with precision.[19]

Role of Foreign Capital

The rightist alliance was a strong supporter of foreign capital, and Alessandri was quite candid in his explanations of why:

It is undeniable that it would be better for the future of the country to have investment, especially in the basic areas, come from national sources. However, to continue trying to do this will only exacerbate the current situation of economic stagnation, and we would have to adopt a policy of profound sacrifice for all, as happened in Russia. . . . I speak of sacrifices for all because, with full knowledge of our economic reality, I firmly believe it is an illusion to think that it is enough to impose them on the richest classes. This was what happened in 1939 [the Popular Front] and would cause a fleeting solution, with consequences a thousand times more serious than the present ones.

To increase the benefits of all, it is indispensable to create a climate propitious to the entry of important foreign capital which can considerably increase our production, thus avoiding greater sacrifices for the current generation even though we thus lower expectations for future generations.[20]

The centrist alliance was also interested in attracting foreign capital. Frei describes the situation:

It is a fact that the country does not have sufficient resources of internal savings to make the investments that are necessary to achieve full development. To give up foreign investment would lead inevitably to economic stagnation and put us in a situation of inferiority with respect to other countries of the world. It is the duty of the government not only to accept, but also to seek—in a manner compatible with the dignity and sovereignty of the nation—this type of investment.[21]

Frei adds that, in areas of high technology (such as chemicals, electronics, and automobiles), foreign investment, accompanied by technological know-how, is not only necessary but indispensable. The distinguishing feature of the centrist, as opposed to the rightist, policy on foreign capital was the emphasis of the former on joint foreign-state ventures. A CORFO publication explains why: "As we had expected, in cases of relatively large investments such as in the fishing, paper, chemical, metallurgical, and automobile industries, foreign capital will only come in when it is stimulated or supported by the state."[22]

This viewpoint was perhaps best exemplified in the plans for the chileanization of copper, which Frei explained in the 1964 campaign:

Foreign investments [in copper] will not be discouraged. On the contrary, we will try to establish with the companies a statute of international cooperation and of solidarity with national interests, expressed in a true association with the Chilean state. We will try to bring this about through audacious and imaginative new formulas, such as have been used in many countries, and such cooperation will be a necessary precondition for giving [the copper companies] the just and rational facilities necessary for the tremendous effort in investment and production which they will carry out in the country's interest. . . . An increase in production of more than 600,000 tons annually demands enormous investments, technical experience, and industrial equipment which Chile still does not have. These production and investment goals will provide a large influx of foreign exchange, high-quality workers for our industries, and thousands of high-paying jobs.[23]

The leftist alliance had a much more complicated position on the foreign capital problem. It simultaneously attacked foreign capital as the cause of many of the country's problems; proposed to nationalize the principal foreign holdings (i.e. the copper mines); declared that it was *not* against foreign investment per se; and solicited economic assistance from a new set of foreigners—the socialist countries.

The first two aspects are well expressed in the decree signed by Allende when the mines were nationalized on July 28, 1971.

In the course of our historical development, our nation has conquered by force the right to control its own destiny and to be owner of its own natural resources. This right is universally recognized today, and Chile is exercising it in nationalizing the large copper-mining companies. . . . It is being done in terms that are socially justified, theoretically founded, and scrupulously executed.

The international economic relations through which our people have suffered are based on a structure that is inherently unjust, that imposes on the dependent countries decisions that have been unilaterally adopted by the hegemonic countries. This unilaterality often violates publicly contracted promises and has gravely damaged the economic interests of Latin America, and of Chile in particular.

The formal equality that law and universal conscience recognize for all states is intrinsically limited, when not made laughable, by the use that some make of their power to subjugate others. It is not possible to speak of freedom and dignity in the relations between peoples when the fundamental means of production, the resources necessary for subsistence, have been appropriated . . . by a small group of large companies that seek their own profit at the cost of the underdevelopment and backwardness of the masses in the countries in which they are located.[24]

On the other hand, Economics Minister Vuscovic told the Alliance for Progress Committee (Comité Interamericano de la Alianza para el Progreso—CIAP) that Chile was not opposed to foreign investment, as long as it was implemented in such a way that the Chilean people would be helped rather than harmed by it.

We are not closed in any sense to the participation of foreign capital in the process we have initiated; on the contrary, we are interested in help that not only augments our own possibilities of capital formation, but that, above all, assists us in access to technological progress and helps us to be more active participants in scientific and technological development.

[On the other hand,] we have continually stressed our disagreement with the methods of participation that have frequently been used by foreign investment in our country in the past. Let me repeat it, with the positive desire to redefine bases that will permit increased participation [of foreign capital] under forms that make it fully in accord with the fundamental interests of the Chilean people.[25]

But, in the final instance, the leftist alliance believed that the vast majority of foreign assistance, whatever its form, would come from the socialist countries, not from the United States.[*]

Our efforts to amplify and strengthen relations of all kinds with the countries of Eastern Europe have been met by them with a clear interest which now has assumed concrete expression. In the increase of trade and collaboration with the socialist countries, our government sees a way of taking care of our own interests and stimulating the economy, technology, science, and culture, as well as a means of serving the working classes of the entire world.[26]

Relationship Between Investment and Consumption

The basic goals of the rightist alliance during the period it was in power were (1) economic growth, (2) stabilization, and (3) institutional reform so as to permit more private initiative and participation in the economy.[†] Higher consumption for the workers was not a goal per se because it was thought that this could only come from an increase in investment and production, rather than redistribution. This was the famous "trickle down" theory, which says that, if resources are provided to the capitalist class, this will encourage the capitalists to invest, which will provide greater employment and —eventually—higher salaries through increased productivity. Alessandri explained it in the following way:

I am the first to recognize that the conditions of life of an immense part of our citizenry are absolutely deficient and that, in general, salaries are low, including those in public administration. This situation forces people to maintain a way of life that makes them feel smothered and creates a climate of rebellion. The only way to escape from this state of affairs is through an increase in production. Nothing is gained from huge salary increases, which inevitably give way to a rapid and constant decrease in the purchasing power of wages and salaries.

[*] Interest was also shown in assistance from other capitalist countries in Western Europe and Japan.

[†] Neither in 1958 nor in 1970 did Alessandri have an electoral platform per se; he preferred to leave his ideas and plans vague. For one discussion of his goals, drawn from a variety of campaign and presidential statements, see Theodor Fuchs and E. Alejandro Yung, "Aproximación al análisis del impacto de la política económica sobre el desarrollo industrial en Chile, 1958–68" (Memoria de Prueba, Facultad de Ciencias Económicas, Universidad de Chile, 1970), pp. III-9-13.

Those who insist that this situation can be resolved immediately through redistributing the current wealth of the country are lying or committing a grave error. The most obvious proof of what I am saying is the impossibility of achieving any type of financing worthy of consideration for any new fiscal necessity based solely on taxing those with high incomes.[27]

This position of the alliance was followed up in two more specific ways—on wage increases and taxes. Alessandri had long maintained that wage readjustments that approached 100 percent of the increase in the cost of living of the previous year would hurt the workers. This theme was reiterated in his November 1960 statement, explaining why the CUT's wage demands would not be met.

I want to react against the grave error that would be committed by raising wages and salaries in the same proportion as the increase in the cost of living, because this would be translated into the creation of a purchasing power greater than the country could support and increases in costs that could not be absorbed by the capitalists, thereby leading to a violent increase in prices. The application of this system produces a situation whereby the purchasing power of the workers is increased considerably above reality in the first months and then decreases at an alarming rate in the following months, placing them in a grave situation.[28]

With respect to taxes, Alessandri said the following:

High taxes on the upper class might appear to be the solution to Chile's lack of capital. In reality, however, the effect would be just the opposite. If taxes are too high, the owners of firms will not invest because it will not be worth their while. This is what has happened in the last twenty years, and the result has been the decapitalization of Chilean industry.[29]

The centrist alliance had a much more ambitious program when Frei was elected President in 1964. The proposed goals included (1) increased economic development (modernizing agriculture, increasing exports, expanding mining, expanding industry, increasing housing); (2) education (literacy, primary, secondary, and university); (3) social justice (agrarian reform, tax reform, reform of the Labor Code, reform of health care, reform of social security, reform of the commercialization policy, and economic stability); (4) participation (increased suffrage, reform of the public administration, creation of neighborhood organizations); and (5) national sovereignty (Latin American integration, protection of prices of raw materials, diplomatic relations with all countries).[30] As was pointed out, however, in a critique of the Frei years made by a member of the Christian Democratic Party, in spite of the potential conflict existing between some of these goals, no system of priorities was established among them.[31]

In particular, with respect to investment and consumption, the alliance saw no inherent contradiction. The compatibility and mutual necessity of the two was stressed by Frei's Minister of Finance, who explained that such a joint effort "has seldom been attempted by any government regardless of its political or economic system."[32]

We have tried to find a harmonic combination of the objectives of economic development and social justice. To have put the accent exclusively on the social aspects, neglecting the objectives of economic growth, would have meant raising the level of income without a complementary increase in the supply of goods and services, which would have created strong inflationary pressures. But, in addition, it would have provoked a strong decrease in the rate of growth of the economy, since social investments do not bear fruit in the short run; on the contrary, they take a long time to mature. On the other hand, an exclusive emphasis on economic development would have meant noncompliance with the clear popular mandate of carrying forward social reforms and of advancing quickly in the redistribution of income and national wealth. Therefore, the decision of the government was to move forward in a parallel way in both areas of national life as the only way of avoiding incompatibilities that would make impossible the fulfillment of the goals that the people have proposed.[33]

An important aspect of this simultaneous increase in consumption and investment was the wage policy, which was explained by Finance Minister Sergio Molina:

In the past, there have been various attempts to stop inflation by reducing the purchasing power of the workers. This government thinks that this measure has been abused in the extreme, and the moment has arrived to stop the deterioration of the economic situation of this large sector of the population. Therefore, in 1965, we will readjust wages and salaries at 100 percent of the increase in the cost of living in 1964, without limiting this readjustment to the minimum salary and the minimum wage, as the existing legislation provides. However, those receiving wages and salaries, like all other Chileans, must contribute to the battle against inflation. Therefore, the government proposes that from today, and until December 1965, the unions renounce all attempts to gain wage increases that are above the increase in [last year's] cost of living.[34]

Another important feature of the program of the centrist alliance was the role of education and technology. Frei discussed this matter during the 1964 campaign:

The goal of our administration will be not only to have the economy grow faster, but also to have the fruits of that growth distributed more evenly among the people. There are two ways this can be done. One is to invest in the education of the people; if every Chilean were to have at least a primary education—and a secondary education would be even better—this would increase productivity, and we could produce more. But it would also decrease the gap between incomes caused by different levels of education. The other road is to increase the use of technology. Technology also increases productivity and so has effects similar to those of improved education.[35]

Finally, however, it became obvious that these "automatic" methods of making investment and consumption compatible were not working. At the end of 1967, the government proposed a new mechanism—a forced savings plan to which both employers and employees would contribute. The resulting funds would be used to establish industries that would belong to the workers. Molina introduced the plan in his report to the Congress:

If the country does not make an effort to limit the growth of its consumption and direct a greater percentage to savings and investment, we will inevitably be faced with an increasing inflationary process and we will return to having a low rate of growth, with the consequent increase in unemployment. . . . Therefore, we have decided to propose a program that permits us to overcome these problems. The program includes voluntary incentives to save and the creation of the National Workers' Fund.

Among the objectives of the Fund will be: (a) Participation of the white- and blue-collar workers in the ownership of national capital, and, consequently their access to property of public or private enterprises, obtaining the benefits they produce either through profits or through the increase of the value of their assets. . . . (b) Achievement of a better distribution of the national income in benefit of the labor sector. . . . (c) Creation of the Fund as a stable structural measure and a permanent national contribution for the achievement of the program of economic development and social reform.

Although an important part of this Fund will be contributed by the workers, we deny that it constitutes forced savings, since in the Fund "the savings of the workers will constitute their property and will be administered by them."

The revolution and the great social and economic transformations are not made by consuming more, but by creating the instruments of power that enable us to influence the national structures. Obtaining this power is not free, nor is it achieved through speeches or words; rather, it must be based on ownership of the means of production achieved through effort and sacrifice, however difficult it may be at a given moment.[36]

The aims of the leftist alliance were broader than those of either of the other two regimes. According to the Basic Program of the UP, they included (1) the creation of the new state (replacement of the Congress by a unicameral Popular Assembly, economic planning, reorganization of the system of justice, incorporation of the military into the social life of the country, with the consequent end of their use to repress the people); (2) the creation of the new economy (the

Social Area and Mixed Areas to complement the existing Private Area; extension of the agrarian reform; economic development—more emphasis on basic consumer goods, jobs for all, rapid growth, end of subordination to foreign capital, monetary stability); (3) social tasks (higher salaries, social security, health, housing, status of women, end to legal division between blue- and white-collar workers); (4) education and culture (democratizing of the education system, use of media and cultural forms to create a "popular culture"); (5) international independence (end treaties, loans, or investments limiting Chile's sovereignty; nationalization of natural resources; solidarity with liberation struggles and countries trying to institute socialism).[37]

With respect to the investment-consumption problem, the leftist, like the centrist, alliance saw no inherent contradiction between the two. The mechanisms involved in avoiding the *potential* contradictions, however, were different. In the UP view, two steps were involved. First, wages would be raised at the expense of profits; this, it was acknowledged, would tend to break the investment incentive of the private sector. Therefore (the second step), it would be necessary simultaneously to expropriate significant parts of the private sector so that the state could take over the bulk of the accumulation process (operating at a lower rate of "profit"). The following citations from the major UP economic leaders explain this process:

With respect to wage readjustments, the agreement signed between the government and the Central Unica de Trabajadores [CUT] has established certain principles. In general, it stipulates a readjustment equivalent to the deterioration experienced by wages and salaries during 1970 due to the increase in the cost of living, and in greater proportions in the case of those with the lowest income and some traditionally backward sectors. The readjustment policy, however, would be useless if its effects were to be transferred into price increases, thus annulling the redistribution intent and causing inflation as a result. . . .[38]

In Chile, it is a fact that income to capital represents an excessively high proportion, even in comparison with many capitalist countries, and therefore the majority of the productive apparatus is capable of absorbing the readjustment by lowering profits rather than by raising prices. The price policy of the government clearly means lowering the profit rate per unit produced, with the effect that income to capital can only be compensated to the extent that levels of production and productivity are simultaneously increased, based precisely on the greater purchasing power of the workers.[39]

The preceding process cannot ignore . . . the requirements and necessities for the expansion of the economy, namely the process of savings and investment. The strategy, therefore, must combine the necessities of redistribution with the generation of savings. To do this, we count, on the one hand, on a system of public income and expenditures that already produces important quantities of savings in order to supplement the low savings propensities of the high-income groups. We also count on the surplus generated by the monopolies and foreign corporations which will pass to the Social Area and, finally, on the new surplus that will be generated by the entire economy when it is functioning at full capacity. Therefore, it is this combination of surpluses that must simultaneously achieve the objectives of redistribution and savings, being careful to maintain the necessary equilibrium so that the objectives of neither demand nor growth are frustrated.[40]

Once the existing idle capacity has been exhausted, it will be necessary to put much more emphasis on increasing the rate of capital accumulation. From the point of view of the private sector, this will be contradictory with the decrease in the profit rate, which means that the extensive and rapid growth of the Social Area must provide the key to the solution [of the investment-consumption dilemma].[41]

Before this discussion is closed, however, an important qualification must be added. At the same time that the UP economic leaders were presenting a theoretical model that would make higher investment compatible with higher consumption, another current was also at work. The inherent logic of the "Chilean road to socialism" meant that the UP must win an electoral majority that implied (or so it was thought) a significant increase in the standard of living of the population. Chilean socialism was thus identified from the beginning—especially in the 1970 campaign and the period preceding the April 1971 municipal election—with higher consumption. This attitude, of course, meshed closely with the type of demands on which the CUT had concentrated in previous decades. The combination would place serious strains on the UP economic strategy.

The ideologies of the three alliances, then, can be summarized as follows. The rightist alliance proposed what was a modified laissez-faire strategy. It advocated a minor role for the state which would be limited to providing infrastructure and credit in order to stimulate the private sector, which would be the motor force of development. Foreign capital would be invited in and given free rein in order to supplement national resources. In addition, foreign competition would be sought to increase the efficiency of national industry. The major aims of the alliance would be stability and growth, with increased investment and production considered essential prerequisites for higher consumption for the workers. Redistribution of income was not considered to be a viable alternative.

The development ideology of the centrist alliance represented an attempt to find a "third way" between laissez-faire capitalism and socialism. It was based on a much stronger role for the state in the economy which included state ownership of a part of the means of production, often in conjunction with the private sector; nevertheless, the private sector was still to be the dominant one. Foreign capital was considered necessary, but it would have to act under government control; this brought about the introduction of the 51–49 percent formula (for national and foreign percentage of ownership, respectively) for certain industries. The centrist alliance had a much broader set of goals than the previous government and seemed to see no contradiction between them. This included the goals of higher worker consumption and higher investment, which could be achieved, partly through direct redistribution from the wealthier to the poorer and partly through increased productivity.

The leftist alliance proposed to transform the economy in such a way as to prepare for a future transition to socialism. A key to this strategy would be a vastly increased role for the state, including the ownership of the "commanding heights" of the economy—the mines, key industries, the financial system, transportation, and communications. The private sector would continue to exist but in nonessential areas and integrated into a system of national planning. Foreign capital would also be allowed but only in minor partnership with the state and under strict controls. Higher consumption and investment were seen as compatible goals through the mechanism of an increased role of the state in the accumulation process and a decreased profit margin. At the same time, however, at least some members of the leftist alliance seemed prepared to sacrifice investment for consumption in the short run if a choice were necessary.

CHAPTER FOUR

The Alessandri Regime, 1958-64

THE PREVIOUS chapter described the three class alliances that governed Chile during the 1958–73 period, and it showed how the development ideologies of the three were related to the interests of the participants in the alliances. In the next three chapters, the purpose will be to show how the three alliances came to power and how their ideologies and political-economic programs were changed in the struggle over their implementation. It is crucial to understand that the three development models were not alternatives that could be selected at random and implemented in order to obtain desired results. Rather, the three were embedded in a specific historical context such that the failure of one model created the necessary preconditions for the appearance of another. In more specific terms, there was a progressive radicalization of the population as the traditional policies of Alessandri failed, making it possible for the more leftist Frei alliance to gain legitimacy and support. The failure of the Frei model, in turn, played the same role with respect to the Allende regime. Along with this radicalization, two related trends were developing over the 15 years: first was the increasing level of organization and class consciousness among both the workers and the bourgeoisie, and second was the increasing polarization between classes.

With respect to the bourgeoisie, three trends could be observed. First was the increasing unity—from the generalized internal squabbling under Alessandri, to the unity efforts among the large bourgeois fractions under Frei, to the unity of both large and petty bourgeoisie under Allende. Second was the increasingly broad, and more openly political, nature of the actions of the industrial bourgeoisie being analyzed here. This is striking, for example, when reading through the minutes of the meetings of the Executive Board of SOFOFA. Under Alessandri, discussion centered on points of economic policy such as tariffs and exchange rates as they affected industry; these topics obviously had strong political implications though a technical veneer. Under Frei, attention turned to the constitutional amendment on property and the agrarian reform. Finally, under Allende, there was frequent discussion of the general state of "breakdown" to which the government had brought the country and the need for general political opposition. Third, then, was the increasing activism of the industrialists. Under Alessandri, they operated through behind-the-scenes persuasion and occasional threats to publish declarations in the press. Under Frei, they took the unprecedented step of a campaign to influence public opinion. And, under Allende, they participated openly in rallies and, ultimately, joined in the campaign to overthrow the government.

The trajectory of the workers was less clear. Their unity ebbed and flowed. Perhaps it was greatest under Alessandri when the enemy was clearest. The greatest period of organizational disunity was the first four years of the Frei administration, when the Christian Democrats purposely tried to divide the labor movement. Organizational unity returned by the end of 1968, but it was followed by a growing disagreement on tactics under Allende—although, when necessary, the workers closed ranks against bourgeois aggressions. Like the bourgeoisie, the workers' tactics changed when they were in and out of power. Under Alessandri and Frei, their influence was primarily through strikes of various kinds and congressional battles by their party representatives; under the UP, their main influence was exercised behind the scenes. Finally, a trend can be seen in the goals of the working class. Under Alessandri, the workers were on the defensive, primarily concerned with trying to maintain their standard of living. Under Frei, their objective economic situation began to improve, and during the last three years, more (though not primary) attention began to be turned to the issue of power. Under the UP, although the workers were temporarily diverted through strong emphasis on increased purchasing power, the focus on power became much stronger until it finally eclipsed the stress on economic demands. The legacy of the CUT's history of economistic orientation, however, still had powerful effects.

Although the clash between workers and bourgeoisie largely determined the activities of the state and the foreign sector, a few separate comments can be made on their roles. The role of the state changed in quantitative terms—it became ever stronger over the course of the 15 years—and in qualitative terms—it changed from primarily serving the interests of the bourgeoisie under Alessandri and Frei to serving the workers under Allende. The role of the foreign sector likewise shifted, from "helping" the government (in its own peculiar way) under Alessandri and Frei to actively opposing it under Allende.

In terms of timing and sequence, there was a strong underlying pattern that recurred during each of the three regimes, even though the content of the programs and the identity of the actors were very different. In each case, there was an initial period of apparent success in implementing a political-economic program that was consistent with the development ideology of the regime (1959–61, 1965–66, November 1970–September 1972). This initial period, however, was followed by a crisis period which caused the breakdown of the program; the breakdowns resulted from contradictions in the programs themselves and/or in the tactics used to implement them (1961–62, 1967, October 1972). The third period was then one of drift on the part of the government and attempts to take stock and realign themselves on the part of the various class forces (1963–64, 1968–70, November 1972–September 1973). These patterns will be followed for each regime, with particular attention paid to events and policies that were of major concern to the industrial sector.

THE BOURGEOIS OFFENSIVE, 1958–61

Presidential Election, 1958

The 1958 election was a major turning point in Chilean history because, for the first time, political forces were clearly divided along class lines. This is not to say that politics had not been organized on a class basis before, but now the various forces had coalesced. The bourgeoisie were strongly behind Jorge Alessandri, who was one of their own in personal as well as ideological terms. Alessandri was running as an "independent," but it was clear that he was an independent of the Right. His candidacy was backed not only by the

Liberal (PL) and Conservative (Partido Conservador Unificado—PCU) parties, but he also received the enthusiastic backing of SOFOFA and the other bourgeois organizations. The working class parties had managed to overcome their differences and unite in the Popular Action Front (Frente de Acción Popular—FRAP) and nominate Socialist doctor and Senator Salvador Allende. The FRAP was the "hard core" Left—the Socialist (PS) and Communist (PC) parties —without coalition partners as they had had during the Popular Front and successor governments. Only the so-called middle sectors were still divided. The 1958 election marked the first serious confrontation between the long-time representative of the petty bourgeoisie, the Radical Party (whose candidate was Luis Bossay), and the new contender for their support, the Christian Democrats (whose candidate was Eduardo Frei).* Nevertheless, the three blocs were clarified as never before. The platforms of the candidates expressed major differences, although the situation was not polarized to the extent that it would be later.[1]

Although the candidates were nominated in August and September of 1957, the character of the campaign was not really established until a March 1958 by-election in Santiago's Third District. This contest was won by the PCU-PL candidate, and many saw it as foreshadowing the outcome of the presidential election. The result was the formation of a Left-Center congressional bloc called TOCOA (Todos Contra Alessandri—All Against Alessandri). The TOCOA formula was also followed in the campaign as Allende, Frei, and Bossay made few attacks on each other but concentrated on Alessandri.[2] The outcome of the election, however, was probably decided not among the four major candidates but by a fifth—the so-called "Priest of Catapilco," Antonio Zamorano. Zamorano was actually a defrocked priest who had been elected to the Chamber of Deputies in March 1957 on the FRAP ticket. Running a campaign attacking the large landowners and generally defending the interests of the poor against the rich, he received 41,000 votes, while Alessandri beat Allende by only 33,500.† The final results were as follows: Alessandri, 389,909 (31.6%); Allende, 356,493 (28.9%); Frei,

---

* Frei came very close to being the candidate of the Right as well. The majority of the Liberal Party were ready to nominate him in their convention in 1957 when the main anti-Frei speaker, Senator Raúl Marín Balmaceda, fell dead of a heart attack. The decision was therefore postponed, and, in the meantime, backers of Alessandri pushed his nomination through the Conservative Party convention. In the interests of unity, the Liberals followed suit.

† Some see Zamorano's candidacy as having been supported by the Right in order

255,769 (20.7%); Bossay, 192,077 (15.5%); and Zamorano, 41,304 (3.3%). (See Table A.1 for all election data.)

The Bourgeoisie to the Helm

The Alessandri government, inaugurated on November 4, led to an attempt by the Chilean bourgeoisie to retake direct control of the state apparatus. It was the first time in 20 years that a member of the bourgeoisie had held the presidency, and the industrialists welcomed the victory enthusiastically. "It constitutes a great honor for our association that such a distinguished man as Alessandri has emerged from our ranks to become President of the Republic," a SOFOFA publication exulted.[3]

Taking advantage of their return to power, members of the bourgeoisie began to occupy important government positions that had previously been held by politicians or técnicos.* These included positions at the level of ministers, subsecretaries, and heads of departments. In the first cabinet were found several industrialists and landowners; the rest of the cabinet was composed of professionals with long experience in working in private corporations. At the subsecretarial level, the situation was perhaps more striking, since several prominent SOFOFA members were named to major economic posts, including Luis Marty in Economics, Jorge Fontaine in Mining, and Patricio Huneuus in Transportation. An example of the close relationship between these new appointees and other members of the bourgeois class can be seen in the case of the important Foreign Exchange Committee of the Central Bank. Upon being named chairman, Abelardo Silva informed SOFOFA of his intention "to direct all his actions to the national interest and therefore to be at the orders of SOFOFA in all activities that have to do with the industrial sector."[4] Relations with the Ministry of Finance were so close that SOFOFA members were told that they should channel all their suggestions directly through the Ministry, going through Congress only when it was indispensable.[5]

Unlike Frei and Allende, who succeeded him, Alessandri did not

---

to take votes away from Allende. See, for example, Fernando Casanueva and Manuel Fernández, *El Partido Socialista y la lucha de clases en Chile* (Santiago, 1973), p. 200.

* In some cases, these posts were automatically vacated when the new government took office. In others, Alessandri defied precedent and forced longtime técnicos out of their positions. This happened both in the case of the president of the Central Bank and the general manager of CORFO. See the analysis in Marcelo Cavarozzi, "The Government and the Industrial Bourgeoisie in Chile, 1938–64" (Ph.D. dissertation, University of California, Berkeley, 1976).

have a detailed political-economic program when he came into office. In the campaign, he had confined himself to talking in general terms, placing major stress on the need for moral leadership in government and the withdrawal of the state from many of its economic functions. The essence of the economic program involved the lowering of taxes and the dismantling of many of the controls that the government had used to regulate the economy for decades. These included the controls on prices, wages, imports, and foreign exchange movements. In addition, the government would restrict its activities in industry and commerce to an absolute minimum, confining its role to providing infrastructure such as roads and power plants. The presumption was that the private sector would quickly move in and take over functions previously performed by the state, thus again becoming the leading sector of the economy.[6] On the other hand, the Alessandri economists were realistic enough to realize that such a transformation could not come about overnight, and two kinds of transition measures were foreseen. First, the government itself was prepared to increase its investment at the beginning of the period in order to stimulate private investment later on. Second, the government would try to attract foreign capital, both to finance some of its own expenditures and to assist in domestic capital formation.[7]

The two main substantive goals of the Alessandri regime were stabilization and growth, both of which were of primary concern for the industrial bourgeoisie as well as the workers. These goals were closely interconnected, since the Alessandri economists saw inflation as being caused by insufficient supply (rather than excess demand as indicated by the Klein-Saks analysis). The basic idea was that, since the Popular Front period, the purchasing power of the population, especially the labor sector, had increased significantly without being accompanied by sufficient increases in production. In addition, the economic policies had placed ever-increasing tax burdens on corporations, along with higher salary costs, without creating the necessary conditions for capitalization. The solution was seen as freeing the economy from the restrictions that had been imposed and reducing the amount of state intervention. Together with giving incentives for buying equipment and so elevating productivity in the factories, this policy would lead spontaneously to stability and growth.[8]

The Alessandri Keystone: Stabilization

The basic economic package of the Alessandri regime was presented to Congress by Economics and Finance Minister Roberto Vergara in November 1958. It consisted of four policies: (1) wage increases only in line with productivity, with the exception of one single increase in 1959 equal to the previous year's inflation rate; (2) elimination of the fiscal deficit through lowering fiscal expenditures and obtaining foreign loans; (3) the establishment of a single fixed exchange rate and the elimination of controls on foreign trade; (4) a general freeing of state controls on foreign and domestic capital, although retaining exemptions from taxes and import duties, with the intention of increasing private sector investment. If there had ever been any doubt about whose interests were represented by the Alessandri government, these were now dispelled; stabilization would be achieved at the expense of the workers.

The CUT was firmly opposed to what it saw as the basic principle behind the stabilization program—that wage increases were the main cause of inflation and that they should, therefore, be less than the cost-of-living increases. Two interviews were held with Alessandri, on November 29 and December 22, and a document was presented to the President, denouncing the "false theory" on which the stabilization program was based. The document also made various economic demands including a 100 percent readjustment, equalization of the minimum wage and minimum salary as well as equalization of family allowances for white- and blue-collar workers, and a quarterly wage readjustment.[9] Alessandri denounced labor opposition to the economic policy as a "call to sedition" and said he would act with "inflexible rigidity" against any attempts to "subvert public order."[10] A CUT convention was called for February 1959; it ratified the positions that had been presented to the government and authorized the National Executive Council to call a general strike in support of the demands when it was deemed convenient. But the Council did not act, and the law was promulgated on April 2, 1959.

The CUT opposition contrasted strongly with the bourgeoisie's satisfaction with the Alessandri program. SOFOFA had been intimately involved in its preparation, presenting 42 recommendations either through the President or through representatives in Congress. The great majority were accepted, including those on the readjustment of wages and salaries in the public and private sectors, financing of family allowances, and unemployment benefits. Recommendations on tax policies that were accepted included avoiding increases in certain types of taxes and lowering the property tax assessment on industrial property.[11] As an expression of their support for the government, the SOFOFA board of directors advised their members that "they had the duty to end the system of calculating their costs of production with excessive margins of protection and security and, on the contrary, they must make sacrifices" in order to assist the government with its stabilization program.[12]

Because of the existing state of recession in early 1959, the program was to consist of two phases: first, reactivation of the economy through increasing demand and, second, a clampdown on policies considered to be inflationary. Phase I took place in 1959. In order to increase demand, workers were given wage readjustments that were approximately equal to the previous year's inflation; at the same time, government investment in housing and public works was greatly increased. These factors, along with its own internal problems and the "collective spirit" that prevailed in the country, generally defused the CUT's protests.[13] At the same time, the industrialists found themselves delighted with their new close relationship with the government and the important stimulus to production. Together with the favorable international situation, these factors made 1959 the honeymoon period of the Alessandri regime.

In 1960, however, Phase II was initiated, and discontent began to mount as Alessandri proposed a 10 percent wage readjustment compared with a 38 percent inflation rate the previous year. The workers demanded a full 38 percent readjustment, and a 24-hour general strike was held to support this demand. It was followed by a series of strikes by individual unions in hopes of breaking the stabilization program: 40,000 workers went on strike from the copper and coal mines; telephone and electricity services; metal, textile, and construction industries; 40,000 teachers also went on strike. The government called the strikes all part of a "subversive plan."[14]

The climax of the 1960 protest efforts by the CUT came in November. The 10 percent readjustment bill was still being debated in the Congress when the Labor Committee of the Chamber of Deputies raised it to 38 percent (the previous year's inflation rate). Alessandri responded by withdrawing the bill altogether and, on November 3, gave a radio address justifying his action. At the same time, the CUT held a demonstration where President Clotario Blest called for a march on the presidential palace. Demonstrators marched toward the center of town, damaging windows and cars on the way. The police opened fire on the crowd, killing two workers and wounding 35.[15] The FRAP and the CUT responded by calling a 24-hour general strike for November 7 and a mass demonstration in honor of the victims, who were described as "martyrs against the stabilization program."[16] The strike was complete in government activities, transportation, mining, and many industries. The CUT emerged considerably strengthened, since the strike exceeded the most optimistic expectations, and it turned to negotiate with the government.[17] A petition was sent to Alessandri demanding a 100 percent readjustment for all workers, the retirement of suits against union leaders (including release of CUT president Blest who was arrested for subversive activities), and the end to reprisals. Alessandri gave a long reply on November 22.

No one who has knowledge of national problems can be unaware that there is no possibility that the economy of this country can afford the readjustments that are proposed. In the public sector alone, they would represent an expenditure of 140 million escudos, and everyone knows the notorious difficulties in financing a tenth of this amount for the teachers' raise. Consequently, it can be categorically stated that this payment can be made only by an increase in the money supply, which will result in a violent and monstrous increase in prices. . . .

The situation that would be created in the private sector is no less explosive, since, in accord with the new policy put into practice by the government, readjustments made by the private sector have been at the cost of profits. Therefore, at this point of the year, employers do not have the funds to pay for a major readjustment and will be forced to immediately raise prices in order to cover the new costs.[18]

The final result was a 15 percent salary increase retroactive to January 1960.

The stabilization program, of course, had been very unpopular among many sectors of the population. The opposition of the workers and the Left in general had been expected, but in addition the Radicals were opposed, as were the Liberal and Conservative parties to a lesser extent. The Radicals were against the program insofar as it hit wages of public sector functionaries, who had long been the main base of support of the Party. The Liberal and Conservative opposition arose mainly because they felt excluded from policy making by the regime, which preferred to work directly with the bourgeoisie and certain técnicos rather than through the party system. The three parties joined in demanding the resignation of economic czar Vergara, who, as the occupant of three ministries—

Economics, Finance, and Mining—was seen as responsible for the government economic policy. Alessandri was forced to abandon his chief economic adviser, since, in the face of growing opposition especially from labor, there was a need to incorporate the rightist parties more fully into the government.*

The March 1961 congressional elections showed that government support had been seriously eroded. The results caused the rightist parties to rethink their positions, saying that support of the capitalist system did not mean that they would not permit some reforms.[19] A more concrete consequence of the electoral losses was the official incorporation of the Radical Party into the government coalition, as a result of the Liberals and Conservatives losing control of the Senate.† Although the Radicals had informally supported the government since 1958, they now accepted four cabinet positions, including the installation of Luis Escobar Cerda as Minister of Economics. Various concessions were made by the government, including the passage of a wage bill of 16.7 percent retroactive to June 1961 and the approval of a 100 percent automatic readjustment, to begin on January 1, 1963, equal to the change in the Consumer Price Index during the previous year. This, in itself, posed a serious setback to the government program, and might have been enough to cause its breakdown. Further problems, however, were also accumulating.

The Test of Laissez-faire

If the Alessandri strategy were to work in Chile, it was obvious that the private sector had to be both willing and able to take the lead in the process of capital accumulation. The government was prepared to do some pump-priming in the beginning, and so fiscal investment was increased by 33.5 percent in 1959 and 23 percent

* Vergara's departure was an example of the occasional differences of opinion between the class organizations and their political party representatives. That is, Vergara had gotten along very well with SOFOFA, which lamented his dismissal as follows: "[When making important decisions], he always listened to our opinions first. The Ministries of Finance and Economics [both headed by Vergara] have always maintained an open-door policy for SOFOFA, expressing at all times great cordiality and welcoming all of our suggestions." See Sociedad de Fomento Fabril, *Memoria* (1960).

† Control, in this case, meant one-third plus one vote. Chilean presidents had additive as well as item veto powers on all laws. After Congress had approved a law, the President could veto a particular article and propose an alternative. Sustaining the veto merely required that the Congress be unable to override it by two-thirds in each house. The tendency was to accept the President's version rather than have no law at all—particularly in the case of wage and salary legislation, where no law meant no increase at all.

in 1960.[20] At the same time, it was announced that the State Development Corporation (CORFO) would stop its direct investment programs and confine itself to providing credits for the private sector. Private sector response, however, was disappointing.

In the key industrial sector, private national investment actually declined in both relative and absolute terms during the Alessandri period, even if public sector credits for private industry are included. This was in spite of the fact that one of Chile's leading industrialists was President of the Republic and that he was offering many kinds of incentives to stimulate private investment. Explanations for the lack of investment may, in part, be traced back to historical causes in the development of the industrial bourgeoisie in Chile; but there were also actions on the part of the Alessandri government itself that exacerbated the problem. For one thing, other types of investment were more profitable and less risky. For example, the founding of the Savings and Loan Associations in the early 1960's gave a tremendous stimulus to the private home-building industry, especially luxury apartments and houses for upper-middle-income families. The Savings and Loan Associations themselves provided an attractive financial investment outlet, since they, unlike other financial institutions, were allowed to readjust deposits according to the inflation rate in addition to normal interest payments. Also the interest paid by the Savings and Loans was tax-exempt. Investment in farmland was another popular alternative, or complement, to industrial investment, since it provided not only social status but also a means of tax evasion.*

A more important factor, however, was the Alessandri policy on tariffs. Alessandri wanted to increase the efficiency of Chilean industry by lowering tariff protection. The idea was that, faced with foreign competition, industrialists would have to lower their costs and increase productivity. Thus, in April 1959, freedom to import almost any kind of goods was decreed, although heavy import deposits were set on many goods that had formerly been prohibited. During the rest of 1959 and 1960, these deposits were gradually

---

* The method involved attributing profits to farms instead of factories because farms were taxed on a presumptive basis in relation to their grossly undervalued property assessments rather than on actual net profits. An industrialist could thus explain a high level of personal expenditure as coming from farm profits but pay little income tax because his factory accounts showed a loss. Finance Ministry personnel believed that this method of tax evasion was quite significant. I am indebted to Professor John Strasma of the University of Wisconsin, formerly of the University of Chile, for this information.

lowered, and the result was a flood of imports. This surely discouraged investment which had to compete. It should be added, however, that different sectors of the industrial bourgeoisie had different views on tariffs; in fact, this was one of the most common sources of intrabourgeois conflicts. An example was the situation in late 1959 when a conflict developed within SOFOFA between representatives of the lumber industry and the capital goods industries. The latter wanted higher tariffs so they could compete with the superior and cheaper products of the United States and Europe; the former wanted lower tariffs so they could afford to buy higher-quality foreign equipment rather than being forced to buy Chilean goods.[21]

The other possible source of private investment in Chile was foreign investment; Alessandri's stated proclivity toward foreign capital has already been discussed. In May 1959, six months after Alessandri took office, Roberto Vergara went to the United States to complete arrangements for loans of $130 million from 11 private banks, the U.S. Treasury, the International Cooperation Agency (predecessor of the Agency for International Development), and the International Monetary Fund (IMF). He predicted that U.S. public and private investment would increase by "several hundred million dollars" in the next three years because of the "climate of confidence" created by the Alessandri regime.[22] In April 1960, the government furthered its campaign to attract foreign investment by enacting a measure giving major incentives in terms of tax exemptions and guarantees of repatriation rights to foreign capital. A second such measure was passed in late 1961.

Foreign industrial investors, however, did not respond any more positively than domestic investors had done. Again there were various possible explanations—lack of tradition of industrial investment in Chile, hesitancy caused by the recent nationalizations in Cuba, recession in the United States—but Alessandri's tariff policy, which reopened the door for exports from the United States to Chile, partially counteracted the incentives he was offering through the new foreign investment laws. It was not until 1964 that large quantities of foreign capital began to flow into Chilean industry.

Perhaps an increased role for the private sector could have been fostered gradually over time, but time was not available. It would have been necessary for Alessandri's strategy to bear fruit rapidly in order to prove that such a project was viable in Chile. Before any such proof could come about, however, crisis overtook the regime through the very policies it had initiated in order to encourage and promote the private sector. Thus, the contradictions of the Alessandri program became apparent.

THE FOREIGN EXCHANGE CRISIS, 1961–62

The crisis that led to the breakdown of the Alessandri program manifested itself primarily in the foreign sector of the economy. The policy on imports was one of the main culprits. With restrictions lifted, or at least lightened considerably, imports began to increase rapidly—by about 86 percent between the first half of 1959 and the second half of 1961.[23] With exports increasing only slightly, this meant that the trade balance was becoming highly negative, as the following data (in millions of dollars) show:[24]

Year	Exports	Imports	Trade balance
1959	$457.2	$414.7	+ $42.5
1960	469.7	545.9	− 76.2
1961	465.4	618.8	− 153.4

There was also another aspect of the problem. As part of the search for foreign capital, the government had resolved to unify the exchange rate and maintain it at a fixed value after an initial devaluation. Thus, in January 1959, the escudo was pegged at 1.05 escudos to the dollar,* and this rate was held up as the chief symbol that was supposed to generate confidence in the government. The stable rate was also supposed to reduce inflation by ending the periodic increase in the prices of imported goods as well as to eliminate the temptation to speculate by buying foreign exchange instead of investing in productive assets. All foreign exchange controls were eliminated, and the establishment of dollar deposits was encouraged in the private banks. In this way, the government hoped to encourage the return of Chilean capital previously sent abroad and to attract new foreign capital. As has already been seen, long-term foreign capital did not arrive in this initial period. Short-term speculative flows, on the other hand, became much more important as foreign exchange reserves disappeared, a deficit built up in the balance of payments, and expectations of a devaluation increased.

The result was a crisis in late December 1961, and all foreign exchange transactions were closed down for three weeks. At the end

* The escudo changed in value drastically over the period being considered, going from one escudo per dollar in 1958 to over 300 per dollar in 1973 at the official rate. On the black market, a dollar brought close to 2,000 escudos in mid-1973.

of this period, there was a retreat back to many of the bureaucratic controls that the Alessandri government had previously abandoned. Import deposits were reimposed, as was the complete ban on imports of many kinds. In addition, a dual exchange rate was reestablished, with one rate for the importation of goods and another for tourism and capital movements. The latter was devalued by 34 percent in January 1962, but this had little effect on inflation. The main question, which still remained to be resolved, was whether the other exchange rate should also be devalued.

This continuing crisis became a source of serious disagreement among the government's supporters. The U.S. government and the IMF put strong pressure on the government to devalue the escudo, as did certain sectors of the industrialists and the rest of the bourgeoisie in a campaign led publicly by *El Mercurio*.[25] Other industrialists who had gone heavily into debt abroad opposed the devaluation, and, since it was clear that a devaluation would immediately accelerate the internal inflation rate, all parties representing salaried workers—including the PR—were also opposed. In the face of these conflicting pressures, the Alessandri government proved incapable of making a decision, and the uncertainty dragged out for the better part of a year. Government popularity continued to decline.* Finally, on October 10, 1962, Alessandri announced that the escudo would be allowed to float, which, of course, meant that there would be a de facto devaluation.

During 1962, the threatened devaluation of the escudo with the consequent increase in inflation caused many unions to strike, hoping thus to preempt the coming inflation by getting wage increases in advance. These included the workers of the copper mines, the State Bank, and the National Health Service. When the devaluation was actually announced on October 10, the FRAP immediately proposed a 40 percent wage increase rather than the government's 15 percent, and the CUT called a general strike for November 19. In the early morning, the response was light. Government offices, commerce, and transportation continued to function, although miners, teachers, and municipal workers, as well as workers in some large factories such as steel, joined the stoppage. Later, however, local demonstrations in support of the strike began in the

---

*In a by-election in September 1962, in Santiago's First District, the government candidate won, but in terms of gains since the previous election, the FRAP and the PDC were the winners.

shantytowns surrounding Santiago. Streets were blocked and private buses were stopped. In the area called José María Caro, a serious confrontation developed when residents attempted to block trains going south. A battle developed between citizens armed with stones and police armed with rifles and tear gas. Six civilians were killed and many wounded (including 30 policemen); 192 persons were arrested.[26] The incident created national concern, and the Minister of Public Works visited the area, where he was besieged by housewives complaining of lack of educational facilities, poor roads, and no garbage collection. With unusual foresight, Eduardo Frei reviewed the events and asked, "Are we building something positive in this country, or are we accumulating a foundation of hate in these people which tomorrow no one will be able to contain, neither one man nor any political party?"[27] The wage bill was quickly passed after the strike and its tragic aftermath. Although the government-sponsored percentage prevailed, it was obvious that the stabilization program—and with it the entire government strategy—was at an end.

PREPARATIONS FOR ELECTIONS, 1963–64

The government tried to combat the inevitable inflationary surge by a cutback in public sector expenditure and in credit to the private sector. This, together with falling real wages, caused increased discontent among many sectors of the population,* which was reflected in the results of the April 1963 municipal elections. The government parties (especially the Liberals and Conservatives) lost heavily while the FRAP gained slightly; the big winners, however, were the Christian Democrats, who went from 16 percent in the 1961 congressional election to 22 percent (see Table A.1). This made them the largest single party as they overtook the Radicals and almost matched the combined vote of the Communists and Socialists. The Party was jubilant, staging major demonstrations to celebrate,

*This discontent appeared within the ranks of the industrialists as well as the workers. SOFOFA's complaints against government actions increased enormously, and many of the bourgeois officials left their posts, to be replaced by politicians. The growing feeling of distance was epitomized by one industrialist who expressed his surprise about "the way in which a government like the current one, *which the industrialists consider as our own*, delays in granting an interview to the SOFOFA Executive Board. What will happen when there are enemy governments in power?" The SOFOFA president, however, said that the officers had immediate access to Alessandri when it was necessary. See Sociedad de Fomento Fabril, Actas de Sesiones del Consejo Directivo, May 7, 1962 (archive of SOFOFA, Santiago).

and a meeting of party leaders announced that the PDC would definitely run its own candidate in 1964.

Realignments

With the government program and coalition in disarray, all political forces began to take stock of their situation and to reconsider their alliances in view of the upcoming 1964 presidential election. Perhaps the key shift saw certain industrialists begin to cast eyes toward the PDC. Many had thought in 1958 that the traditional Right was being given one last chance to show it could govern the country. Now, with the failure of the stabilization program (the cost of living was up 9.2 percent during the first three months of 1963 in comparison with 2.5 percent for the same period of the previous year) and the election results as concrete evidence (Liberals and Conservatives together polled 23 percent in the 1963 elections, as compared with 32 percent in 1961), many Rightists were beginning to be worried.

Several types of moves were involved. First, there was an attempt to bring the Christian Democrats into the government coalition. Even before the April elections, the Liberals had issued such an invitation; the Conservatives were less specific but favorable.[28] Second was the participation of bourgeois representatives in pro-Frei groups, such as the Movement of Christian Democratic and Independent Professionals and Técnicos, which operated during 1963 and 1964 and prepared the Blue Book which became part of the Frei platform.[29] Third was another group that, although it claimed to have no political connections, surely supplied some of the Frei support among the bourgeoisie—the Union of Christian Businessmen (USEC).*

The candidates themselves were officially named. Radical Senator Julio Durán would be the candidate of the Democratic Front, the coalition of Conservatives, Liberals, and Radicals. His five-point platform emphasized "spiritual dignity" and "responsible democracy capable of meeting man's aspirations." Also included were the reforms that the Radical Party had insisted on when the Front was

---

* USEC was an organization of several hundred "capitalists with a conscience." Some were Christian Democrats, a few were members of the Liberal and Conservative parties, and many were independents. The main function of USEC seemed to be the organization of seminars on possible changes in Chilean enterprises in order to increase the motivation and skill level of the workers and thus to increase productivity—and, of course, profits as well.

formed: agrarian reform, tax and tariff reforms, and wage increases to keep up with the inflation rate.[30] Frei was named by the PDC Executive Committee, subject to confirmation by the party's national convention. PDC president Renán Fuentealba attacked the "capitalist regime" of Alessandri and rejected *rapprochement* with the Democratic Front.[31] Allende was again endorsed by the FRAP convention as its candidate. His program had eight points: (1) end unemployment; (2) boost consumer purchasing power; (3) overcome educational, health, and housing deficits; (4) nationalize all mines; (5) nationalize banking, credit, foreign commerce, the stock exchange, and public utilities; (6) "profound" agrarian reform; (7) promotion of economic development through industrialization and planning; (8) "profoundly democratize" the nation.[32]

The tenor of the campaign was foreshadowed as early as April 1963, when Frei was interviewed by the *New York Times*. The FRAP and the PDC had essentially the same objectives, he said, but the FRAP would rely on dictatorship while the PDC favored democracy.[33] Soon after the candidates were named, the FRAP met with Alessandri to outline complaints on certain campaign procedures, including anti-Communist leaflets and wall paintings, which they said were instigated by the U.S. embassy. *El Mercurio*, on the other hand, said the leaflets and paintings were the work of a far-right "patriotic" group called Chile Libre (Free Chile). The FRAP also protested the formation of the Guardias Blancas (White Guards)—right-wing shock troops that were to hassle the Left.[34]

The next eight months (July 1963–March 1964) were primarily ones of conflict and confusion in Chile. There were a large number of strikes, including the copper and coal miners, telephone workers, bus drivers, National Health Service, and the State Technical University.[35] More dominant, however, were intra- and interparty conflicts. For example, the PADENA (Partido Democrático Nacional), a small party that belonged to the FRAP, broke into three factions: pro-FRAP, pro-PDC, and pro-Jorge Prat (an independent ex-Nazi).

The Radical Party ministers resigned over a National Health Service controversy, when Congress passed a bill obliging the Central Bank to provide funds for the strikers and Alessandri vetoed it. Altercations (including physical ones) developed within the Democratic Front over support for the Front candidate Durán. The Liberal Party was forced to expel members who insisted on supporting Alessandri for a second term over Durán. Conservative Party President

Francisco Bulnes resigned in protest over members abandoning Durán, though his resignation was rejected. The Radicals continued divided, and former Radical President Gabriel González Videla reportedly saw Frei as the only alternative to a divided Democratic Front for preventing an Allende victory.

Similar divisions broke out within the FRAP. The anniversary of the Chinese Revolution in September provided the occasion for a public demonstration of such splits when three mutually critical gatherings were held. The Communists divided their time between expelling pro-Chinese members from the Party and attacking the Christian Democrats as lackeys of imperialism, recipients of foreign money, and tools of the Catholic Church. The always latent quarrels within the Socialist Party broke into the open in the form of divisions between groups headed by Secretary-General Raúl Ampuero and party ideologue Clodomiro Almeyda. The Trotskyites joined in, showering criticism on all.[36]

The economic situation became worse, and Alessandri was finally forced to clamp a price freeze on some 300 basic items in late February of 1964. More strikes occurred as Alessandri sent a wage bill to Congress, calling for a 25 percent readjustment (in comparison with a 45 percent inflation rate in 1963). The CUT called for 24- and 48-hour strikes against the bill and got a large response.[37] Later, transportation and municipal workers went out on strike.

Presidential Election, 1964

The presidential campaign can be seen as beginning with a by-election in the southern province of Curicó. This province was 90 percent agricultural and dominated by large landowners, who had traditionally sent fellow landowners or their representatives to Congress. This had been possible because, as in many rural areas in Chile, the Curicó landowners had bribed and threatened their workers and tenants to make sure they voted for rightist parties; they also manipulated literacy requirements so as to disenfranchise those known to support the Left.[38] In the last election (April 1963), the results had been the Democratic Front, 48.6 percent; the FRAP, 29.4 percent; and the Christian Democrats, 21.8 percent. All three presidential candidates visited Curicó. The FRAP ran a strong campaign in the by-election although not expecting to win; the PDC did likewise. Durán, on the other hand, was confident of victory and spoke of the election as a national plebiscite. The final result was a stunning victory for the FRAP, which received 40 percent, trailed by the PDC with 27 percent. These results completely changed the 1964 presidential election.

Alliances among the bourgeoisie and petty bourgeoisie quickly shifted in accord with events. Durán withdrew his candidacy to prevent Chile from "going Communist," and the Liberals and Conservatives decided to support Frei, thus opening the way for a two-way electoral battle which would pit Left against Right, workers against bourgeoisie.* Durán was renominated by the Radical Party itself, which hoped to become kingmaker in Congress if neither candidate should get an absolute majority.† The Left was euphoric over the victory, and Allende and Oscar Naranjo (the Curicó winner) embarked on a national tour that one leftist publication compared with Castro's cavalcade from the Sierra Maestra to Havana. Allende spoke to thousands of people when the group arrived in Santiago on March 19. He called the by-election an indication of the "failure of a social class, a regime, and a system." It was a moderate speech, however, urging Radical Party support. Allende said his government would not be socialist but "democratic, nationalist, and popular" on the road to socialism.[39]

Although the Durán candidacy continued, it was definitely a two-way race between Frei and Allende. The stakes were high for all concerned, for those outside as well as those inside Chile. The candidates' positions sounded similar on most issues: both supported agrarian reform, greater Chilean control over natural resources, and a greater share of income for the workers; both attacked unemployment. Debate, therefore, centered on the means to achieve these goals, and here the campaign became vicious. Frei himself said his campaign would not be based on "fear of Communism," but immediately thereafter said his election was "the only road for the

---

* Frei insisted that his program would not be compromised by his new supporters, but the FRAP thought otherwise, saying, "The wolf has taken off his sheep's clothing." See Foreign Broadcast Information Service, *Daily Report*, April 27, 1964.

† An alternative explanation of the Radicals' nomination of Durán focuses on two other factors. First, the traditional anticlerical stance of the PR made it likely that many Radicals would vote for Allende rather than Frei as the lesser of two evils. Second, the PR had big campaign debts, which it had no way to pay if Durán left the race. After announcing his intention to withdraw, Durán played golf with the chargé d'affaires of the U.S. Embassy, and the following day announced to his surprised Party that he would stay in the race. His participation, although only drawing 5–10 percent of the vote, could be expected to assure a Frei victory. (Information from John Strasma of the University of Wisconsin, formerly of the University of Chile.) Whether some of the U.S. funds coming to help the Christian Democrats actually were funneled to Durán is a question to be investigated.

country to take in order not to fall into Communism."[40] His supporters, however, sank to a lower level as a true campaign of terror was unleashed. In the shantytowns, for example, mothers were told that, if Allende won, their children would be taken away from them and put into concentration camps.[41] Cuba also became a big issue which the PDC used against Allende, quoting alleged interviews with the foreign press, saying that Chilean socialism would be like that in Cuba.[42] Durán showed film clips on TV of Castro saying he was not a Marxist, and then saying that he had been one all his life. Durán said this proved that Allende could not be trusted—even though he claimed he was not a Communist.[43] Former Cuban President Manuel Urrutia also wrote Allende an open letter, imploring him to "choose Chile over Russia."[44] In the last days of the campaign, a tape recording by Juana Castro was broadcast, discussing the "horrors" of Cuban socialism under her brother.*

The Left was not above demagoguery either, although they practiced far less of it. Their main contribution was to quote some statements made by Frei when he worked on the newspaper *El Tarapacá* in the 1940's. These statements were apologies for Mussolini, on the one hand, and statements about wage increases, labor legislation, and university reform, on the other, which the FRAP said were pro-Fascist and proved that Frei was the reactionary enemy of reform. The PDC said these statements were taken out of context and, furthermore, only reflected views in vogue at the time.[45] Frei emphasized these themes a few days before the election, saying, "There are two Lefts—the Marxist Left and the Democratic Left. We are the Democratic Left. Chile wants reform, but it does not want reform under dictatorship."[46]

The election was also of interest to those outside the country. The PDC accused the FRAP of receiving money and support from "international Communism," and probably there was some Soviet money used for campaign purposes. This, however, could not begin to match the U.S. contributions. U.S. policy makers were originally divided over whether to support Durán or Frei. The CIA, high-level echelons of the State Department, and the U.S. Ambassador to Chile, Charles Cole, favored Durán, while most other influential policy makers within the Kennedy Administration were oriented

---

* The tape was broadcast on several radio stations during the evening of September 2 (i.e. two days before the election), after the campaign had been officially closed. Allende requested and received national radio time to protest; the other candidates were also given time.

toward Frei.[47] After the Curicó election, however, support was unified behind Frei.*

A Frei victory was considered so important to U.S. interests that over $20 million of U.S. money was reportedly spent on the campaign, and at least 100 "special personnel" were sent from Washington and other Latin American countries to provide assistance.[48] A key U.S. intelligence official recalls, "U.S. government intervention in Chile in 1964 was blatant and almost obscene. We were shipping people off right and left, mainly State Department but also CIA with all sorts of covers."[49] An important U.S. policy maker on Latin America at the time of the election described the activities this way:

The State Department maintained a facade of neutrality and proclaimed it from time to time. . . . Individual officers—and economic counselors—would look for opportunities. And where it was a question of passing money, forming a newspaper or community development program, the operational people would do the work. AID found itself suddenly overstaffed, looking around for peasant groups or projects for slum dwellers. . . . Once you established a policy of building support among peasant groups, government workers and trade unions, the strategies fell into place.[50]

An ITT document adds, "The U.S. government sponsored and paid for special political polls, analyzed Frei's campaign, gave him extraordinary consolation and comfort, all under the friendly aegis of the U.S. Ambassador."[51]

Extra military personnel were also sent to Chile, but this kind of assistance proved unnecessary since the propaganda campaign had been so effective. The result was that Frei became the first Chilean President in over 20 years to receive an absolute majority of the votes. The results were: Frei, 1,406,002 (56.1%); Allende, 975,692 (38.9%), and Durán, 124,869 (5.0%). (See Table A.1.)

* But see p. 94n with respect to Durán.

CHAPTER FIVE

The Frei Regime, 1964-70

THE FREI PERIOD can be divided into three subperiods. First was the initial two years, when the government, trying to maintain its autonomy from the social class structure, successfully implemented many of the reforms called for in its program. This was followed by a crucial year of decision when the government was strongly pressured by both workers and bourgeoisie to take sides and either speed up or slow down its program. The government's solution to the conflict was a turn to the Right and a general drift as the momentum of its policy thrust was lost. As the government drifted, however, activity by social class organizations increased. Militancy and polarization also increased until, in 1970, the centrist PDC had no chance of maintaining control of the presidency.

REFORMS BY THE "NEUTRAL" STATE, 1965–66

The coalition of parties and groups that ultimately supported Frei in the 1964 election was very broad. For all practical purposes, it included everyone except supporters of the Communist and Socialist parties,* which meant that widely diverging views on policy matters were hidden under the façade of apparent unity. Three key groups could be identified in the leadership of this original broad coalition. First were the leaders of the Liberal and Conservative

---

* The Radicals had their own candidate, but even they did not support him wholeheartedly. Thus Durán received less than 5 percent of the vote, although the PR had regularly received at least 20 percent in elections over the previous decade.

parties, who supported Frei only because he was preferable to Allende, and who favored a continuation of Alessandri's policies. Perhaps their views can best be characterized in negative terms: they wanted the state to stay out of the economic sphere as much as possible, and they were especially against any kind of structural reforms. On the other hand, a small minority among the bourgeoisie were more farsighted; they realized that Chilean capitalism could benefit from a series of modernizing reforms, especially those of a sort designed to expand the market and to bring the state into partnership with certain new industries.* The third major sector of the Frei coalition consisted of progressive members of the petty bourgeoisie. They favored a set of reforms that appeared to coincide with the views of those who were called above the farsighted bourgeoisie. As events were to prove, however, there were at the very least serious differences between the two groups on how far these reforms should be carried. The Frei program was, therefore, enthusiastically supported by the latter two factions of his electoral coalition and reluctantly by the first. Very soon after the election, in fact, the Liberals and Conservatives began to oppose the government.

The program called for a wide spectrum of change in the Chilean economy and society. The "chileanization" of copper was the keystone of the program, since it was to provide additional resources for other items. Chileanization was to involve the purchase of 51 percent of the shares of the large copper mines currently owned by U.S. corporations. In addition, it would lead to a vast expansion in the production of copper, refining of all copper locally, production of copper products for sale abroad, and an expansion of international markets beyond traditional buyers. Economic growth was also singled out as a principal goal. The connection between chileanization and increased growth was obvious. A second crucial input to more rapid growth was an increase in agricultural output, which

---

* This division within bourgeois opinion was reflected within SOFOFA, where pro- and anti-government factions quickly appeared. For the first time, there was a contested election for the association's presidency, which showed that about one-third of the board of directors supported Frei and two-thirds were against. (Sociedad de Fomento Fabril, "Actas de sesiones del Consejo Directivo, April 21, 1965," archive of SOFOFA, Santiago.) There seems to have been slightly more support for Frei among the SOFOFA board members than among industrialists as a whole. According to one study, only 28 percent of a sample of industrialists claimed to have voted for the PDC in 1965 (19 percent said they voted for Frei in 1958). In terms of support for Frei's program (agrarian reform, wage increases, price controls, tax reform, etc.), 4 percent were very favorable, 14 percent gave moderate support, 26 percent gave limited support, 47 percent were generally opposed, and 8 percent were totally opposed. See Dale Johnson, "Industry and Industrialists in Chile" (Ph.D. dissertation, Stanford University, 1967), pp. 176, 229–32.

was closely connected to the agrarian reform to be discussed below. Other methods identified for increasing the growth rate included increasing industrial production, expanding the construction sector, and conquering new foreign markets.

Another category of goals involved social welfare. The expansion of construction already touched on this area, since it was primarily to be aimed at resolving the housing shortage. In addition, extension of education (basic, technical, and university) was foreseen, as were reform of the social security system and expansion of the health service. Increased social justice was to be obtained through an agrarian reform that would create 100,000 new proprietors (plus providing them with credit, technical assistance, seeds, fertilizer, marketing facilities, etc.); reform of the tax system to extract more from the wealthy; reform of the Labor Code to institute an open shop; a remunerations policy that would redistribute income toward the workers as well as equalize wages and salaries and family allowances between white-collar and blue-collar workers; a slowing down of inflation in order to maintain the value of wages and to order the economy; and full employment. Finally, greater political participation for all was called for.[1]

The advent of the Frei regime meant a major change in state personnel. The bourgeoisie and conservative politicians who had manned the Alessandri government were replaced by a group of relatively young, highly competent, and generally idealistic técnicos, most of whom represented the petty bourgeois wing of the PDC. Some members of this group received ministerial posts (e.g. Sergio Molina), but generally the ministries went to founders and longtime members of the Christian Democratic Party. The young técnicos were mostly placed in middle-level jobs in the ministries and the decentralized agencies (e.g. the Development Corporation or the Agrarian Reform Corporation) and other key places such as the Central Bank.

The enthusiasm and sense of mission of the PDC administration were strong, and they increased with the results of the March 1965 parliamentary elections. The Party won 82 of the 147 seats in the Chamber of Deputies and increased its representation in the Senate from 12 to 21 seats. (It could not win a majority of the Senate's 45 seats because only one-half were up for renewal; see Table A.1). On the basis of this majority, the Christian Democrats set out to do something quite new in Chilean politics. They sought to avoid identification with either the bourgeoisie or the working class, but demanded sacrifices from both in the name of a "communitarian" solution to national problems.* In terms of the earlier theoretical discussion, the Frei regime sought a much greater measure of relative autonomy than was the norm in class-dominated Chilean politics. During the 1965–66 period, this approach achieved substantial success, as will become clear in the following discussion of the industrial sector; there and elsewhere, many of the reforms called for in the Frei program were implemented. By the end of the biennium, however, opposition to the "neutral" state was beginning to build up on all sides.

Property Rights Amendment

The reforms of greatest interest to industry were the constitutional amendment on property rights, the proposed reform of the union system, and the stabilization program with its corresponding effects on wages and prices. The property rights amendment was introduced as part of a package of constitutional amendments in November of 1964. It proposed four major types of changes with respect to the previous article on property. First, it introduced the concept of the "social function" of property and the goal of "making it available to all." Social function was defined as (1) serving the general interests of the state, (2) improving public health and welfare, (3) providing better use of productive resources and energy in service of the collective, and (4) raising the living standards of the population. Second, the amendment strengthened the constitutional basis for state-owned property, saying, "When the interests of the community demand it, the law can reserve to the state the exclusive domain over certain types of property." Third, it empowered the legislature to establish the norms for the expropriation of and payment for property (rather than specifying these items in the constitution itself). And, finally, the amendment provided for a much broader system of deferred payment for expropriated property. Formerly, only in the case of uncontested claims, or property expropriated because it was abandoned or notoriously badly exploited, could deferred payment be employed.[2]

The essential purpose of this constitutional change was to establish the legal basis for the agrarian reform. The vagueness of many of the provisions, however, meant that it opened the possibility of

---

* The meaning of the term "communitarian" was always very vague, but the basic idea seemed to be an emphasis on the common interests of workers and owners. In negative terms, it was the rejection of the process of class struggle that the Marxist parties stressed.

much wider application. This was what worried the industrialists; they saw the amendment as an attack on private property in general. According to one member of the SOFOFA board, "This is a problem that will come down on us with all its force when it will no longer be possible to stop it. Everyone is convinced that it only affects agriculture when what is really at stake is the right to property itself."[3] In discussing tactics, many of the board members agreed with one who said,

The only thing we can do is to get as close as possible to the government with the greatest quantity of information and try to explain our point of view and bring about a change in the position of the government with respect to private property. We can't expect any other defense because the political parties that defend private property [i.e. the Liberals and Conservatives, now fused into the National Party] have been discarded and their action annulled.[4]

Others, however, were more militant, saying there was no reason for SOFOFA to simply accept the bill when everyone was aware that it opened the possibility for the current Congress or another later to expropriate all private activity. Also discussed was the possibility of tying up expropriations indefinitely through use of the courts.

This discussion intensified the conflict between the pro- and anti-government factions within SOFOFA (see p. 98n). Julio del Río Berthoud, a representative of the former, questioned whether the board was representative and strongly attacked the majority, saying, "Opposing the reform of property rights such as the Executive proposes is an attempt similar to trying to plug a volcano in full eruption." Pointing out that not all citizens currently had access to property, which was accumulated in a few hands, del Río said that the primary task of the industrialists should be to facilitate the access of property to those who had none. Not only should the amendment be accepted but it should also be supported.[5]

The quarrel became public in July, when the newsweekly *Ercilla* published an interview with Andrés Feliú, member of the so-called "rebel" faction. Feliú explained that Chilean industry had always operated with a large amount of idle capacity because of lack of demand. The Frei-sponsored wage increases, plus the new consumer credit policies, were helping to resolve this problem. The agrarian reform was crucial in this respect; if the peasants could be incorporated into the national market, industry not only would eliminate its idle capacity, but would have to expand rapidly to meet this new demand. "It is obvious that rapid progress toward modernization requires modification of the classic concepts about private property. I don't see how one can attack the idea of increasing the number of owners. The more there are, the better. There will be more who will have to defend it [private property]."[6]

SOFOFA made various attempts to change the bill, although realizing that it was necessary to act with "great reserve." The view of its members was that declarations or activities that became public knowledge would simply have turned opinion further against the bourgeois position. Work with respect to the Congress was concentrated on obtaining the passage of the least prejudicial bill at any given point. Finally they convinced Frei to consider vetoing the final bill, even though he had originally been against this procedure. SOFOFA was told to negotiate with the Minister of Justice, and the Minister's position would then be adopted by Frei. Working in conjunction with the Confederation of Production and Commerce (CPC), SOFOFA prepared a substitute bill, and a series of attempts were made to talk with the Minister and with Frei himself. Both the SOFOFA and CPC representatives were put off for several weeks and were finally informed that the Frei veto would affect only one portion of the bill; the intention would be to put the Executive in charge of the initiative for expropriations when deferred payment was involved.* The acting president of SOFOFA complained that the association "had been defrauded at the last minute when the President decided not to consult with us."[7]

Two months later, the breach between the industrialists and the government grew even sharper as the SOFOFA president openly attacked the government in a speech at the annual trade fair. Citing the property amendment, wage and tax increases, price controls, and other measures, he claimed that "in few periods of history have conditions been so difficult with respect to investment."†

Relations with Labor

Relations with the working class became equally as tense as with the bourgeoisie. The main characteristic of the labor movement during the 1965–66 period was a series of interrelated conflicts between the CUT and the government, on the one hand, and the

---

* This Frei proposal is said to have been requested by the copper companies to make sure that the Congress could not initiate any action against them based on the amendment.

† This attack brought an immediate angry response from the pro-Frei sector of SOFOFA. See declarations by eight SOFOFA board members and several member associations, as well as the speech itself, in *El Mercurio*, Nov. 16, 1966.

CUT and the Christian Democratic union groups, on the other. In fact, many observers considered that the PDC was anti–organized labor.[8] The emphasis was on those sectors of the population that had been left out—especially the peasants and "marginal" urban groups.* In addition to the government's general ignoring of the workers, when it was not denouncing them as a privileged group, there were three specific actions that illustrate this view. First, although stressing the need for the people to organize themselves, the government refused to recognize the CUT as a legal entity representing the workers. Thus under Frei, as under Alessandri and Ibáñez before him, the CUT remained a de facto organization. Second, there was an attempt to reform the Labor Code to permit more than one union per plant and to eliminate obligatory membership (the closed shop). This was seen by many Christian Democrats, as well as the Marxists, as an attempt to weaken the labor movement in general and the CUT in particular. Third was the repeated attempt to form rival labor confederations which the Christian Democrats could control.[9]

The first such attempt to form a rival labor movement was the drive to attract Christian Democratic workers by AISCh (Acción Sindical Chilena), a Catholic union movement formed in the early 1950's. William Thayer, Frei's Minister of Labor, was a leading member of AISCh and a strong proponent of the drive. Second was the formation of MUTCh (Movimiento Unitario de Trabajadores de Chile) by one section of the PDC immediately after the 1964 election. At the same time, the Comando Nacional de Trabajadores was formed by Santiago Pereira, PDC deputy and former leader of the CUT. None of these organizations had much success in attracting members; their main activity was agitation and propaganda. In fact, their only real achievement seems to have been the sponsoring of 1965 and 1966 May Day rallies where Frei was the main speaker. These rallies were copies of the traditional CUT demonstrations that had been held in Santiago's Plaza Bulnes every year since the CUT's founding. All of these rival organizations faded away, but not until they had further alienated the CUT from the government.

The conflict between the CUT and the Christian Democratic unions was closely connected to the government labor policies,

---

* The cynical explanation for the Christian Democrats' behavior, of course, was that organized labor was already controlled by the Communists and Socialists, while the peasants and marginal sectors were still available as potential PDC supporters.

especially during the 1965–66 period, when the PDC union members still strongly supported the government. The first clash occurred shortly after the 1964 election, when the CUT demanded an extra month's pay [the so-called "thirteenth month"] to make up for the rapid increase in the cost of living. Opposition came not from the government but from the Christian Democratic members of the CUT, whose representative said:

The FRAP has put the CUT in charge of creating the first obstacles to the government of Eduardo Frei. They insist on a thirteenth month and a large readjustment of the family allowance. Through use of this apparently economic demand, they are trying to create a breach between the workers and the new government before the latter has even announced its remuneration policy. . . . The Marxists do not seem to understand that a new correlation of forces now exists within the labor movement: on the one hand is a force in decline [the CUT], outdated and without perspective or vision of the new conditions of the country; on the other hand is Christian Democracy, an advanced revolutionary force which has clear and precise aims that represent union freedom of choice and the rights of the workers.[10]

More conflicts developed around the organization of the Fourth National Congress of the CUT, which was originally scheduled for May 1965. The Comando Nacional de Trabajadores refused to participate in the Congress. The MUTCh, however, did participate in both the organizing committee and the Congress itself, which finally took place in August. Quarrels quickly developed in the commission meetings with respect to the Frei policies in general and the chileanization of copper in particular. The real crisis, however, came when it was time to elect the new national executive committee of the CUT. The Communists proposed a slate of seven Socialists, six Communists, five Christian Democrats, and three Radicals, to be unanimously elected; but the Socialists refused to go along and said that the board should be divided according to the real strength of each party. Finally an election was held, with only the Communists, Socialists, and the MIR (Movement of the Revolutionary Left) participating. This marked the effective withdrawal of the PDC from participation in the CUT.[11]

Perhaps the most profound breach between the CUT and the government did not directly involve the industrial workers, but they were certainly affected indirectly. Soon after the CUT Congress was over, the copper workers went on strike. The strike lasted on and off until March 1966, when the government declared a state of emergency in the mining areas, charging the local and national leaders with infractions of the Internal Security Law, and turned over the maintenance of order to the military. On March 11, under the pretext of dissolving a meeting in the union local at the El Salvador mine, troops opened fire and killed six men and two women and wounded more than 30 others. The CUT called a 24-hour general strike to protest the "El Salvador Massacre," which became a symbol of government contempt and brutality toward the workers.[12] If the death of the miners was not enough to cause further deterioration of the CUT-government relations, Frei aggravated the situation by defending the troops and accusing the Marxist parties of inciting the trouble.

In spite of, or because of, the internecine quarrels within the labor movement and the CUT-government conflicts, 1965–66 was a period of tremendous activity in labor terms. Large amounts of organizing were done, by both the Marxists and the Christian Democrats, such that the increases in union membership were greater than at any other time in the period covered by this study. Membership increased by 8.2 percent in 1965 and by 20.1 percent in 1966. The number of strikes also greatly increased during these two years: a 30 percent increase in 1965 and 48 percent in 1966 (see Tables A.3 and A.4). The strikes, in turn, resulted in wage increases that far outstripped the increase in the cost of living and had the effect of lowering the profits of the bourgeoisie. This is one indication of the fact that the major gains scored by the workers in this period, as well as during the rest of the Frei administration, were not due to government benevolence toward the workers but to the strength of the workers' movement.

The Stabilization Program

A third area where the government attempted to remain above the class struggle and to maintain its autonomy from both the bourgeoisie and the working class was the stabilization program. Unlike the Alessandri government, which tried to stop inflation at the expense of the workers, Frei expected both capital and labor to share the necessary sacrifices. Inflation was to be halted gradually; the announced goal was to lower the rate from 40 percent in 1964 to 25 percent in 1965, to 15 percent in 1966, to 10 percent in 1967, and to minimal levels thereafter. Workers were to receive a 100 percent readjustment based on the previous year's inflation rate. The return to capital would decline by 5 percent in real terms, but this could be eliminated by increasing productivity by 2 percent. Agricultural prices were to rise 25 percent and industrial prices by only 19 percent, but industrialists could recoup their relative losses by increasing productivity and production, which was completely possible because of the excess capacity available. All of these calculations were based on a model constructed by one of the PDC técnicos, Jorge Cauas (formerly Minister of Finance for the Junta and Ambassador to the United States). According to these estimates, inflation would begin to decline in 1965, but, as the economists were aware, everything depended on gaining the cooperation and confidence of both workers and owners. This was the key aspect, since, if the workers demanded more than a 100 percent readjustment or if owners refused to accept price rises that were less than the increases in costs, then the plan would fail.[13]

Another aspect of the stabilization program, which followed the same approach of workers and bourgeoisie sharing sacrifices, was the 1965 tax reform. This had the effect of increasing government revenue so that it was not necessary to finance such a large part of government expenditure by printing money. In general, the reforms hit the wealthiest sectors of the country hardest, but all income tax payments were made readjustable by the cost-of-living index, which affected white-collar workers and professionals as well as the bourgeoisie. During 1965 and 1966, relative success was achieved as the inflation rate fell in spite of large wage increases. This combination was possible because of increased use of excess capacity and some squeezing of profits. How long the trend would last remained to be seen.

Copper and Foreign Investment

The United States helped to make Eduardo Frei President of Chile and, once he was safely inaugurated, poured money and other types of assistance into the country to make Chile the "showcase" for the Alliance for Progress and an attractive alternative to Cuba. U.S. government loans during 1965–66 reached $251 million, making Chile one of the highest per capita recipients of U.S. aid in the world.[14] In addition, Frei was allowed to renegotiate the Chilean foreign debt (also one of the highest per capita in the world) on extremely favorable terms.

Private foreign capitalists indicated that they thought they could work with Frei in spite of the fact that he had been elected on a platform advocating various structural changes, including greater control over Chilean natural resources. As the *Engineering and Mining Journal* explained in November of 1964,

Washington remains hopeful of getting along well in Chile with the new moderate-leftist Frei government even though problems are apt to crop up. The feeling is that any problems created will probably be minor compared to those that would have resulted if the Marxist Allende had won. . . . Privately, top Washington officials admit Frei's election was greatly helped by the "serious efforts" of U.S. copper interests aiding the U.S. Information Agency.[15]

Since around 60 percent of foreign investment in Chile was in copper, the treatment accorded the mining companies was obviously crucial, and the Frei program of chileanization left the companies ecstatic. The key plank in this program provided for the government to purchase 51 percent of the Kennecott mine, El Teniente. The purchase price was over twice the book value of the mine, and the company received major tax breaks, plus being left in control of administration and sales and having a veto over major decisions. In return, Kennecott agreed to a major investment program in cooperation with the government—though, as it turned out, none of Kennecott's own money was involved. The company's share came from the Chilean purchase funds plus a loan from the Export-Import Bank. Anaconda refused to sell any stock in its major mine, Chuquicamata, but agreed to sell 25 percent of a new mine, La Exótica, plus a 25 percent share of any future mines and to increase investment and production. In return, Anaconda too received major tax breaks.* The smaller Cerro Corporation also sold the government 25 percent of its Río Blanco mine and had its taxes lowered.[16]

As the copper deal was being negotiated, foreign investment was flowing into the industrial sector. The large inflows that had finally begun to appear in the last year of the Alessandri administration increased under Frei. The Christian Democrats continued the highly favorable treatment accorded foreign investment under the two Alessandri laws and, in addition, proposed to go into joint ventures with foreign capital in a number of large-scale industrial projects. Chief among these were two new paper-processing plants (in conjunction with U.S., British, and French capital) and a huge petrochemical complex (with Dow Chemical).

During 1965–66, then, the foreign sector contributed to the un-

---

*In 1969, Anaconda was forced to sell part of Chuquicamata and to sign a contract providing the government with an option to buy the rest later. This was the so-called pacted nationalization.

usually favorable situation enjoyed by the Frei administration. Although the new loans and investment coming in would soon begin to take their toll in terms of amortization, interest, and profits, this had not yet begun. In addition, higher copper prices further increased the favorable foreign exchange situation, which, in turn, increased the ability of the administration to carry out its program.

THE GOVERNMENT DECIDES, 1967

Although it was a crisis in the foreign sector that effectively ended attempts to implement the Alessandri program, it was primarily domestic pressures that caused a breakdown under Frei. Both workers and bourgeoisie pressured the government to give up its attempts to remain above the class struggle. In addition, economic difficulties also tended to limit the government's room for maneuver; as long as the economy was growing, benefits could be distributed to the workers, peasants, and marginal sectors without taking away from the bourgeoisie. Without such growth, continued increases for the former implied *re*distribution.

As the economic policy for 1967 was being planned, the decision was made that it would not be possible to continue increasing public expenditure at the same rate as during the 1965–66 period. Various reasons were suggested—the impossibility of further tax increases, the drop in copper prices, the desire of the government to limit the foreign debt—but the most important consideration seems to have been the increasing inflationary pressures that were beginning to recur. Three concrete changes resulted: a low budget for 1967, a slowdown in monetary expansion, and a change in the structure of public investment. During 1965–66, there had been heavy emphasis on construction investment, which provided an important stimulus to the industrial sector and increased employment; this was changed toward more long-term investment in copper and in certain capital-intensive industrial projects such as the petrochemical and paper sectors.[17] The effects of these changes began to appear almost immediately; industrial output, as well as GDP in general, dropped sharply, and unemployment began to increase.

These new economic policies only increased the already growing opposition from both the workers and the bourgeoisie. The first clear evidence of this disenchantment came from the results of the April 1967 municipal elections, when the PDC declined from 42.3 percent of the vote in the 1965 parliamentary elections to 35.6 percent (see Table A.1).

A much more serious blow to the government, however, came in July, when the left wing of the PDC won a majority on the executive board of the Party. The left-wing faction represented many of the government técnicos as well as the youth and labor sections of the Party. They were the ones who had been trying to implement the "Revolution in Liberty," and they had become increasingly frustrated by the structural barriers that were preventing the reforms. Therefore, they demanded that the reforms be greatly speeded up and proposed their own program, which called for a "noncapitalist road to development." The program was vague and was characterized in the following way: (1) democratic planning of economic and social life, (2) rapidly increasing communitarian forms of production, (3) extending community control over centers of economic powers and basic activities, (4) restructuring the state to facilitate the process of noncapitalist development, and permitting the active participation of the people in decision making, and (5) defining a statute for private enterprises and foreign capital so that these would be subject to state planning and the political power of the people.

In order to carry out this program, certain conditions were seen as necessary: (1) preparing for a confrontation with the Right, (2) making members of the middle class understand that their interests were opposed to those of the Right, and (3) carrying on a dialog with, and gaining support from, the Left (more among the base than the political parties).[18]

The government view of this process was described by the Minister of Finance:

Criticisms arose from one faction of the PDC, which, under the influence of the propaganda and pressures of the parties of the extreme Left, argued that the changes that had been initiated should be accelerated and extended to the financial and industrial sectors, in the process of which they expected to destroy the centers of power of the economic Right and mobilize the popular sectors. They put these objectives ahead of the fulfillment of economic goals, whether these were growth or stability. . . .

The criteria of the Christian Democratic group were contained in a report titled "A noncapitalist road to development," which was composed of a series of declarations on general policy but no coherent model; nor were the majority of these declarations adapted to the economic measures being applied. In addition, many of the technical solutions proposed were insufficient and superficial. Because of the context of the report and the discrepancies existing between the government and the members of the commission that authored it, its publication had the political effects that would be expected, and the opposition knew how to exploit it skillfully.

The extreme Left increased the internal controversy, trying to divide the Christian Democrats into two sectors: the good progressive sector which supported the report and the bad reactionary sector which rejected it. In the latter were placed the representatives of the government, and especially the President of the Republic, in order to provoke a breach between them and their party, creating the image of the government "turning toward the Right."[19]

As a result of the economic downturn, plus the increasing criticisms from both the Left and the Right, the government decided to make one last attempt at a "communitarian" solution. In November of 1967, a formal proposal was made to create a forced savings program. This scheme had been advanced as early as December 1964, but had been continually rejected within the PDC itself for fear of its political repercussions. By late 1967, however, few alternatives were left. The program, formally known as the "Workers' Capitalization Fund," was presented in conjunction with the 1968 wage readjustment bill. Workers would be given a 20 percent increase (the usual 100 percent of the previous year's inflation), but 5 percent would go to the Fund. Employers would also contribute the equivalent of 5 percent of the salaries of their employees. The funds would be managed by a council composed of representatives of the workers and the state and used to create new enterprises or to buy old ones, which would then become the property of the workers. The amount that would be put into the Capitalization Fund could not be withdrawn except for unemployment or death. However, this was not the only objection to the bill; it would also suspend (during 1968) the rights to collective bargaining and to strike, with infractions to be prosecuted under the Internal Security Law.

The CUT immediately attacked the project, labeling it the *chiribonos* (a contraction of the slang expression *chirimoyo* meaning bad check and *bono* meaning bond). They described the bill as one that

gives a readjustment of less than the cost of living, imposes forced savings, threatens social security, lowers taxes on business, increases various indirect taxes, and suppresses the right to negotiation, petition, and strike. . . . Such a law should be called a financing project, since what it tries to do is to collect money from the workers and turn it over to the capitalists. Foreseeing protest, they try to eliminate the right to strike. It has nothing to do with development—quite the contrary; what they really want to do is to find resources to fulfill government obligations and reactivate the private corporations.[20]

In an interview, CUT Secretary-General Hernán del Canto further explained the political meaning of the project:

[We are against the chiribonos because,] more than a project of wage and salary readjustments, this is the expression of a policy that tries to reconcile the social classes through the creation of the famous Savings or Capitalization Fund, destined to create corporations in which theoretically the workers are in charge and can develop our own country. We say that the workers will be the owners of the means of production when we are in power, and we do not want to share the direction of a company with our class enemies.[21]

The CUT and the Confederation of Private Employees (Confederación de Empleados Particulares de Chile—CEPCh) together elaborated a comprehensive series of demands known as the "platform for struggle against the chiribonos." These demands not only called for the absolute rejection of the savings plan but also included a 40 percent readjustment (which they said was the real increase in the cost of living), a price freeze, tax reform, speed-up of the agrarian reform, new taxes on copper and private enterprises, and recognition of the CUT, its federations, and the CEPCh.[22] A general strike was called for November 22 in support of this platform. The response was much greater than usual; even government sources admitted the participation of almost 150,000 workers. In addition, shantytown dwellers on the outskirts of Santiago tried to stop private buses from circulating, producing various confrontations with the police. In the process, four workers were killed as well as one child, dozens wounded, and some 300 arrested. Charges were brought against the president and secretary-general of the CUT for infractions of the Internal Security Law.[23]

Although relations between the government and the industrialists warmed up considerably after their all-time low at the end of 1966, this did not mean that SOFOFA was in agreement with all government policies or even the general trend. It was concerned with the economic downturn and blamed this on erroneous government policies: (1) excessive increases in public expenditures, (2) uncontrolled labor pressures, which provoked a larger number of strikes than ever before, (3) a remunerations policy that went beyond compensation for inflation, (4) a restrictive credit policy, (5) excessive increases in taxes, and (6) a rigid price policy that, in many cases, did not even cover increases in inputs.[24] Beyond these specific policies, SOFOFA was also concerned about the general increase in the state's role in the economy.

Like the workers, the industrialists also decided to pressure the government; the SOFOFA strategy was to work together with the CPC in planning a major campaign to influence public opinion in

favor of free enterprise. This direct public role was new for the bourgeoisie and reflected the failure of the old methods of behind-the-
scenes influence which had worked so well, especially under Alessandri. It also reflected their newly discovered recognition that the
various fractions of the bourgeoisie must act together in order to
protect themselves in what was perceived as a hostile environment.
This implied two types of unity—among the different fractions of
the large bourgeoisie and between the large and petty bourgeoisie.

The best example of the former was the new feeling of unity between the industrial and agricultural sectors. When the agrarian reform law was being debated in 1965–66, SOFOFA did not even take
a stand. The CPC finally came out in late 1966 with a protest statement, but by then it was too late, and the law was promulgated
early in 1967. Then the bourgeoisie saw that they would have to
fight together at the implementation stage. As the SOFOFA president put it:

Finally the SNA [National Agricultural Society] . . . convinced construction
and industry that the agrarian reform would seriously affect industry in the
way it was being carried out. At the same time they [SNA] saw that they
would have to fight harder and more openly. For three years of Christian
Democratic government, each sector looked with indifference on the
others' problems. Now we realize the interdependency of the private
economy.[25]

It was decided that a primary tactic in this fight would be a general
campaign in favor of free enterprise, avoiding directly political con-
notations. The preliminary steps involved a mass propaganda campaign, discussing the characteristics of free enterprise and the history of its contributions to Chile's development. Spot interviews on
radio and television were used, together with posters and newspaper
ads. In addition, there was wide diffusion of an Argentine film called
"The Branch and the Cage," which "compared the liberty, risk,
work and happiness of the free bird on the branch with that of the
entrepreneurs while the bird in the cage, a socialist regime, withered
and died."[26]

The second type of unity that the campaign sought to promote
was that between the large and petty bourgeoisie. The idea was to
emphasize the concept of the small entrepreneur and eliminate the
identification of the entrepreneur with big business. The technique
used here was also based on publicity. The most effective part was
large picture ads of small entrepreneurs—taxi drivers, owners of
small stores, artisan producers; the series even included an ad show-

ing a peanut vendor who takes the risk of roasting his own peanuts without a government guarantee. The basic message was that there were 600,000 entrepreneurs, not just 50,000.[27]

The propaganda campaigns were to culminate with two national conventions—one of leaders of the empresarial organizations in December 1967, and the second, much larger, of individuals in April 1968. The entire campaign was the most costly nonelection campaign in Chile's history (up to that time) and probably second only to the 1964 election campaign. It was financed by "voluntary" contributions and cost close to $400,000.[28]

As a result of the various kinds of pressures—the publicity campaign of the bourgeoisie, the strike of the workers, and the leftist takeover of the PDC—the government was forced to change its policy. The "communitarian" solution, in the end, had proved to be incompatible with Chilean reality, and the government was forced to choose sides in the intensifying conflict between the workers and the bourgeoisie.

DESCENT TO THE RIGHT, 1968–70

The Realignment

Once the turning point was reached, the government wasted little time in charting a new course. On January 6, Frei convened the National Assembly of the Christian Democratic Party and, in an all-night session, forced the Party to determine whether it was with the government or the opposition. The result was the defeat of the left-wing majority of the executive board, headed by Rafael Gumucio, and the installation of a new board with a pro-Frei majority, headed by Party ideologue Jaime Castillo. This was the beginning of a three-year period that would be characterized by two main features: an increasing unity within both the labor movement and the bourgeoisie and an increasing polarization and violence between the two. The government had been forced to descend from the position it was trying to occupy above the class struggle and to take sides openly. It went with the bourgeoisie, but not in a way that was sufficiently firm to regain the support of that class or to end the new mass mobilization that the government itself had encouraged but now wanted to harness.

The retaking of the Party was followed closely by a reorganization of the cabinet and other government posts, which also indicated a shift to the Right. With respect to the economic situation, the most important change was the resignation of reform-oriented Sergio Molina from the key Ministry of Finance. Molina was first replaced by Raúl Saez, who had the confidence not only of the Chilean bourgeoisie (he was the key person with whom SOFOFA had decided to work at the beginning of the Frei administration) but also of foreign capital (Saez was one of the "nine wise men" of the Alliance for Progress as well as the chief Chilean negotiator in the chileanization program, which left the copper companies so delighted). After a few months, however, Saez decided to leave Chile to work in Venezuela, and the Ministry of Finance was occupied by Andrés Zaldívar, who also had the complete confidence of the bourgeoisie.[29] Other key switches saw Jacques Chonchol, leader of the left-wing Christian Democratic faction, resign as head of the Agrarian Reform Institute (INDAP), and industrialist Edmundo Pérez Zúcovic move from the Ministry of Economics to the Ministry of Interior, which controlled law enforcement, including tasks such as breaking strikes and demonstrations. Pérez was replaced in the Ministry of Economics by a series of right-wing officials who were also closely linked to the bourgeoisie.

The period 1968–70 was characterized by a complete dearth of new reforms or even maintenance of the old ones. The forced savings plan was withdrawn early in 1968, and a bill calling for the usual 100 percent readjustment was presented in its place. Inflation increased and production fell, but the government seemed to have neither the will nor the capacity to do anything about it. Contacts were increased with the bourgeoisie, beginning with Frei's appearance at the CPC Convention in April, and decreased with labor; the latter included the labor section of Frei's own party. As one expert explained, "Relations between business and government had changed considerably. . . . Partly this was because of the influence of Freista businessmen, but it was also due to the political environment which found government, like business, increasingly isolated from support."[30] But these new relations were not enough; the bourgeoisie saw Frei as vacillating, indecisive, and thus opening the way to a potentially unmanageable situation. More repression, however, did begin to be used. The *Carabineros* (national police) were sent in to break up strikes. The MIR (Movement of the Revolutionary Left) was forced underground. Increasing numbers of incidents took place in which people were wounded or killed, the most notorious occurring on March 9, 1969, when the Carabineros fired on a group of squatters in the southern city of Puerto Montt, killing nine.[31]

These actions on the part of the government had the effect of accentuating the polarization, which began to increase significantly in 1968.* The polarization at the national level was reflected within the PDC itself in the split between the left-wing faction which had been ousted in January and the official faction. By mid-1969, it was clear that the disagreement could no longer be patched over. This was reinforced at the 1969 Party congress in the discussion of strategy for the 1970 presidential election; the PDC Left wanted to run a joint candidate with the FRAP while the Right looked toward the PN. On May 6, 1969, Party founder Rafael Gumucio resigned from the Christian Democracy, leading the group that would soon form the MAPU (Movimiento de Acción Popular Unitaria). Gumucio's letter of resignation stated: "The most advanced current of Christian thought is no longer picked up by us and in fact, rather than an instrument of revolutionary change, we are an instrument of the status quo, an administrator of the system, guarantor of the established order."[32]

Polarization Increases Between Bourgeoisie and Workers

The year of unification of the labor movement in Chile was 1968. The first of a series of related events came with the leftist takeover of the PDC labor section in September 1968. The union congress, in a vote of 44 to 5, decided to reenter the CUT. It also condemned UTRACh (Unión de Trabajadores de Chile), the latest and only surviving attempt to set up a rival labor federation, and sent UTRACh's leaders, including Emilio Caballero, who was Frei's labor adviser, to the Party's disciplinary tribunal. In a final move, the congress asked the PDC national assembly to require all Christian Democratic industrialists to hand over their enterprises within six months to be run by their workers.[33] In an interview in *El Siglo*,

---

*A quantitative indication of the increase in polarization can be seen in the following data on illegal occupations in the period 1968–70:

	1968	1969	1970
Occupations of industries	5	24	133
Occupations of farms	16	121	368
Occupations of land (for building shantytowns)	8	73	220

Unfortunately it is not possible to determine from these data what percentage of the 1970 occupations occurred after the presidential election. (See Joaquín Duque and Ernestro Pastrana, "La movilización reivindicativa urbana de los sectores populares en Chile: 1964–72," *Revista Latinoamericana de Ciencias Sociales*, No. 4, Dec. 1972, p. 268.)

the new head of the union department, Alejandro Sepúlveda, said, "The CUT should be made the instrument of the vanguard in the fight against the national oligarchy and American imperialism in order to realize a noncapitalist road to development."[34]

Because the Communists were anxious to have the Christian Democrats participate in the Fifth National Congress of the CUT, the meeting was postponed until November of 1968. The congress took place in a general atmosphere of unity, which was broken only by quarrels between Communists and Socialists. The final unity event of 1968 occurred when the CEPCh congress, meeting in December, voted to join the CUT. The two organizations had agreed on joint proposals and actions for the 1967 general strike, but now the union would be official. With the CEPCh decision, all of the major labor organizations were united into one federation.

In a somewhat paradoxical way, at the same time that the labor hierarchy was being unified, grass-roots activities were beginning, which produced potential divisions within the CUT at that level. The first and most dramatic event was the occupation (*toma*) of the Wagner-Stein (SABA) electronics factory by its striking workers; this was followed by a fire in the factory. The trouble at SABA began on January 4, 1968, when a list of salary demands was presented to the owners. In mid-June, the workers claimed that the owners still had not bargained in good faith, and a strike was called. On July 22, in order to prevent the owners from removing equipment and materials from the factory and establishing another plant elsewhere, the workers occupied the buildings. The owners appealed to Pérez Zúcovic, the new Minister of Interior, and the Carabineros were sent to evict the strikers. According to the workers, the police threw tear-gas bombs which caused a small fire; the officials, however, claimed that the workers set the fire to prevent the owners from returning. As a result, 28 workers were jailed. They were finally released on bail in May 1969, after a long hunger strike by wives and mothers, and given sentences in October. These ranged from 17 years for the strike leader, to 11–15 years for the workers accused of setting the fire, to two to three years for the others, accused of trespassing.[35]

The bourgeoisie viewed the incident as little less than a declaration of war by the workers. Workers had long ago adopted the tactic of "outside takeovers" (camping in front of the factories); but this was the first actual occupation of the buildings themselves. The fire, of course, increased the drama. SOFOFA demanded an interview with Frei "to express its alarm about the climate of indiscipline and violence which have now gone to such an extreme that they must be brought under control."[36] Frei assured the industrialists that the government was firmly resolved to prevent the occurrence of similar events in the future.

In an extraordinary session of the SOFOFA board of directors, the representative of the electronics industries attacked the SABA incident as follows:

An attempt is being made to alter our institutionality, replacing juridical norms and moving toward the position where rule by law is replaced by rule by the strongest. Never before in the history of Chile has something like this happened—but then there is always a first time. If we don't react valiently, and if necessary violently, right now, we will soon have a second use of force, and then another and another—until this type of thing becomes customary, just as the [outside] occupation of factories is now customary. I am not just talking about punishing those who are guilty, though they must be severely punished. It is also necessary that we, the industrial sector, become conscious that we are faced with methodical and patient plans that, step by step, are transforming and modifying the mentality of the country to produce a climate of hostility and violence which undermines the basic institutions. It will be necessary for us to have a plan too, perfectly studied and coordinated, not only to defend ourselves from the things that have happened, but to foresee and prevent them from occurring.[37]

SOFOFA called the event "a criminal attack . . . without precedent up to now . . . which provoked the repudiation of all sectors of the population, including labor organizations."[38] The CPC talked of "a national plan of subversion to destroy the productive resources of the country."[39]

The SABA incident was important for several reasons. First, it encouraged the polarization as no other event could have. This could be seen through the increasing unity and organization of the bourgeoisie. For one thing, a series of meetings resulted between SOFOFA and the SNA. The first took place in August 1968. The subject came up for full discussion again the following year. SOFOFA President Heiremans stated:

We cannot consider that industry is excluded from the anguished situation to which the agricultural sector is subjected. To expect that the shots are going to stop by themselves and not hurt the industrial enterprises and other sectors of production would be to ignore the tragic experiences of other countries and, because of passivity, run enormous risks. We cannot fool ourselves; what is happening now in agriculture is the problem of industry and involves the entire concept of private activity. It is not enough that the presidents of the various business associations (*gremios*) send messages of solidarity to the president of the SNA. . . . There is no other way to defend democracy, dignity, and the legitimate rights of citizens than to oppose these undermining elements with the greatest energy, including drastic and violent actions.[40]

In addition to the discussions with the agricultural sector, the other main result of the SABA incident was the Campaign for Entrepreneurial Solidarity. This was initiated by the SOFOFA board "upon observing that a new form of pressure is developing in social conflicts—violence and destruction together with political actions designed to belittle the importance of the private enterprise, creating a climate favorable for its destruction and expropriation."[41] The campaign, which was soon taken over by the CPC, was similar to the previous one—public relations in the external aspect and an attempt to shore up the gremios internally. On the one hand was the task of instilling "entrepreneurial mentality" in the petty bourgeoisie, and on the other was the attempt to force all to join and actively support the gremio organizations. "It is unquestionable that individual entrepreneurs, acting by themselves, are not capable of confronting the pressures of all kinds which they are suffering; but acting in unity, they constitute a powerful force whose voice is important among those who run the government."[42] The most significant advances were the strengthening of employer syndicates in agriculture and commerce. Less progress was made in industry because of the strong competition between SOFOFA and the government for the allegiance of the small industrialists. Also SOFOFA was still opposed to fully incorporating the small industrialists into the gremio.

The second way in which SABA was important was that it represented the beginning of a grass-roots movement among workers which had little or no support from the CUT. SABA itself was essentially an isolated event, but it occurred at the same time that other similar experiences were beginning to develop. All had the common characteristic of taking place in small or medium-sized factories where the workers felt themselves alienated from the CUT and the other labor organizations whose main base was in the large factories and public administration. The next major occupation took place in December 1968 in a factory originally called Andrés Hidalgo y Cía. Ltda., which made cement posts for electric wiring. This factory had a history of problems, with Hidalgo (the owner) falling behind in wage and social security payments, and the courts had twice ruled in favor of the workers. This did not affect Hidalgo's behavior, and, in September 1968, a strike was declared; Hidalgo responded with a lockout in December. The workers were in a desperate situation; they had been two months without wages, and it seemed unlikely that they would recover this money or keep their jobs, since Hidalgo's debts were far more than the value of the factory. Given this situation, a decision was made on December 22 (in spite of the SABA experience) to occupy the factory. This time, however, the intention was to maintain control of the factory and to have the workers run it themselves. With aid from university students and professionals, the legal and technical problems were overcome. The factory took the name Cootralaco and began to operate. The final step came when the workers bought the factory at auction with money raised from unions, neighborhood councils, and other organizations throughout the country.[43]

Cootralaco thus became one of a group of self-managed factories that were formed during the late 1960's. By 1970, there were 21, united in the Federación de Empresas de Trabajadores y Cooperativas de Producción y Trabajo. Some had been established as a result of occupations like Cootralaco; others were formed by unemployed workers with private or state credits; a few resulted from arrangements between workers and owners; and the rest were promoted by the Federation after its formation in 1969.[44]

These enterprises got little help from the Frei government, although self-managed factories (empresas de trabajadores) were the ideal "communitarian" enterprises championed by Christian Democratic ideology. They also had a fragile relationship with the CUT, as the following comments by the president of the Cootralaco administrative council (looking back from 1971) indicate:

Although it is painful to us, there are those who try to isolate us from the workers' struggle for the sole crime of having invented a new means of struggle in 1968. Last year Compañero Pedro Vuscovic [Allende's first Minister of Economics] said to us here: "You predated the UP by two years." But it seems that some compañeros of the CUT do not see things in this way and refuse any dialogue. . . . In one of the first conversations we had with Compañero Luis Figueroa [president of the CUT], he said, "Your movement will only make sense when there is a popular government." We think our movement has always made sense, and now, more than ever, all workers must unite . . . to face the common enemy: capitalism.[45]

The problem between the CUT and these factories was that the CUT did not trust organizations outside its direct control, seeing such movements as threatening its own plans for moving toward socialism via the electoral route.

The Tacnazo

The polarization trend continued and was clearly demonstrated in the March 1969 congressional election, which took on a private enterprise vs. state socialism tone. Both the Right and the Left made major gains at the expense of the PDC, which fell to its lowest point since Frei won the presidency. The only significant lull in the polarization occurred in October, when a strange event transpired—the so-called Tacnazo. The Tacnazo was an uprising of the Tacna regiment of the supposedly apolitical Chilean military. The exact nature of the uprising was never clear. Was it merely an attempt to increase wages and other benefits among the military? Was it a personalistic move by its leader, General Roberto Viaux? Was it part of a larger plot aimed at a military coup? These questions have never been satisfactorily answered.[46]

The events began on October 16, when General Viaux, commander of the Army's Division I, was asked to resign. The reasons apparently had to do with previous insubordinate behavior.[47] On October 20, Viaux arrived in Santiago and, the following morning, led an uprising of the Tacna Army regiment. He insisted that the move was a pressure tactic, designed to achieve certain economic demands, and had no relation with any political activity or party. The demands made were the resignation of the Minister of Defense and the Commander in Chief of the Army, an increase in salaries for the military (which the government had promised the previous year but had not implemented), and improvement of equipment. Frei responded by putting the country under a state of emergency and called for support. The call was answered primarily by the Communist Party and the CUT; a general strike was called, including the occupation of factories, farms, and other work places. In addition, a rally was held on the afternoon of the uprising, at which, in spite of protests of independence and criticism of the government, the latter received conditional support for maintaining constitutionality.[48] The bourgeoisie also rallied to the support of the government, although complaining angrily about the CUT president being given access to radio networks to call on workers to take over their industries.

The most logical explanation for the workers' support for the government during the Tacnazo was that the Communist Party (and through it the CUT) was committed to one final attempt to win the presidency and was therefore stuck with shoring up the system until 1970.[49] This analysis is compatible with another surprising event that took place a month and a half later. For the first time in Chilean history, the CUT negotiated an agreement with the government on wage readjustments. Generally the proposal was for the usual 100 percent of the previous year's increase in the cost of living; but the minimum wage and family allowance for blue-collar workers (as well as agricultural workers) were raised by approximately twice the inflation rate. The arrangement evoked outrage from the MIR, which pointed out that the agreement maintained the differential between blue- and white-collar workers and that, although the National Health Service had calculated that a family of four needed at least 20 escudos a day just for food, the CUT had settled for a minimum of only 12 escudos.[50]

The bourgeoisie, however, were pleased with the agreement. *El Mercurio*, the leading right-wing newspaper, said:

At other times we have been able to accuse the union leaders of intransigence and even of acting with the clear proposition of blocking governmental action. . . . On this occasion, the directive of the CUT has contributed to avoiding the climate of agitation that normally is incited when discussing the bill concerning readjustments. Certainly, it has obtained the greater part of what it asked for, but also it is true that the original demands were more realistic than those of other years, and that it has been flexible in some important respects. . . . For our part we applaud the example given by the CUT in this opportunity to other sectors. . . . It constitutes a first step toward constructive participation of unions in the elaboration of responsible wage and salary policies.[51]

The Minister of Interior commented, "It is an example for many other sectors which haven't had the appropriate understanding in the difficult moments through which we have lived."[52]

The approval was temporary, however, for the CUT called another general strike in July 1970 with the purpose of "defending the democratic electoral practice, denouncing coup and terrorist adventures, and obtaining solutions to urgent economic problems." Also the CUT wanted to restrain what it saw as "escalation of repression and terror by the government and the Right, designed to prevent the people from full freedom of expression." The government called the strike "political" and made veiled references to the dilemma of "law or violence." The strike itself was carried out with less violence than usual, since only one person was killed in confrontations with the police.[53]

Presidential Election, 1970

The onset of another presidential election year meant that, as usual, activities in all sectors gave way to the campaign preparations. As it turned out, the election was, in many senses, a repeat of the 1958 contest. In the selection of candidates, two key decisions were made. The first was the Left's decision to form the Popular Unity (UP) alliance, which was composed of the Communists and Socialists (the old FRAP), plus the MAPU, the Radicals, and two other minor parties. The alliance was the creation of the Communists; the Socialists, as always, were against the Radicals' participation. They agreed to go along, however, because of the pressure of the Communists and certain changes in the Radical Party itself. The latter had elected a left-wing directorate and expelled some of its more reactionary members.[54] In addition, it was clear that the alliance candidate would be a Socialist.

The other main decision was that, unlike the situation in 1964, the Christian Democrats and the National Party would run separate candidates. This was mainly due to the serious split that had developed between the PDC and the sectors of the bourgeoisie represented by the PN. Although the latter's dislike was mostly directed against the Party rather than the government, there was also strong dislike for the Frei government. On the one hand, even with its mild reforms, it had trod upon many toes, especially in the agricultural sector; on the other hand, the PN viewed the PDC as a party of indecision. This indecision, in turn, had paved the way for all kinds of radical activity of which the government might not have approved but could not or would not prevent.[55] The decision not to run a joint candidate was strengthened because such a candidate would surely have had to be from the PDC, and the person most often mentioned was Radomiro Tomic, leader of the Party's left wing who himself favored a coalition with the FRAP. Also the PN was convinced that it would win the election on its own, with former President Jorge Alessandri as its candidate.

Thus the election turned out to be a three-way race between some very familiar candidates. The Right was backing Alessandri; the UP nominated Salvador Allende; and the PDC finally chose Tomic. In terms of platforms, many of the positions advocated by Allende and

Tomic appeared similar.[56] Both called for the enlargement of the state sector of the economy, for a rapid increase in the agrarian reform, and for the immediate nationalization of the copper mines. The basic difference was that Allende specifically stated that the UP would prepare for a move toward a socialist mode of production while Tomic was more ambiguous. An indication of this ambiguity was Tomic's failure to say what would be incorporated into the state sector other than copper. Allende, on the other hand, said the UP would include industrial monopolies, the financial system, distribution agencies, and foreign trade, as well as the entire mining resources of the country. With respect to social policies, both Allende and Tomic advocated redistribution of income and increased social benefits for the working class. Both also called for greater international independence for Chile. According to one analysis, the difference between the international proposals was that Tomic envisioned "neutralism," whereas Allende championed "autodetermination for all peoples and solidarity with liberated economies."[57] In any case, the surface differences appeared minimal.

Alessandri, on the other hand, never announced a platform per se, although it was apparent that his views were substantially different from the other two candidates. He went along with certain ideas that had become almost compulsory in Chilean politics, e.g. increased social benefits and agrarian reform, although he gave a different interpretation to the latter, emphasizing technical changes. Basically, however, Alessandri supported the capitalist system in Chile and believed that the state should decrease rather than increase its role in the economy. The state should devote itself to restoring order and tranquillity so that the private sector could take the lead. In terms of international politics, Alessandri believed that Chile must remain within the world capitalist system and limited himself to advocating greater integration of Latin America—although not as a means of confronting the United States.

The campaign itself was a lower-key repeat of 1964. Alessandri's supporters played up the horrors of communism, referring especially to Allende, but also including Tomic. Alessandri himself was portrayed as an independent, above politics, "the honest strong *patrón* fighting against the forces of corruption, egoism, evil and destruction."[58] The candidate's public appearances were minimized in view of his age and health problems. Tomic ran a slick media-oriented campaign, although greatly hindered because the PDC had no large-circulation daily newspaper. The Left, as usual, limited itself mostly to stumping from one end of the country to the other and relied on a grass-roots organization around the UP committees.[59] U.S. money again poured into Chile, although in much lesser amounts than in 1964, since it was assumed that Alessandri would win. According to testimony by CIA Director William Colby, the CIA alone was authorized to spend $1 million in anti-Allende election efforts during 1969 and 1970.[60] It can be assumed that other government agencies, as well as private corporations, donated much more, though these figures have not yet been publicized. Most of this money went to support Alessandri, although probably some also went to Tomic.

The campaign reflected the polarization that had been created during the Frei years. Although Tomic had the government apparatus behind him, it was clear from the beginning that he had little chance; the election would be won either by the Left, which promised radical change, or by the Right, which promised to reorder society and take it back to a previous period. As it turned out, Allende won by a narrow margin. The final totals were: Allende, 1,075,616 (36.6 percent); Alessandri, 1,036,278 (35.3 percent) and Tomic, 824,849 (28.1 percent). (See Table A.1.)

Since no one had won an absolute majority, the final choice had to be made by the Congress on October 24. Although it was customary for the Congress to ratify the plurality winner, various tactics were tried by the Chilean Right and their U.S. allies to prevent this. First was the attempt to persuade the Christian Democratic Congressmen to vote for Alessandri, who would then resign and new elections would be held with Frei as candidate.* The PDC, however, after forcing Allende to sign a set of constitutional guarantees, agreed to support him. Although the U.S. government budgeted $350,000 for bribe money, the money was probably not used since the task appeared hopeless.[61] The second tactic was to try to provoke a military coup. When creating "economic chaos" in line with the ITT plans[62] failed to produce the desired effect, the Right went even further and planned to kidnap René Schneider, Commander in Chief of the Army, and blame the kidnaping on the Left. The attempt was bungled, however, and Schneider was killed. Since it was apparent that the Right was to blame for the incident, public opinion rallied around Allende and assured his confirmation.[63]

---

*According to the Chilean constitution, a President could not succeed himself. If Alessandri were to be chosen by the Congress, however, and served even a few minutes before resigning, then Frei would have been out of office and could run in a new election.

CHAPTER SIX

The Allende Regime, 1970–73

Iɴ ᴀ ꜰᴏʀᴍᴀʟ sense, the chronological structure of the Allende administration was similar to its predecessor. The Allende years could also be divided into three subperiods: an initial span (of almost two years) in which the government took the initiative in trying to implement its development strategy; a short period (a month in this case) in which Right and Left battled each other, reaching something of a stalemate; and finally a period in which the government merely struggled to keep afloat, wracked by internal divisions. As was also the case with the Frei administration, the final period was marked by growing polarization, although in the Allende case this polarization was much more complete and profound.[1]

THE ''PEACEFUL ROAD'' BEGINS, NOVEMBER 1970 –
SEPTEMBER 1972

As a coalition of the Communist, Socialist, and Radical parties, plus several smaller groups, the Popular Unity (UP) was characterized as an alliance of the working class and the petty bourgeoisie.* Given the nature of this alliance, the Basic Program of the UP represented a radical statement indeed, indicating that in 1970 (unlike superficially similar situations in 1938, 1941, and 1946), the working class dominated the alliance. The key economic section of the program made it clear from the beginning that the UP would not be

---

* But see analysis of coalition in Chapters Three and Ten.

content merely to administer the economy or to make a series of reforms. Rather, the intention was to move as rapidly as possible toward a change in the mode of production itself. Thus, the opening sentence of the economic program stated, "The central objective of the united popular forces is to replace the current economic structure, ending the power of national and foreign monopoly capitalists and large landowners, in order to initiate the construction of socialism." Implications of the program were that Chilean socialism would be characterized by (1) state ownership of important sectors of the economy, (2) state planning, and (3) popular control.

The economic goals were divided into what might be called structural changes and economic development objectives. The first type of structural change would be the formation of a dominant state (social) area of the economy. The Social Area would consist of those firms already owned by the state and others that would be taken over, including the large mines, the financial system, wholesale distribution, foreign commerce, strategic industrial firms, and some parts of the economic infrastructure, such as energy production, transportation, and communications. The second structural change dealt with agrarian reform. The objective here would be to expropriate all farms over a certain (unspecified) size, perhaps including animals and machinery, and to put unused state land into cultivation. Cooperatives would be the main organizational form for the expropriated land.

Economic development goals included (1) reorientation of production from luxury goods to basic consumer items; (2) guarantees of employment for all Chileans of working age at adequate salaries; (3) liberation of Chile from subordination to foreign capital (expropriating some firms and setting conditions for the operation of others); (4) rapid economic growth; (5) development of exports and new markets, reduction of technological dependency, and the ending of devaluations; and (6) control of inflation and the rationalization of commerce and distribution. These goals were to be implemented through the national planning system as well as through state control of credit, taxes, technological assistance, foreign trade, and the state sector of the economy.

In addition to these economic objectives, the UP was also committed to a number of social goals, including (1) a new wage policy which would eliminate discrimination between workers as well as increase their remunerations; (2) the extension and amplification of the social security program; (3) the guarantee of free medical care for all; (4) the extension of the housing program for low-income families; and (5) the end of discrimination against women. The democratization of education and the development of "popular culture" were also seen as important aims. In political terms, two related goals were established. One was a call for greater participation by all citizens at the local level (neighborhood, factory, school, etc.). The other was a restructuring of the national political system which would build on the increased local participation. Thus, there would be municipal and provincial assemblies, culminating with a one-chamber Popular Assembly at the national level which would replace the existing two-chamber Congress. Finally, at the international level, the UP demanded independence from military and economic ties to the United States and announced its intention to foster strong relations with the socialist countries and to defend other nations that were also involved in the anti-imperialist struggle.[2]

The first concrete demonstration of the new status of the working class was the change in the role of the National Workers' Confederation (CUT). The CUT became the main organizational base of the government and, in exchange for this support, received a major voice not only in labor policy but in the entire public sector. To begin with, Allende appointed three workers or labor leaders as members of his first cabinet: Américo Zorilla as Minister of Finance, José Oyarce as Minister of Labor, and Pascual Barraza as Minister of Public Works. In the shifts that followed, caused by the opposition-controlled Congress impeaching ministers, other workers were installed in the cabinet, including Hernán del Canto, secretary-general of the CUT, who assumed the top cabinet post as Minister of Interior. In addition, the CUT was recognized as the legal representative of the working class, and its representatives became important members of the major governmental economic organs, including the National Development Council, the National Planning Office (ODEPLAN), and the State Development Corporation (CORFO). Members of the working class were also incorporated into the administration of the principal state enterprises, such as the steel company (CAP), the oil company (ENAP), and the electricity company (ENDESA). Finally, the workers were made part of the tripartite committee (government-workers-owners) to determine wage policies.

Economic Gains for the Workers

The workers not only occupied new positions in the state apparatus; they also received concrete economic gains with the advent of the new government. These gains were embodied in a number of agreements (*convenios*) that the government negotiated with the CUT. The most important of these were the 1970 and 1971 convenios on remunerations and related matters and the convenio on participation. The first was signed on December 7, 1970, with the following introduction:

The Basic Program of the Unidad Popular and the Declarations of Principles and Resolutions of the Congresses of the Central Unica de Trabajadores coincide in affirming that the definitive solution of the problems of the workers will be achieved only through profound transformations in the economic and social structures of the country, including nationalization of basic resources, realization of an effective agrarian reform, elimination of the industrial and commercial monopolies, nationalization of the banks and insurance companies, and control of foreign commerce.

The direct and active participation of the workers in the elaboration and realization of these transformations will be the best guarantee that they will be carried out rapidly and effectively. It is necessary, therefore, to create mechanisms that permit this participation on all levels. This will signify the responsible and patriotic commitment of the workers to contribute their continuing efforts to attain increasing productivity. . . .

While these fundamental changes are being carried out, it is necessary to establish a remunerations policy for 1971 that will bring about improvement of the living standard of the workers, especially those who have the lowest remunerations and those who lack stable jobs.

Therefore, in order to define the remunerations policy for 1971, and to proceed toward incorporating the workers into the responsibilities of national transformation, we sign this Act of Accord.[3]

The wage scales established included a 66.7 percent increase in the minimum industrial wage, compared to a 34.9 percent inflation rate in 1970, and a 34.9 percent increase in the minimum salary. In addition, the general readjustment contained a redistributive clause whereby workers earning less than one SV* would receive the cost of living plus 5 percent more (i.e. 39.9 percent); those earning between one and two SV would receive an additional 3 percent (37.9 percent), while those earning more than two SV would receive increases equaling the inflation rate (34.9 percent). (The inflation rates referred to here are the *previous year's* rates; since the 1971

---

* SV (*sueldo vital*) is used in Chile to mean both minimum salary and a unit of measure.

rate declined to 22 percent from 35 percent in 1970, this meant that the 1971 salaries represented large increases in purchasing power even for those who received only a 100 percent readjustment.) Those workers subject to collective bargaining were left free to negotiate their wage increases, but with an important new factor. Since wage disputes were settled by arbitration boards consisting of representatives of employers, workers, and the Ministry of Labor, the change in government meant, as CUT President Luis Figueroa said: "We went from a two-to-one majority against the workers to a two-to-one majority in their favor."[4]

The second agreement, for the year 1972, was quite similar to the first. The minimum industrial wage was increased by 50 percent while all other wage increases were to be equal to the 1971 increase in the cost of living, i.e. 22 percent.[5] Although the remunerations set by the previous year's agreement had been substantially exceeded (on the average, wages and salaries increased by about 50 percent in nominal terms in 1971), it soon became apparent that the 1972 union demands would bear no relation whatsoever to the 22 percent established in the agreement with the CUT. The main reason was that the union leaders at the plant level did not believe that inflation could be kept down for another year and so were determined to protect their members by asking for larger increases. An important secondary reason, however, was that the Christian Democratic labor leaders were demanding higher wages in an attempt to create problems for the government, and so the UP leaders had to counter these demands in order to maintain the allegiance of their followers. This was the tragic legacy of many years of CUT concentration on economistic demands; now the UP was to be plagued by what its own supporters had fostered.

The third major agreement between the CUT and the government in this period concerned worker participation in the administration of the state-controlled factories. A committee had been established soon after the election to work on this problem, and, in June 1971, it presented a document called the Normas Básicas de Participación. These rules established a two-tier participation structure with a coordinating committee in between. At the shop-floor level, workers would meet in an assembly to make major decisions and elect a production committee, which would be both executive committee and representative to the coordinating committee. At the factory level, there was an administrative council, composed of five representatives elected by the factory-wide assembly and five representatives appointed by the government. The chairman of the council would be the government-appointed administrator (*interventor*) of the factory. The administrative council had control over all decisions relating to the functioning of the factory. The third organ established was the only one in which the unions per se participated; the other organs were composed of directly elected representatives who could not be union leaders. The coordinating committee was presided over by the head of the largest union in the factory, and its membership consisted of the presidents of the production committees and the five labor representatives on the administrative council. As its name implies, the coordinating committee coordinated functions between the other two organs. By June 1972, the participation structure was functioning in complete or modified form in 76 percent of the Social Area firms.[6]

The Social Area

A second area in which the UP moved against the bourgeoisie and in favor of the workers was in the establishment of the Social Area, which, as explained in the Basic Program, would consist of the "commanding heights" of the economy. The Social Area would be complemented by a Mixed Area, consisting of jointly owned state-private property; most of these firms would be state-foreign ventures in sectors where foreign technology was essential. The vast majority of firms, in numerical terms, would remain in the Private Area.[7]

An initial problem arose over how to define the Social and Mixed Areas; what firms would be incorporated and how? A bill was introduced by the government in October of 1971 that would establish the three areas (Social, Mixed, and Private). All companies with capital exceeding 14 million escudos in December of 1969 ($1.34 million) would be put in the Social or Mixed Area; this was a total of 253 firms. Payment would be at book value in long-term readjustable bonds. Smaller companies would be given absolute guarantees that they would not be expropriated. The Christian Democrats, however, introduced a rival bill (the Hamilton-Fuentealba bill) that would require congressional authorization for each individual expropriation; in addition, it provided that all firms which came under government control after October 14, 1971, would be returned to their owners. The other major difference was the establishment of a fourth area of the economy—the Self-Management Area (Empresas de Trabajadores). This area would consist of firms owned by their workers, in a plan similar to that in Yugoslavia. The Congress passed the PDC bill in the form of a constitutional amendment, the President vetoed it, and the Congress, in turn, claimed to have overridden the veto, based on a constitutional ambiguity. Although a two-thirds majority was necessary to override a veto on an ordinary bill, the argument was that only a majority was necessary for a constitutional amendment. Since there was no way to resolve the conflict, it was temporarily tabled.[8]

In the meantime, firms were being put under state control through the use of an old law, decreed during the 12-day Socialist Republic in 1932, whereby the government could "intervene" or "requisition" firms where labor or other problems were causing production declines that seriously affected the economy.* However, there was still no way of deciding which firms should be taken over, and finally, in February of 1972, the government published a list of 91 that would be incorporated into the Social and Mixed areas.† Further efforts to resolve the dilemma and give the Social Area a firmer legal status occurred in two sets of conversations between the government and the Christian Democrats, in March and June of 1972. During the latter, an agreement was reached and ready to be signed when it was vetoed by the right wing of the PDC and the left wing of the Socialist Party. Such problems did not arise with respect to the nationalization of the banks, since they had been brought under state control through the purchase of shares from individual owners.

Therefore, the Social Area basically went ahead in an ad hoc fashion. By the end of 1971, over 150 industries had been put under state control; 104 were intervened, 35 requisitioned, four expropriated, and others purchased. Their importance to the economy can be seen by the fact that they included 12 of the 20 largest industrial firms in Chile.[9] In addition, the majority of the 23 private national

* There was a rather subtle, and not very important, difference between requisition and intervention. Requisitions were carried out by the Ministry of Economics, based on Decreto Ley 520 of 1932. Legal causes for requisition included speculation, hoarding, or failure to produce goods of basic necessity as defined by the Executive. Interventions were carried out by the Ministry of Labor, based on Article 26 of the Labor Code or Article 38 of the Internal Security Law. The main cause was a factory's ceasing to function, whether through a strike or a lockout. Most of the large firms were requisitioned and the smaller ones intervened, but the form that was used depended on a wide variety of factors.

† The list was later cut to 90 with the elimination of the distribution firm CODINA (Compañía Distribuidora Nacional). This firm had been owned by one of the large financial groups, but, to avoid its requisition, 75 percent of the stock was transferred to various organizations of retail merchants. More information on all 91 firms can be found in *Libro de las 91* (Santiago, 1972), pp. 59–154.

banks were in state hands, and three of the four major foreign-owned banks had also been purchased (including Bank of America and First National City Bank). This meant that the state controlled over two-thirds of the credit of the entire banking system.[10] By October 1972, another 24 industries had been requisitioned and 37 more intervened.[11]

The Allende Doctrine

The government also moved against the foreign bourgeoisie through the nationalization of certain foreign corporations in the industrial, financial, commercial, and mining sectors. In many cases, agreements were reached by the parties involved and compensation was paid; in a few instances, however, no agreement was possible. The best-known case involved the copper mines owned by the U.S.-based Anaconda and Kennecott corporations. The mines were expropriated through a constitutional amendment unanimously approved by the Chilean Congress on July 11, 1971. Compensation was to be paid, but the President was authorized to deduct from the value of the mines the "excess profits"* of the companies over the previous 15 years. On September 28, it was announced that these excess profits amounted to more than the total value of the mines; thus the companies would receive no compensation. This was the so-called "Allende Doctrine."[12]

U.S. officials were quick to grab onto the measure as an excuse for their economic and diplomatic aggressions against Chile, but it seems likely that, even if Chile had acted differently on the compensation question, U.S. actions would probably have been the same.† A few days after the Allende announcement, Secretary of

---

* Excess profits were defined as those resulting from profit rates above the average of the companies in all of their international subsidiaries. This was calculated on the basis of the companies' own books for the period since 1955 (the beginning of the Nuevo Trato law).

† Testimony presented at congressional hearings, for example, indicates that Nixon and Kissinger saw the Allende election as a major blow to U.S. interests in South America, threatening the stability of Peru, Argentina, and Bolivia as well as Chile. Kissinger's statements only twelve days after the election give an indication of these views: "I don't think we should delude ourselves that an Allende takeover in Chile would not present massive problems for us, and for democratic forces and for pro–U.S. forces in Latin America, and indeed to the whole Western Hemisphere." (See *Multinational Corporations and United States Foreign Policy* [hearings before the Subcommittee on Multinational Corporations of the Committee on Foreign Relations, U.S. Senate, 93d Congress, 2d sess., 1974], Part 2, p. 543.) Kissinger personally chaired the interdepartmental working group on Chile (the 40 Committee), which ruled out new economic aid to Chile well before the copper dispute arose.

State William Rogers met with representatives of major American firms with investments in Chile—Anaconda, Ford, ITT, Ralston Purina, First National City Bank, and Bank of America—to assure them that aid would be cut off unless Chile provided compensation.[13] Finally, on January 19, 1972, President Nixon formally announced the government policy:

When a country expropriates a significant U.S. interest without making reasonable provision for [prompt and just] compensation to U.S. citizens, we will presume that the U.S. will not extend new bilateral economic benefits to the expropriating country unless and until it is determined that the country is taking reasonable steps to provide adequate compensation or that there are major factors affecting U.S. interests which require continuance of all or part of these benefits. In the face of the expropriatory circumstances just described, we will presume that the United States government will withhold its support from loans under consideration in multilateral development banks.[14]

After 1970, Chile received no new loans from U.S. government sources—AID or the Export-Import Bank—and investment guarantees were eliminated for private corporations investing in Chile by the government Overseas Private Insurance Corporation.[15] To the annoyance of hardliners such as ITT, however, disbursement was continued on loans that had previously been approved.

But it was not only the U.S. government agencies that cut off funds. The multilateral agencies followed suit—under U.S. pressure. The World Bank, which had loaned Chile $235 million since it was founded in 1944, gave Chile no new loans during the UP government. The denial of funds extended even to an electrification project that had been supported by the Bank for 20 years.[16] The Inter-American Development Bank (IDB) had also granted large loans in the past —$310,000,000 since it began operations in 1961. Under Allende, only two loans were made, and both went to opposition-controlled universities.[17] Only the International Monetary Fund (IMF) continued to provide Chile with credit; this was because Chile was entitled to certain credits under existing rules, with no special decisions required. Through this channel, the UP received $148 million in compensation for fallen copper prices and its normal allotment of drawing rights.[18]

The other source of finance that followed the U.S. government lead was the private banks. Whereas Chile had formerly received an average of $220 million in short-term credits, this was down to $35 million by 1972. In addition, all supplier credits were cut off, which meant that Chile had to pay in advance for anything that was imported.[19] It should be noted in this context that supplier credits are no special favor to underdeveloped countries; all international trade operates on the basis of short-term credits. On the other hand, the private banks had their own reasons for shutting down credit, which did not necessarily derive from government pressure. As one banker explained: "The Banco de Chile [formerly Chile's largest private bank] wasn't just the dull grey building off Huerfanos Avenue. It was the board of directors that I knew personally. As each bank was taken over, we cut credit. We didn't know if the new director would be an experienced banker or a political hack."[20] In essence, the private bankers were worried about Chile's "creditworthiness"—though it must be pointed out that it was not so much Chilean government actions that were casting doubts on Chile's creditworthiness as the actions of the U.S. government. As bilateral and multilateral aid was withdrawn, Chile's ability to service its debts declined by definition, surely part of the Nixon-Kissinger plan.

This cutoff of credit of various kinds hit industry harder than any other sector of the Chilean economy. The historical development of Chilean industry, as seen in Chapter Two, meant that the majority of firms were highly dependent on foreign imports of various kinds —raw materials, technology, spare parts, and even new machinery, since it was hard to integrate different types of equipment in the short run. Thus the credit blockade began to cause supply problems in certain sectors of industry, and the interrelated nature of the industrial sector itself, as well as its key role with respect to the rest of the economy, meant that these problems soon had a ripple effect elsewhere.

Left Opposition: The Demand for Greater Speed

As was patently obvious would happen, opposition to government policies soon began to develop. This opposition came from two sources—from the Left and from the Right. The leftist opposition came from within the UP coalition itself, especially the Socialist Party, with support from the MIR outside the coalition. At the same time, but not in any mechanically related fashion, pressure began to build from the grass roots of the working class. Both groups wanted to speed up the move toward socialism.

The first rumblings from the political party structure began to be heard after the UP won an absolute majority in the April 1971 municipal elections. Some Socialists hesitantly suggested that a plebiscite be held to approve a new constitution that would change the structure of the state. Later the leftist opposition began to focus more specifically on the economic sphere, as the short-term economic policies, which had been successfully combined with the structural transformation programs during most of 1971, began to encounter difficulties in early 1972. With the appearance of inflation, shortages of goods, and lack of foreign exchange, different analyses and recommendations began to be put forward by the two main factions within the UP. The moderates, composed of the Communist Party, the Allende wing of the Socialist Party, and the Radicals, argued for the need to consolidate the gains made during the first 18 months and to reorder the economy before moving ahead further. Chile was still a capitalist society, the argument ran, and so capitalist mechanisms must be allowed to function until they could be replaced. According to this analysis, the following steps should be taken: (1) limit the Social Area to 90 firms and stop bringing in smaller firms with no economic importance; (2) define the three areas of the economy and give guarantees to the small and medium bourgeoisie so as to gain their support; (3) raise prices to more realistic levels and reorder the relationship between prices; and (4) hold down wage increases and the government deficit in order to reduce inflation.[21]

The left-wing faction—the Altamirano wing of the Socialists, the MAPU, the Christian Left, supported from outside the coalition by the MIR—believed that the economic problems existed because the government had moved too slowly with respect to gaining control over the economy. The recommendations of this group involved (1) rapid completion of the Social Area; (2) greater control over the private sector through vigilance committees; (3) control of distribution mechanisms; (4) strong discrimination in prices, raising prices on luxury goods and freezing them on basic consumer items; and (5) periodic wage increases to keep up with the inflation rate in basic consumer goods.[22]

These two positions formally clashed at the UP conference held in the Santiago suburb of Lo Curro in June 1972. The main exponent of the former was Orlando Millas of the PC, and the latter was primarily defended by the Minister of Economics, Pedro Vuscovic. Vuscovic was an independent at the time, though he worked closely with the leftist faction of the UP and was the main force behind the requisition and intervention of industries. Although, in typical UP style, no explicit decision was made, an implicit decision emerged when Vuscovic was removed from the Ministry of Economics to become head of the Economic Coordinating Committee. He was replaced by an Allende Socialist, Carlos Matus, and Orlando Millas was made Minister of Finance.*

At about the same time that the leftist party opposition first surfaced with the April 1971 municipal elections, what was called above a grass-roots movement began to appear among the workers. This time the movement was not limited to workers in small and medium-sized factories, as had been the case during the Frei regime, but reached up to the largest factories in Chile, which were the CUT's main base of support. Although the movement began in a relatively spontaneous fashion, oriented around local issues, it soon became the nucleus of the left-wing faction, which was pushing the UP to move much faster in the structural transformations, especially with respect to the construction of the Social Area and its use to support and instigate further changes.

The first major action in this process was the occupation (*toma*) of the Yarur textile plant by its workers on April 25, 1971. There were two basic reasons for the occupation—sabotage by Amador Yarur, who represented the Yarur family in this particular enterprise, and his refusal to deal with a noncompany union. The main demand of the workers was that the factory be nationalized and incorporated into the Social Area. The idea of the occupation was supported by Economics Minister Pedro Vuscovic and the left faction of the UP; it was opposed by Allende and some Communists because they were afraid it would take the process out of their control and ruin the timing of their strategy. Nevertheless, the occupation of Yarur lasted only three days and, on April 28, the factory was requisitioned by the government. Although this was not the first factory to be taken over by the government, it was the first to be requisitioned or intervened because of a worker occupation demanding nationalization. The incorporation of the Yarur plant was important in and of itself, since it was one of the largest factories in the country and was owned by one of the most powerful financial groups in

* The Matus/Millas team came in early in July and tried to implement a series of policies along the lines of the moderates' recommendations. They had little success, however, because the policies were based on a faulty analysis of the political-economic situation in Chile at that time. The analysis failed to realize that the class struggle had brought the opposing forces to such a level of polarization that, until the question of political power was resolved, conventional economic measures could only make the situation worse.

Chile. In this sense, it marked the beginning of the struggle with the national bourgeoisie. In addition, however, it had exactly the effect that Allende and others had feared—it served as a demonstration effect for the workers and set off a wave of occupations in other factories.[23] The next month, for example, eight other large textile factories were occupied by their workers, demanding nationalization.

Even more upsetting for the strategy of the UP moderates was the eventual spread of the occupations to smaller factories that were not on the list of 91 firms to be put in the Social and Mixed areas. In June 1972, in the Santiago suburb of Maipú, a small food-processing plant called Perlak went on strike and demanded to be taken into the Social Area. The government refused, saying that the factory was not on the list of 91 and therefore would not be nationalized. The Perlak workers insisted, however, and the other factories in the Maipú area united to back the demand, taking the name Cordón Cerrillos. This was the first of the *cordones industriales*, the geographical groupings of factories that were to play an important role during the rest of the UP period and to become the key to the strategy of the leftist faction of the UP. The cordón united with other groups in the area, and blockades were set up on the roads. In addition, demonstrations were held in downtown Santiago, including the occupation of the Ministry of Labor. It became apparent that the government had to either send in the police to evict the striking workers or requisition the factory. The latter course was chosen and, in mid-July, Perlak became part of the Social Area through the first decree signed by Carlos Matus, who had come to office on a program designed, among other things, to limit the size of the Social Area and keep small firms out.[24] The process was beginning to escape from the government's control.

Right Opposition: Sabotage

Turning to the other end of the spectrum, opposition also began to develop among the Right.[25] The initial reaction of the industrial bourgeoisie to the new government alternated between panic and paralysis. A number of industrialists simply left the country, abandoning their factories; others lowered production and laid off workers. With nothing very clear about the timing or terms of expropriation, owners refrained from putting any of their own money into their firms, and they took out all they could. This semiparalysis was maintained for the first seven or eight months of the new gov-

137

ernment. The bourgeoisie's political representatives remained divided, with the Christian Democrats and the National Party each blaming the other for the Allende victory. There was general confusion about what would happen and how to defend against it. As one industrialist said:

There exists a great disorientation among the entrepreneurs and a sensation of fear that worries me. The result of this fear is that the industrialists search individually for conditions that will secure the future, absurdly believing that the current problems will be resolved in that way. In reality, the only thing they accomplish is to weaken the gremios and thereby destroy the only weapon that can strengthen the industrialists in Chile.[26]

When former SOFOFA President Eugenio Heiremans returned from a trip abroad in mid-March, he reported that foreign financial circles were shocked at the lack of reaction by the Chilean industrialists to the increasing state intervention in the economy: "rapid elimination of private enterprise, growing public expenditures which take resources from the private sector, concentration of savings in state institutions, complete economic dictatorship."[27]

Finally, in June, an event occurred that seemed to shake the bourgeoisie out of their lethargy. Edmundo Pérez Zúcovic, industrialist and former Frei Minister, was assassinated by the VOP (Vanguardia Obrero Popular), a far-left group that had broken with the MIR because the latter was considered too conservative. Pérez Zúcovic's death catalyzed a new alliance between the two bourgeois parties, the PDC and the PN. The first open evidence of the renewed alliance was the fielding of a joint candidate in the July 1971 by-election in the province of Valparaiso. This alliance was continued throughout the rest of the UP regime.

In a manner somewhat analogous to the workers' movement, events among the bourgeoisie also began to escape the traditional political framework. In the latter case, the principal manifestation was the growing importance of the class associations. SOFOFA itself began to make major changes to deal with the new situation in which it found itself. It streamlined its organization and, more important, dismissed its newly elected president and brought in a young aggressive industrialist named Orlando Sáenz. The SOFOFA old guard did not really approve of Sáenz: "He is not one of us," as one of them put it.[28] But they realized that they and their methods of behind-the-scenes bargaining were not capable of dealing with the changed circumstances, and Sáenz was both an able politician and ingenious at devising ways of combating the government. This talent had been shown when he instigated the later much-used tactic of siphoning capital out of a firm about to be nationalized and channeling it into a shadow corporation. Sáenz also had previous personal contacts with Allende so that he seemed the ideal person for the job. He took office on June 2, saying that he was aware he might be the last SOFOFA president but that he would do everything possible to prevent this. He served notice to the board that SOFOFA would have to change its traditionally elite-oriented policies and practices. "We have to broaden our bases and carry the mystique and struggle of SOFOFA to all the industrialists in Chile in order to defend what we believe in and what we have learned to honor and love in life."[29]

Sáenz also took the industrialists beyond their own organization. Just as unity with the SNA and other gremios of the large bourgeoisie had been seen as necessary during the difficult period under the Frei administration, now, since problems were even more serious, the unity had to be broader. SOFOFA became a founding member of FRENAP (Frente Nacional del Area Privada), a coordinating organization of all the large and petty bourgeois gremios. Sáenz was organizer and main speaker at the first FRENAP public event—a mass rally held in the Caupolicán Theater in Santiago on December 2, 1971. There Sáenz delivered a major speech, saying:

We have here the workers of the Private Area who want to discuss their problems in their work places and their anxieties as Chileans! We have here the Private Area which today meets in the most transcendental act in its history to speak to Chile and tell her of its fears and hopes! For it is true that today we meet under the pressure of a difficult present and an uncertain future, which oppresses us as much in our status as Private Area workers as in our status as Chilean citizens. . . . In spite of our attempts, reflected in serious productive endeavor, a national economic picture has developed that is so bleak that the efforts of the bureaucrats who try to hide it are pathetic. In spite of our firm goal of national conciliation, a civic panorama has developed that is so full of tensions and abnormalities that even the most indifferent realize that the country is in danger of a social crisis, with unpredictable, and certainly ominous, results. . . . The hour has arrived to say ENOUGH to abuse, injustice, and plunder, and because of this, we have met here today.[30]

FRENAP continued to mount its campaign, but the December 2 rally was the last time that SOFOFA took such a public role. The decision was made that it was better to let the petty bourgeois gremios take the lead so that the movement did not take on the appearance of the large bourgeoisie against the workers. In February,

SOFOFA contributed by financing a three-month publicity campaign at a cost of about $400,000. The campaign, which was designed by the advertising firm Cruz y del Solar, aimed specifically at the defeat of the UP proposal to incorporate the 91 firms into the Social and Mixed areas. It also had a broader aim, which was to generally influence public opinion against state ownership. Techniques used in the campaign included newspaper and magazine advertisements, articles by "independent journalists," radio and television programs, films, and talks.[31]

In March of 1972, planning began to take on serious dimensions. The right-wing political parties and the gremios began to plan a long-range strategy that would result in the overthrow, or at least the serious weakening, of the government, probably through a national strike. The beginning of the campaign was a meeting of 33 right-wing leaders, who stated that "our liberty, our democracy, and our human rights are seriously threatened." All who agreed with this analysis, they added, had the obligation "to act with decision and courage," since, "faced with this situation, we cannot afford cowardice or hesitancy. It is the hour of action."[32]

The rightist opposition inside Chile quickly found itself in contact with its natural allies in the United States. Long before the 1970 election, certain sectors in the United States had decided that an Allende presidency would pose a serious threat to their interests in the hemisphere. When the attempt to keep Allende from taking office failed, a consensus emerged between the U.S. government (as represented by President Nixon and his adviser Henry Kissinger) and certain U.S. corporations (ITT being the most prominent among them) with respect to a long-term strategy. One prong of the strategy was represented by the so-called "invisible blockade," i.e. the cutoff of loans and credits, described earlier. A second prong involved the Central Intelligence Agency, which was authorized to spend up to $8 million to "destabilize" the Allende government during the 1971–73 period[33]—although because of the black market in dollars, the real value of this money was closer to $40 million. President Ford later claimed that the funds went to support the opposition press and political parties, adding, "I think this was in the best interests of the people in Chile and certainly in our best interest."[34] Intelligence sources, however, say that less than half of the money actually went to opposition parties and press. Rather, it was used to support strikes by the opposition, especially the general strike called by the bourgeoisie in October 1972 in order to try to overthrow the

Allende government.[35] The third prong of the U.S. strategy involved maintaining and strengthening ties with key groups in Chile that were opposed to Allende. The most important of these groups, of course, was the military. While economic aid almost disappeared, aid to the Chilean military was actually increased. In addition, officer-training programs for all branches of the armed forces continued. Aid was also maintained for anti-Allende civilian groups.[36]

THE BOURGEOIS STRIKE, OCTOBER 1972

The right-wing opposition reached crisis proportions in October of 1972. Just as the year 1967 was the turning point for the Frei regime, so was the month of October 1972 for the UP. Before October, the Allende government was on the offensive, generally in control of the situation; after October, the government essentially limited itself to reacting to the initiatives of others. October was also important because it clarified the struggle between the government and the opposition. Its nature as a class struggle between the bourgeoisie and the workers became even more obvious than before. People were forced to take sides; and hatred between those two sides increased to the point that communications were almost totally shut off.*

The October events began on the night of October 12, when the truckowners' gremio declared itself on strike and blocked the roads leading into Santiago.[37] The strike was supposedly in support of demands for higher rates and better access to spare parts, and in defense against an alleged government threat to nationalize the trucking industry. In reality, it was what had been planned months earlier —a general strike by the bourgeoisie, an attempt either to bring the government down immediately (the PN aim) or simply to weaken it to the point that it could no longer act (the PDC goal). Within 48 hours, the truckers had been joined by the retail merchants' gremio, so that the majority of the stores (including food stores) were closed throughout the country. In addition, the professional gremios (including doctors) ordered their members to stop working, and SOFOFA called on its members to institute lockouts in their factories. The National Party and the Christian Democrats endorsed

---

* Many Christian Democratic workers put class position ahead of party affiliation and refused to go on strike. This is not to say, of course, that the divisions were 100 percent clear; there were exceptions and the petty bourgeoisie were divided as usual. But the situation was clear enough that *El Mercurio* felt it necessary to run an article denying that Chile was witnessing the class struggle that Karl Marx had written about a century earlier.

the strike, and the strikers came together to form the Frente Gremialista, with León Vilarín, head of the truckers' gremio and probably on the payroll of the CIA, at its head. With U.S. money flowing in freely, the strikers seemed prepared to hold out indefinitely.

The workers, however, had no intention of seeing their government fall. The CUT put its members in a state of emergency and called on all supporters of the government to do voluntary work. Workers joined with students, housewives, farmers, and shantytown dwellers to solve the most urgent problem, which was transportation. Cargo was piled double- and triple-load on railway cars to carry it up and down the country. In the cities, voluntary workers gathered at the stations to unload food and vital raw materials from the railway cars and to reload them into buses, trucks, private cars, or whatever else was available. They were then taken either to warehouses for later distribution or directly to factories or those stores that were open. In addition, farm products were brought in from surrounding areas.

At the same time, the industrial cordones began to multiply throughout the country. The initial task was to seize the factories where owners' lockouts were in force and to make them produce without the aid of their owners and managers. The SOFOFA strike attempt turned out to be an almost complete failure; few, if any, factories were closed.* On the other hand, many had serious problems with inputs, owing to the transportation situation. But other tasks were also urgent—food and transportation for individuals had to be provided. To solve these problems, the cordones joined with other local groups—neighborhood councils, mothers' centers, peasant unions, student associations, petty bourgeois groups that were opposed to the strike—to form *comandos comunales*. These comandos coordinated tasks in their own geographical areas. The economy was still functioning, and the working class and its allies were gaining confidence in their own ability to resolve problems.

Both sides presented their positions—the bourgeoisie in their *Pliego de Chile* and the workers in the *Pliego del Pueblo*. The former demanded the elimination of all sanctions against those participating in the strike, the complete freedom of the opposition press to

* SOFOFA, however, seems to have been more successful at another kind of role. Jonathan Kandell, former *New York Times* reporter in Santiago, claims that SOFOFA members told him they received $200,000 from companies in Mexico, Venezuela, and Peru. This money (around $1 million when exchanged on the black market) was distributed to the strikers. See *New York Times*, Oct. 15, 1974.

publish any kind of information including subversive statements, the submission of all structural changes to the opposition-controlled Congress, participation of the opposition gremios in planning and other activities, promulgation of an arms control law, the end of certain bureaucratic requirements involved in leaving the country, and elimination of neighborhood organizations, such as the Price and Supply Committees.[38] The overall effect of implementing the demands would have been to end the UP program.

As a response, the *Pliego del Pueblo* demanded the nationalization of the wholesale distribution firms, large retail chains, the major transportation companies, industrial monopolies, the large construction firms, and the rest of the banks and insurance companies; the nonreturn of firms occupied by their workers during the October strike; the expropriation of all farms over 40 hectares; the expropriation of all U.S. investments in Chile and the end of payments on the foreign debt; more taxes on capital and higher wage readjustments for workers, including discriminating readjustments (whereby those earning less would get higher readjustments); increasing facilities and local control of health, education, and distribution; and more just treatment of women.[39] The effect of implementing these demands would have been to greatly speed up the UP program and to increase the conflicts with the bourgeoisie.

Although the workers had risen to the occasion, the government per se seemed to be foundering. It could do nothing to break the truckers' strike; neither threats nor bribes would work. The situation was made more difficult owing to the nature of the trucking sector. Many trucks were individually owned; others were held in fleets of two, three, or four; very few were part of large companies. In addition, most of the trucks were hidden, and/or vital parts had been removed so they were immobilized. The commerce problem was similar in that a large percentage of the sector was also composed of individually owned small stores. With respect to industry, the government limited itself to ratifying the worker occupations by intervening and requisitioning factories where lockouts had occurred. More than 50 factories were put under state control during this period.[40] The only initiative taken by the government was to declare a state of emergency and put the military in control of maintaining law and order.

As the days passed, however, Allende devised a plan—to bring the military directly into the government in order to end the strike and, he said, to strengthen the regime. At first he could find no support for this tactic, not even from the Communist Party, while the Socialists declared themselves totally opposed. But it seemed that there were only two possibilities—incorporate the military or rely on the workers and drastically increase the speed of changes. Faced with this choice, the PC came around to support the Allende plan and the PS gave in as usual.

Thus, on November 2, Allende announced a new cabinet, which included three military men: General Carlos Prats, Commander in Chief of the Army, as Minister of Interior; Admiral Ismael Huerta as Minister of Public Works; and Air Force General Claudio Sepúlveda as Minister of Mining. In an attempt to mollify the workers, the two top leaders of the CUT— President Luis Figueroa and Secretary-General Rolando Calderón—were also given cabinet positions as Ministers of Labor and Agriculture, respectively. Prats ordered the striking bourgeoisie back to work and they responded immediately. Negotiations were carried on in which the bourgeoisie won many concessions that they had not been able to gain during the strike itself. Both sides claimed victory, but it seemed clear that few major changes would be made with the military in the government.

"HASTA LAS ULTIMAS CONSEQUENCIAS,"
NOVEMBER 1972–SEPTEMBER 1973

Contradictory Government Initiatives

It is somewhat difficult to characterize government policy during the last year of the UP because it had little coherence or focus.* Rather, it consisted of trying to survive on a day-to-day basis, of reacting to the initiatives of others, of floating some trial balloons and pulling them down as soon as they encountered rough going. Differences within the UP continued, leaving the government helpless to act as production fell, inflation increased, and terrorism mounted.

With the military in the cabinet between November and March, there was little expectation that the structural changes would go forward very rapidly. In fact, the first major initiative after the end of the strike was an attempt to pull back. The so-called Millas Plan, presented by the Minister of Finance in January of 1973, called for a "reexamination" of the industries currently within the Social

---

* The literal translation of the phrase *"hasta las últimas consequencias"* is "to the ultimate consequences." It continually appeared in speeches of both the government and the opposition in 1973, indicating a general hardening of line.

Area. The implication was that many of the smaller firms would be returned to their owners. The cordones mounted strong opposition to the plan; in addition, the Socialist Party leaders claimed they had never been consulted on the plan, which they said was elaborated by Allende, the Communists, and the military. Eventually the plan was withdrawn.[41]

At approximately the same time, however, the government also launched an initiative toward the left. In early January, Minister of Economics Fernando Flores announced a proposed rationing plan to combat the scarcities being caused by the black market, sabotage, and production declines caused by the invisible blockade and other problems. According to this plan, some 27 basic commodities would be distributed at official prices through the neighborhood-based Price and Supply Committees (Juntas de Abastecimiento y Precios —the JAP); the products included such items as sugar, flour, rice, noodles, cooking oil, coffee, and tea. This program, however, encountered immediate opposition from the Right, which claimed that the UP was "trying to control Chile through the stomach." A major campaign was mounted in the bourgeois newspapers against the rationing scheme, which then was also withdrawn. The only aspect of the plan that survived was the establishment of a Distribution Secretariat, but this was also tied to the military with the appointment of Air Force General Alberto Bachelet as director.

Although the above measures may seem to move in contradictory directions, both were actually quite compatible with the main goal of the military officials who were friendly to the regime (the "constitutionalists"). What they wanted was to increase the *order* of the process. Most of these officers supported the government because they believed that a constitutionally elected government should be alllowed to finish its term, although a few were authentic supporters of the UP program per se.[42] The priority on order was also inherent in the strategy of the moderate faction within the UP, while the left faction was more interested in increasing the UP's political control over the economy and thought that order could be sought later.

The March Election

Most of the country's attention in the months immediately following the strike was concentrated on the March congressional election, which, like all of the by-elections since mid-1971, was fought as a two-way battle between the bourgeois parties and the UP. The former were hoping to gain a two-thirds majority in the

Congress so they could impeach Allende (PN aim), or at least take control of the country through their ability to override a presidential veto (PDC). The UP, which had originally hoped to gain a congressional majority in this election in order to carry through the "peaceful road to socialism," had now scaled down its goal to preventing the opposition from attaining two-thirds.

The PN-PDC alliance hammered on the themes of shortages and the difficulties in obtaining goods, as well as generally on anticommunism. The UP dwelt on the improvements in the living standards of the workers, but their biggest pitch was a call to defend the workers' government against those who were trying to destroy it. This was best captured in the MAPU slogan "This government may be shit, but at least it's ours." Thanks in part to the new level of class consciousness achieved through the October strike, the workers did rally to the support of the government, and, for the first time in memory, the party in control of the Executive branch increased its percentage of the vote in the mid-term election. Thus, the UP went from 36 percent in 1970 to 44 percent in 1973. The UP was jubilant about the results, which far exceeded their expectations. The bourgeoisie also claimed victory on the basis that they had won a majority (56 percent) of the votes. But this was far short of the 67 percent they had counted on, and their last chance to eliminate the UP legally before the 1976 elections was gone.

Infighting Within the Left

The results of the election generally served to increase the divisions within the UP. The moderate faction said that the increased support justified the policies in force since June of the previous year; the Left said that advantage must be taken of the increased support to move ahead more rapidly. The schism was both symbolized and intensified by a split in the MAPU immediately after the election. Two new parties resulted; one continued to be called MAPU and supported the left wing of the UP, while the other took on the name MAPU-Obrero y Campesino (MAPU-OC) and backed the UP moderates. The PC, which was generally acknowledged to be behind the split, hoped it would lead to a similar break within the Socialist Party, thus giving the moderates a clear majority within the UP.[43]

Within the labor movement, the growing conflicts between the two factions of the UP were reflected in the relationship between the CUT and the cordones. The main problem arose because the CUT was dominated by the Communists, whereas the cordones had been founded and were led by the Socialists and the MIR. A secondary reason, however, was merely that a large bureaucracy, like the CUT, will try to avoid losing any of its power. Originally the CUT and the PC had both ignored the cordones. When they began to prove themselves useful in practical terms as well as a potential power base, then the CUT and the PC changed their attitude and began to move in. Since they were obviously going to keep on existing, the question became one of the proper relationship between the cordones, on the one hand, and the CUT and the government, on the other.

In general, the leaders of the cordones tried to avoid open conflict with the CUT. The long delay in attempting to form a national coordinating committee of the cordones was, in large part, due to fear that such a committee would be interpreted as an attack on the CUT. Thus, it was not until late July 1973 that the cordones were united on the national level, and the structure was never very strong. The head of the committee immediately made a statement denying any rift or intention of creating an organization parallel to the CUT:

Our coordinating committee, or, if you prefer, our meeting of cordón leaders, has no other purpose than to share experiences, to avoid the self-centeredness that has developed in some cordones, to avoid the development of parallel cordones, and to avoid infantile leftist deviations. We are basically talking about coordinating the struggle. We do not aim to replace the CUT or the political parties, which are the organizations that should lead the struggle of the working class in our country.[44]

The main mobilization of the cordones in 1973 occurred during the abortive coup attempt on June 29. The cordones were the key to the seizure of factories in response to Allende's call to protect the government. Over 350 factories were occupied by their workers; defense organizations were quickly formed, and buses and trucks operating in the vicinities of the factories were requisitioned to assure transportation facilities. The importance of the worker organizations was reinforced, since, early in the morning of June 29, when the dimensions of the coup attempt were still unclear, the UP parties made the decision to distribute arms to the workers so they could defend themselves and the government if necessary. In the days that followed, as rumors of more military conspiracies in other parts of the country continued, new cordones were formed, and attempts were made to combine forces with students, peasants, and other groups to constitute new comandos comunales.

At the superstructural level, however, things were different. As soon as the immediate threat was removed, the government decided to stabilize the situation. Thus, although the workers, backed by the cordones, were prepared to assume the management of the factories they had taken over, they could not obtain the support of the CUT for their incorporation into the Social Area. The CUT promised only to study the matter, and decision making was turned over to a CUT-government commission, leaving the workers and cordones out of the process. The result was that all but 15 factories were eventually returned.[45]

While the cordones were intent on increasing the power of the UP by increasing its control over the means of production and by providing an organizational base that the government could use to decrease its reliance on the military, the CUT continued its more traditional tactics of mobilization. The main CUT weapons were rallies and demonstrations, with the idea that if the bourgeoisie saw concrete proof of the number of government supporters, they would be afraid to attempt a coup. Rallies were also, of course, supposed to raise the morale and increase the enthusiasm of the workers themselves. As the situation got more and more tense, the CUT responded by calling more and more rallies.

Rightist Opposition Hardens

The bourgeoisie, meantime, was marshaling its own forces. The March congressional election was a key turning point. The opposition's failure to attain the two-thirds majority necessary to impeach Allende meant that it would be three more years before there would be another opportunity to remove the UP by constitutional means. In the meantime, if UP strength kept growing at the same rate, it might even win a majority in 1976. Although many industrialists had favored a military coup long ago, this now appeared the only possible way of maintaining the capitalist system and their own rapidly vanishing economic power and privileges. Sáenz's post-electoral speech to SOFOFA members previewed this situation in its praise of the armed forces and its talk of "imminent change":

An imminent change is due that will determine the course of our future. In a few more months, Chile will have been subsumed in a Marxist dictatorship or will have emerged in the full light of liberty. The most recent attempt to control the process set loose by President Allende has been closed off in these days. The armed forces, which in November put aside their whole tradition and patriotically risked their most cherished values in order to try to save Chile, today leave the government, convinced that the tasks of democratic administration are impossible when it is necessary to work together with those who are determined to submit the country to blood and fire.[46]

In the events that followed, the industrialists generally let others take the lead. In May, for example, copper workers who supported the opposition were persuaded to go on strike.[*] Because of careless drafting of the October 1972 readjustment law, the miners were formally owed a 150 percent salary increase rather than only 100 percent like everyone else. Obviously a strike by any sector of the workers was worth a thousand protests by the bourgeoisie in terms of influencing public opinion. The word went out, in Chile and throughout the world, that the workers were rejecting the government that claimed to act in their name. The industrialists and their friends limited their role to contributing a few items from their hoarded supplies to the miners and congratulating them on their patriotism—probably the first time the bourgeoisie had ever supported a workers' strike.

Behind the scenes, the industrialists were much more active. Sáenz himself was widely believed to be involved with the right-wing terrorist group Patria y Libertad. He made several visits to Buenos Aires to consult with Roberto Thieme, head of Patria y Libertad in exile. In addition, a letter was confiscated from Pablo Rodríguez, head of Patria y Libertad in Chile, to Sáenz. The letter was sent from the Ecuadorian embassy, where Rodríguez took asylum after the June 29 coup attempt in which the right-wing group confessed to being involved. The letter said:

As you know, there are few among us who consider what happened [the putting down of the coup attempt] a defeat. Many people remain ready and willing and on the job. We need to guide them and help them in these difficult moments. . . . The previous services you have rendered to our cause make us realize that we can count on your disinterested collaboration, not only now but also in the future. This help also confirms your allegiance to the principles that guide our actions. . . . I can give the most complete assurances that your help in the defense of liberty and democracy will be duly acknowledged after our triumph.[47]

---

[*] UP workers also briefly joined the strike at the beginning. This can mainly be attributed to the failure of the UP to keep track of what was happening at the base level and the failure to make adequate explanations to the workers with respect to government policies. The UP workers, and the blue-collar workers in general, returned to work after a couple of days. The main body of strikers then became opposition supporters among the white-collar workers.

The industrialists and other members of the bourgeoisie were also in the best position to lobby with the top military hierarchy in fa ɔr of military intervention, as well as to lobby with the U.S. government and corporations for financial and other kinds of assistance.

The Second Bourgeois Strike

On July 29, the bourgeoisie declared a second general strike. Again spearheaded by the truckers, this second strike was much lower-key than the previous one. Commerce was interrupted only occasionally, and the industrialists did not attempt to close the factories on a large scale. In fact, the industrialists maintained a low profile in general, with SOFOFA's actions limited to a statement supporting the truckers "and vigorously condemning the brutal repression by the government."[48] "What else could we do?" asked a key SOFOFA member. "Our attempt to close down the factories in October was a total failure. We can't close down industry if the workers don't want it. All we can do is to support the others."[49] Support also came from the United States, as money again poured in to sustain the strike.*

Although the strike itself may have been low-key, the terrorist activities that accompanied it were not. Between July 29 and the middle of August, 20 persons had been killed; there had been 71 attacks on trucks that were still functioning, 77 against buses, 16 against service stations, and 37 against railroad lines. In addition, two major oil pipelines were blown up. Potentially the most serious attack occurred on August 13, when terrorists blew up many high-voltage electricity towers, causing blackouts in eight provinces that lasted for several hours. The government estimated that if all parts of the plan had functioned, the entire country could have been without electricity for at least a month.[50]

Although the workers were willing to come to the aid of the government, Allende hesitated to call on them, thinking that this would be interpreted as a direct provocation by the Right and even by some of the "constitutionalist" military. In part also, Allende's hesitancy surely derived from the realization that the workers had not been adequately prepared for an open confrontation with the military.† Whatever the reasons, failure to rely on the workers

---

*An extra $1 million was appropriated in August for destabilizing activities, although the money apparently did not get into circulation before the coup. See the *New York Times*, Oct. 21, 1974.

†A confrontation would have had to pit workers against the military, perhaps with some proportion of the latter on the side of the former, because the Right itself

meant the necessity of relying more and more on the support of the military. The latter were given ever-increasing powers, the most important of which was the authorization to conduct searches for arms whenever a denunciation was made. Theoretically, these searches were designed to disarm both the Right and the Left, but over 90 percent of them were carried out in homes, factories, or party headquarters of UP supporters. In many parts of the country, the military were in effective control long before September 11. The stage was thus set for the end.

EPILOGUE: THE COUP

On September 11, 1973, the UP experience came to an abrupt halt as the armed forces and police carried out the most brutal coup in recent Latin American history. Although Chile had been rife with coup rumors for months, and especially in the weeks before the 11th, very few people foresaw the nature the coup would take. Much of the Left expected a *golpe blando*, a soft coup, whereby the armed forces would be invited to occupy many of the key government posts, and even some Christian Democrats might join the coalition. With this would come a crackdown on both the far Right and the far Left as well as a revised UP program. At most, there might be a military pronouncement, with elections then called within a few months. But, as had been the case since the very beginning, the bourgeoisie understood the process unleashed by the UP far better than the latter itself did.

They realized that the perspective of the working class had changed during the three years of the Allende government. The workers had participated in the exercise of power; their families had grown accustomed to a new standard of living; and both had experienced a new sense of dignity. At the same time, the workers had increased their understanding about who had been denying them these things during previous years and how it had been done. As the level of class consciousness increased, so the polarization increased between classes, and the hatred increased between classes. Chile, in the winter of 1973,* was not one nation but two, and the

---

had no significant civilian base that was willing to engage in armed struggle. The whole strategy of the Right had been oriented precisely toward convincing the military to intervene. This interpretation of Allende's actions is supported by comments of his personal political adviser. See Joan Garcés, *Allende y la experiencia chilena* (Barcelona, 1976), chap. 10.

* The southern winter, i.e. June–August.

only communications between the two were messages of hostility. As many people warned, the civil war had already begun. Finally, in addition to perspective and consciousness, the working class had changed in terms of organization and strength. The regional organizations, the cordones, had increased their combat potential, and the parties had guns that could be used. If these workers combined with some sector of the armed forces, they might very likely be able to win a civil war in combination with the active help of large portions of the population.

Therefore, a half-way coup would not work. The only way to success (defined by Air Force General Gustavo Leigh as erasing the last 50 years of Chilean history) was by speed, surprise, and overwhelming force and brutality. This was the only way to break the working class—and to prevent a split in the armed forces. So, on September 11, the military called out not only their tanks but their bombers. By 6:00 A.M., the main port of Valparaiso was under military control. By 8:00 A.M., the bombers had silenced all but one UP radio station. At 10:00, they bombed the presidential residence of Tomás Moro. At 11:00, they bombed the Presidential Palace itself after Allende refused to surrender. In the afternoon, they bombed areas of stubborn resistance in the factories and shantytowns. In areas of lesser resistance, tanks and troops, with orders to kill, were sent in to eliminate resisters.[51] At 6:00 P.M., people were ordered to their homes on pain of death; but the next 42 hours of continuous curfew meant death for thousands in any case. In the weeks and months that followed, murder, mass arrests, concentration camps, and torture became commonplace.[52]

The violence used was only the logical culmination of the level to which the class struggle had progressed in Chile. A standoff was no longer possible—either the workers had to impose their control or the bourgeoisie had to impose theirs. The divisions within the former, plus the strong commitment of many of the leaders to constitutionality, meant that the workers would not take the first step. The bourgeoisie, long used to using violence when it was necessary and more committed to the capitalist system than to its democratic trappings, had no such hesitations.

In the aftermath, more logical consequences followed. In government, the bourgeoisie shared office with the military and implemented policies to benefit both. Military salaries were quickly raised and their privileges were increased. Factories were returned to their former owners. The agrarian reform—of both Frei and Allende—was undone. Those collectives that have not been returned to their former owners have been divided into individual holdings. Agreements were made to compensate the copper companies. At the other end of the spectrum, the workers saw their purchasing power drop by an estimated 50 percent, as wages were held down while prices were allowed to rise to whatever level the bourgeoisie chose. Unemployment also added to the workers' problems as mass firings were undertaken for political reasons. Hunger and cold once again became problems for Chile's workers and their families. In an ironic twist of events, however, the workers were not the only ones who suffered from the Junta's economic policies. The small and medium bourgeoisie, and especially the petty bourgeoisie, found themselves squeezed between increasing costs and the absence of demand due to falling real wages. Thus, the rate of bankruptcies skyrocketed— precisely among those groups who had become convinced that their interests lay with the large bourgeoisie.[53]

No definitive evidence about a U.S. role in the coup itself has come to light, although it seems likely that the American military provided technical assistance. Certain crucial facts, however, are very clear: the U.S. government and corporations provided massive aid to the Allende opposition, and they made it clear that they would welcome the downfall of the UP. The economic and diplomatic aid that followed the coup provides the base on which the Junta currently rests. This is not to say that U.S. forces "caused" the coup, but that their assistance was important in supporting the efforts of the internal opposition; the interests of the internal and external bourgeoisie coincided and each played a crucial role.[54]

The current policies, which favor the Chilean and foreign bourgeoisie and the military at the expense of all others, are being maintained by fear and repression. How long this can go on, before a new stage of the class struggle is reached, remains to be seen.

CHAPTER SEVEN

Economic Policies: Differences Among Regimes

As WAS DEMONSTRATED in Chapter Three, there were major differences among the Alessandri, Frei, and Allende regimes in terms of the class base of their support and their development ideologies and political-economic programs. A basic hypothesis of this study predicts that these differences should, in turn, produce significant variations in the policies followed by the three. This chapter will review a series of policy areas where the differences among regimes were indeed substantial.* Such policies include those relating to public vs. private control of resources, investment, distribution, and relations with the foreign sector. This list is by no means exhaustive; it merely illustrates some important areas where the three governments succeeded in carrying out policies that were more or less in line with the development ideologies they espoused. On the other hand, there were also aspects of economic policy where the similarities were more important than the differences. Examples include policies leading to the stop-go cycles to which the Chilean economy has long been subject, and areas where the three governments tried to carry out policies in line with their development ideologies but were frustrated by the actions of domestic or foreign groups that felt their interests were being threatened. Policy similarities will be discussed in Chapter Eight.

---

* The policies that will be discussed are *implemented* policies. That is, two stages are being combined: policy proposals and implementation. Policy areas where implementation was problematical will be discussed in Chapter Eight.

CONTROL OF RESOURCES

Property Relations

At the very heart of the differences between development ideologies was the issue of public vs. private control of resources. The uses to which these resources would be put was a separate question, which will be dealt with below; but the basic question of control was a crucial issue in its own right. The importance of who controlled real resources (i.e. the means of production) is obvious because of the relationship to the mode of production that would be dominant in the country. State ownership of basic industries would permit, though not necessarily lead to, the transition from a capitalist to a socialist mode of production. Control of financial resources —through such mechanisms as the public sector budget and bank credit—offered another, if more indirect, way of controlling the economy. That is, through use of its financial power, the state could exert strong influence over the activities of those sectors of the economy remaining under private ownership.

The views of the three regimes about the proper division between state and private property—and, within the private sector, between national and foreign capital—varied greatly. Alessandri thought the state should own as little as possible; but, on the other hand, he was not in favor of excessive protection for domestic industry and tried to induce foreigners to invest in Chile. Frei believed that the private sector (national and foreign) should be dominant but subject to certain controls. He put particular emphasis on joint state-private ownership schemes, especially for large-scale projects. Allende believed that the state should own all key industries, as well as those in monopoly positions, and that private capital should operate only in nonessential areas. (See Chapter Three for an elaboration of these themes.)

When Alessandri came into office in 1958, the state owned a number of industrial corporations, especially in the intermediate goods sector. The most important included the National Oil Company (ENAP), the National Sugar Company (IANSA), the Army and Navy metal works (FAMAE and ASMAR, respectively), the Sulfuric Acid Company (FASSA), the Chilean Fertilizer Company (SOCHIF), part of the Pacific Steel Company (CAP), and several fish-processing companies.[1] Although he was opposed to state ownership and did not increase the state share of industrial property, it is interesting to note that Alessandri did not undertake the "desocialization" process that many industrialists wished.[2] The traditionally strong role of the state in the economy was simply too well established. There was not much change with respect to foreign ownership either, although the Alessandri regime tried hard to attract foreign investment. Two laws were passed that offered strong incentives to foreign industries, guaranteeing them the right to repatriate any amount of profits, free access to foreign exchange markets, tax exemptions, and import privileges. Response was slow, however, until the final year of the administration.

Frei, on the other hand, moved to increase state control over industrial property, mainly by the formation of new enterprises. The most important of these were a petrochemical complex, formed jointly with Dow Chemical, and two new paper plants. Frei was also interested in attracting foreign capital and was more successful in the attempt than was Alessandri. Foreign capital, however, tended to buy out existing industrial facilities rather than establishing new ones and thus adding to productive capacity.[3] As was explained in Chapter Five, the main controversy over property under the Frei regime came with respect to the constitutional amendment on property rights in connection with the agrarian reform. This amendment introduced the concept of the "social function" of property and made expropriations easier, which aroused strong opposition from the industrial bourgeoisie and their organization SOFOFA. In spite of their pressure tactics, the industrialists were not able to significantly water down the property amendment.

The Allende policy called for the creation of a Social Area of the economy which would become the dominant economic force. It would be composed of wholly state-owned firms and complemented by a Mixed Area of joint state-private firms where the state would own at least 51 percent of the capital. The Mixed Area was to consist primarily of state-foreign companies and be confined to those industries where foreign capital and technology were considered vital. In addition to the 43 industrial firms owned by the state in 1970, the UP expropriated seven industries, founded eight new enterprises, bought 85 existing industrial firms, and intervened or requisitioned 250 more by December 1972.[4] Of these 250, only 70 were formally scheduled to be in the Social or Mixed Area. The rest were taken over in response to the demands of their workers, who occupied them. Another large number of factories were taken over, formally or de facto, during the aborted coup attempt of June 29,

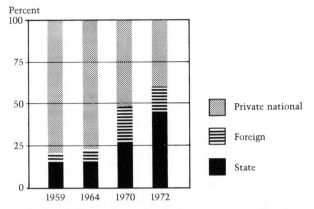

Fig. 7.1. Ownership/control of industrial capital, 1959–72, including industries intervened or requisitioned during 1971–72. These estimates are based on a CORFO study of property ownership covering the period 1967–69. (See Luis Pacheco, "La inversión extranjera y las corporaciones internacionales en el desarrollo industrial chileno," in Oscar Muñoz, ed., *Proceso a la industrialización chilena* [Santiago, 1972].) Extrapolations are then made backward and forward. The 1972 figures add to the 1969 totals for state property *only* those industries taken over by the government which were on the list of the 90 firms to become part of the Social or Mixed Area. Therefore, the state totals are an underestimation of the property under state control. Data on the 90 firms come from "Notas e informaciones," *Panorama Económico*, No. 278, July 1973, cuadro 3, p. 8. The 1959 and 1964 figures are extrapolations based on the 1967 data plus investment trends.

1973, when Allende called on the workers to occupy their factories in order to defend the government.

Precise data on the ownership of property do not exist, but Figure 7.1 gives some rough estimates. Private national ownership dropped from 80 to 77 percent during Alessandri's term, to 52 percent at the end of Frei's term, and finally to 40 percent by 1972. Foreign investment, during the same years, rose from 5 to 8 percent, then to 20 percent, and then dropped to 15 percent. State participation stayed constant under Alessandri at 15 percent, rose to 28 percent by 1970, and to 45 percent by the end of 1972.*

*The only indication of what happened in the state sector between December 1972 and the coup comes from an article by Pedro Vuscovic in *Las Noticias de Ultima Hora*, June 7, 1973. According to this source, the *number* of industrial firms under state ownership increased from 103 in December 1972 to 165 in May 1973. Industrial firms that were requisitioned or intervened rose from 99 to 120. Thus the total number of firms under some form of state control increased by over 40 percent in this period. Since the size of these firms is not known, however, the effects of the changes on the pattern of ownership of industrial capital cannot be determined. (See Stefan de Vylder, *Allende's Chile* [Cambridge, 1976], p. 145.)

157

Public Sector Budget

Turning to control over financial resources, the first item concerns the evolution of the public sector budget as a share of the gross domestic product. The public sector in Chile was composed of the fiscal sector (the ministries), the decentralized institutions (those agencies that carried out the direct state intervention in the economy, e.g. the Development Corporation, the Agrarian Reform Corporation, the Copper Corporation), and, after 1970, the state-controlled industries. Before 1970, the last two categories were combined. The relative importance of these sectors varied over time, with the fiscal sector declining in importance as the role of the state expanded. In 1961, the fiscal sector was 55 percent of the total public expenditure, whereas, by 1972, it had decreased to only 28 percent.[5] In a trend similar to that observed with respect to ownership of property, the state came to control a growing share of the GDP during the 1958–73 period. As can be seen in Figure 7.2, the average share of the public sector during the Alessandri administration was 38 percent, rising to 43 percent under Frei and to 53 percent under Allende.

To understand what the public sector budget meant in terms of the Chilean economy, it is necessary to look at its component parts. The budget was divided into current and capital expenditures. Current expenditures accounted for about three-quarters of the total and mainly consisted of remunerations and social security payments to public sector employees. These outlays tended to maintain a fairly steady upward trend, regardless of changes in the size of the budget as a whole. Capital expenditure, on the other hand, experienced much greater fluctuations, depending on whether the government in any given year wanted to expand or contract economic activity. In addition to fluctuations in the total amount of capital expenditure, changes were made in the type of expenditures. These latter trends also formed a pattern during the three regimes: Alessandri concentrated on infrastructure investment (especially transport and energy); the Frei regime gave more or less equal priority to the productive sectors (agriculture, industry, and mining) and social services (health, education, and housing); and the Allende administration focused expenditure primarily on the social services.[6] These priorities fit, in general terms, with the development ideologies of the three.

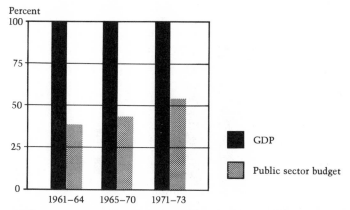

Fig. 7.2. Public sector budget as percentage of GDP, 1961–73. Calculated from Mini: terio de Hacienda, *Balance consolidado del sector público de Chile*, various years.

The budget provided the state with two types of control over the economy. First, the budget constituted the most important tool for regulating the level of activity of the economy. This Keynesian function and its consequences will be discussed in greater detail in Chapter Eight. In addition, use of capital expenditures—both direct and indirect investment—was a way of influencing both the amount of investment and the sectors to which investment was directed. Obviously, the larger the budget as a percentage of the GDP, the larger the influence of the state would be.

Credit

Bank credit was related to the budget, since the portion of credit going to the public sector then became part of the public sector budget per se. As would be expected, credit to the public sector became an ever-larger share of the total, increasing from an average of 41 percent under Alessandri to 54 percent under Frei to 79 percent under Allende. See Figure 7.3.

The banking system was regarded by all groups in Chile as crucially important in the operation of the economy. The system consisted of the Central Bank, the State Bank, and 26 major commercial banks (including branches of First National City Bank, Bank of America, and two European banks). Prior to 1971, the vast majority of the credit from the State Bank and the commercial banks went to the private sector or, more specifically, to the large bourgeoisie,

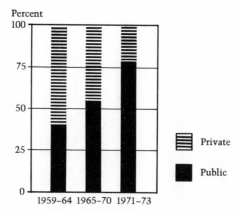

Fig. 7.3. Comparison of public and private shares of bank credit, 1959–73. Calculated from Banco Central, *Boletín Mensual*, various numbers.

since credit was highly concentrated.* This access to credit, which was generally not available to small and medium firms, was an important source of economic power for the large bourgeoisie. Its importance was increased by the situation with respect to interest rates. Because of the traditionally high inflation rates in Chile, the real interest rate was generally negative, such that, instead of having to pay to borrow money, borrowers actually made money through loans because less was paid back in real terms than was borrowed. Inflation exceeded the interest rate in all but three of the 15 years (1960, 1961, and 1971). On the other hand, the interest rate was not the only cost of borrowing; there were also a number of taxes that increased the cost. During the Frei period, the taxes had the specific aim of making the interest rate positive; that is, they were a function of the inflation rate. When the taxes were added, the *real* cost of credit was negative only in 1959, 1963–64, and 1972–73. Very low real costs, however, were still quite common.[7] Under the Allende regime, special attempts were made to funnel credit to the small and medium producers. For example, interest rates for these groups were 12 percent in 1971–72 and 18 percent in 1973 (as compared with 15 and 30 percent for other borrowers).

The operation of the credit system was one of the most blatant

*Near the end of the Alessandri period, 3.8 percent of all borrowers received 56 percent of all credit; this situation changed very little during the Frei period. (See Ricardo Ffrench-Davis, *Políticas económicas en Chile, 1952–70* [Santiago, 1973], pp. 137–52.)

examples of the bourgeoisie using their political power to increase their economic benefits. In this case, they did not even need to rely on the state to serve their interests—they could do it directly. The board of directors of the Central Bank, which established monetary and credit policy, was composed of 11 persons. Of the 11, three were representatives of the private banks, two of the empresarial associations, one of the private shareholders; of the other five, four were appointed by the President of the Republic and one represented the bank employees.[8] Frei tried to change the lineup to increase the power of the Executive, but was blocked in Congress by the representatives of the bourgeoisie. Allende, however, realized that the only way to gain real control over credit was to take over the private banks rather than trying to devise ways of controlling the actions of the private sector. By the end of 1971, the majority of the private national banks were in state hands, and the four private foreign-owned banks had also been purchased. This meant that the state controlled over two-thirds of the credit of the entire banking system.[9] The following year, the government also gained a majority on the board of directors of the Banco de Chile, the largest private bank in the country.

INVESTMENT

Aggregate Level

A second important set of policies, which varied substantially among the three regimes, concerned investment, both the amount of money invested and its sectoral distribution. Investment in Chile, in the economy as a whole as well as in industry, had traditionally been low, which, in turn, led to slow growth in capacity. The period being considered in this study was no different in this respect. As can be seen in Figure 7.4, gross industrial investment under Alessandri averaged E°368 million per year (9.4 percent of industrial output). During the Frei regime, the average increased to E°520 million (10.0 percent of output), but under Allende it dropped to E°312 million (5.0 percent of output).*

In addition, there were important differences in who was doing the investing over the period. The vast majority of investment (71

*Calculating depreciation on the basis of a 30-year life for capital equipment, *net* investment as a percentage of industrial output averaged 5.5 percent under Alessandri, 5.8 percent under Frei, and 0.7 percent under Allende. Using these same calculations, the increase in the capital stock in industry was 3.9, 4.5, and 0.0 percent, respectively.

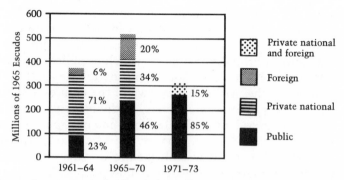

Fig. 7.4. Investment in fixed capital in industry, 1961–73. Source: Table A.7.

percent) during the Alessandri administration was carried out by the private national sector. Foreign investors contributed only 6 percent, while the remaining 23 percent was done by the state. Under Frei, both foreign and state investment increased at the expense of private national investors. State investment averaged 46 percent of the total in the 1965–70 period, while foreign investment accounted for 20 percent. Private national investment was 34 percent. The Allende period saw almost all investment (about 85 percent) done by the state, while the private sector—national and foreign—contributed only about 15 percent.

It might be expected that investment rates (gross investment to output) would be correlated with the emphasis that a regime put on investment as compared to consumption. Since, at the level of development ideologies, Alessandri put the highest stress on investment, followed by Frei and then Allende, investment might have been expected to follow this same pattern. This did happen in the private national sector, but trends in the public and foreign sectors were sufficiently different that they offset private national investment trends, producing higher investment rates under Frei than under Alessandri. That is, both state and foreign investment increased substantially in the Frei period as compared with the previous administration. Under Allende all private investment dropped off heavily, and state investment could not increase enough to offset the drop. State investment in industry increased in 1971, but fell off substantially in 1972 and only began to recover in 1973. As will be seen, the fall was due both to investment being squeezed by consumption and to problems with planning.

Sectoral Distribution

Turning to sectoral trends in investment, it is necessary to divide investment according to its source because state, foreign, and private national investors did not act in the same way.* To begin with state investment, it must first be pointed out that the majority of state investment (especially direct investment) went into the intermediate goods sector because these were the industries—petroleum, chemicals, steel—where large amounts of capital were required and where the state owned more of the means of production. This was true in all three regimes, but, beyond this base, there were the usual distinctions.

Alessandri thought the state should confine itself to direct investment in intermediate goods as an aid to the private sector and, with indirect investment, lend money in accordance with the wishes of the private sector (as opposed to any system of state planning).[10] Frei put strong emphasis on state investment in export industries—especially paper and petrochemicals; these projects were to be carried out as joint ventures with foreign capital. Indirect investment was to favor these same areas as well as the durable consumer goods sector.[11] During the Allende period, there was serious disagreement over investment policy. One group within the administration wanted to concentrate state resources on the basic consumer goods sector; the other group agreed that this sector was important, but believed that it needed only small amounts of investment to break bottlenecks, and that emphasis should be placed on five basic areas in order to increase foreign exchange. These areas were copper, iron and steel, wood and paper, fishing, and agro-industry. Both groups were agreed, however, that state investment in durable consumer goods and petrochemicals must stop.[12]

Data on the sectoral breakdown of industrial investment are quite difficult to find, but Table 7.1 gives some approximations for the Alessandri and Frei periods. These data show that state industrial investment under Alessandri was heavily concentrated in two areas: the oil and fish-processing industries. Oil investment went into the

---

* Here only state and foreign investment will be discussed because of lack of data on the private national sector. Some data are available on credit from the banking system to private industry (from the Statistical Bulletin of the Superintendencia de Bancos), but this credit was short-term and used for operating expenses rather than investment.

TABLE 7.1
Sectoral Distribution of Public Investment in Industry, 1961–70
(Millions of 1965 escudos and percent)

Sector	1961–64		1965–70	
	Annual average	Percent	Annual average	Percent
Food	E° 2.4	3.0%	E° 5.1	2.1%
Sugar	1.0	1.2	27.5	11.5
Fish products	25.1	31.0	5.8	2.4
Textiles	—	—	6.7	2.8
Wood/paper	3.2	4.0	31.3	13.0
Chemicals	1.0	1.2	21.7	9.0
Oil	33.6	41.5	83.8	34.9
Construction materials	0.2	0.3	0.5	0.2
Metal/metal products	0.6	0.7	22.4	9.3
FAMAE/ASMAR[a]	6.6	8.2	5.1	2.1
Other	5.0	6.2	9.6	4.0
Technology[b]	2.2	2.7	20.9	8.7
TOTAL	E° 80.9	100.0%	E° 240.4	100.0%

SOURCE: Table A.8.
NOTE: Direct and indirect investment as presented in Table A.7.
[a] Army and Navy metal works.
[b] Includes feasibility studies and money for the Technical Cooperation Service (SERCOTEC), the National Training Institute (INACAP), and the Technological Research Committee.

National Oil Company (ENAP), while both public and private fish-processing companies received state funds. Under Frei, investment became more diversified. Oil was still the most important state investment sector, but the sugar, paper, chemical, and metal industries (basic metals and consumer durables) also received significant amounts of state investment. Investment in paper and cellulose was principally channeled to the two new companies that the Frei government founded jointly with American, French, and British capital. Investment in chemicals focused on the new petrochemical complex that the government established in partnership with Dow Chemical. Important investment funds also went into technology and training programs through the Technical Cooperation Service (SERCOTEC) and the National Training Institute (INACAP).

No quantitative data exist for industrial investment during the 1971–73 period because of the destruction of documents by the military after the coup. Some qualitative ideas, however, can be given about the overall approach of the Allende government. First was the shift in the sectoral allocation of investment. The principal change was the new emphasis on agro-industry, especially pork, chicken, and fruit; together with fishing, these investments were designed to feed the population. A related emphasis was on construction materials (cement, bricks, and prefabricated materials) to satisfy housing needs. More traditional investments were in energy, especially oil and coal, as well as paper and cellulose for export. Steel also continued to be a priority area. Investments were cut in petrochemicals and durable consumer goods, with the exception of automobiles. Of greater importance, however, was the change in the nature of the investment process. CORFO was no longer restricted to approving individual projects but began to take an integral view of the entire economy to see which areas needed to be developed. In addition, an integrated approach was taken within sectors. For example, in the fishing industry, CORFO investments ranged from the fishing stage through processing to transportation and commercialization. This new approach obviously required time to analyze the economy and plan projects properly; this was one reason for the drop in industrial investment during 1972, with the trend beginning to reverse itself in 1973.[13]

As will be explained below, foreign investment in industry entered Chile via two legal channels during the Alessandri and Frei periods—DFL 258, which was controlled by CORFO, and Article 16 of Decree 1272, which was controlled by the Central Bank. In 1971, the Allende government repealed these two laws and promulgated another that put much more stringent controls on foreign capital. Table 7.2 shows DFL 258 foreign investment by sectors during the Alessandri and Frei periods. The largest investments during both periods were in paper, constituting 60 percent of all foreign investment during the Alessandri years and 37 percent under Frei. Other important investment sectors during the Alessandri period were food products (17 percent), durable consumer goods (9 percent), and chemicals (8 percent). These same areas were also dominant under Frei, although chemicals rose in importance, accounting for 24 percent of total foreign investment in industry. Food products (16 percent), durable consumer goods (11 percent) and basic metals (8 percent) were other major areas. It should be pointed out that the investment in food products was mostly in fishmeal and frozen seafoods. These, together with paper, chemicals, and copper products, were Chile's chief industrial exports. Much less information is available on investment via Article 16. What data there are, however, show paper again dominant under Alessandri. Under Frei, steel and copper products were more important; paper and oil were secondary investment areas.[14]

Under Allende, foreign investment virtually ceased during the

TABLE 7.2

Sectoral Distribution of Foreign Industrial Investment Entering Chile via DFL 258, 1959–70
(Millions of dollars and percent)

Sector	1959–64		1965–70	
	Annual average	Percent	Annual average	Percent
Food and beverages	$0.83	17.1%	$1.14	15.7%
Textiles, clothes, shoes, leather	0.10	2.1	0.03	0.4
Wood	0.16	3.2	0.07	0.4
Paper	2.84	59.5	2.78	36.7
Chemicals, oil, rubber, plastics	0.38	7.9	1.82	24.0
Construction materials	0.05	1.0	0.30	4.0
Basic metals	0.01	0.2	0.59	7.7
Durable consumer goods	0.43	8.9	0.83	11.0
TOTAL	$4.80	99.9%	$7.56	99.9%

SOURCE: CORFO, Gerencia de Promoción Financiera, Departamento de Inversiones Extranjeras, *Análisis de las inversiones extranjeras en Chile amparadas por el Estatuto del Inversionista* (1972).
NOTE: DFL: Decree with Force of Law (Decreto con Fuerza de Ley).

first two years. By 1973, however, negotiations were being carried out with various East and West European countries, although the nature of the foreign investment process, like that of state investment, had changed. Foreign investment, loans, and technical assistance were requested from countries and/or firms that were particularly efficient in priority sectors of the economy. Examples included Peugeot, Citröen, and Pegaso (automobiles and trucks); Japanese firms (iron and steel); Finland (wood and paper); Spain, Poland, and the USSR (fishing); Bulgaria, Holland, and Belgium (agro-industry); and West Germany and various socialist countries (copper products).[15]

Technology

A third important aspect of investment is the kind of technology it embodies. There is often more than one technology that can be used to produce any given product; these technologies can be classified according to whether they employ relatively large amounts of labor and small amounts of capital (labor-intensive) or vice-versa (capital-intensive). There are strong reasons to believe that capital-intensive technology increased much more rapidly during the Frei years than under either Alessandri or Allende. One reason is that much more foreign investment came into Chile under Frei, and foreign corporations tend to use more capital-intensive technology than Chilean companies. This is primarily because technology is expensive, and the foreign firms obtain it through their parent companies and/or through credit from public and private international financial institutions. In fact, one reason for trying to attract foreign investment is precisely because it gives Third World countries increased access to technology. Another reason for believing that capital-intensity increased faster under Frei was the situation in the two main areas of investment between 1964 and 1970 (in terms of both state and foreign investment); these were highly capital-intensive paper and petrochemical complexes. A third reason is that much larger amounts of machinery were being imported. A final reason is simply the emphasis put on capital-intensive technology by the government as a way to resolve the Chilean problems vis-à-vis both growth and distribution.

The Alessandri regime would certainly have been glad to have more capital-intensive technology, but this did not materialize in practice to the extent that it did under Frei. That is, much less foreign investment came in, and the 1962 foreign exchange crisis limited the possibilities for imports. Allende, on the other hand, specifically tried to concentrate on labor-intensive projects in order to increase employment. From the negative point of view, he was "aided" by the decline in foreign investment and the lack of foreign exchange with which to import machinery.

DISTRIBUTIVE POLICIES

The main distributive policies to be dealt with here concern wages and employment, although some brief comments on the issue of nonmonetary distribution will be made at the end of this section. Distributive policies are closely related to the question of the sectoral distribution of investment, which was just discussed. That is, if a redistribution of monetary income is to have effects other than merely increasing the rate of inflation, it must be accompanied by a change in the production structure. For example, a redistribution of income toward blue-collar workers and other low-paid groups must be accompanied by an increase in the production of basic consumer goods, such as food and clothing.* Likewise, redistribu-

* If sufficient foreign exchange is available, a short-term solution might be to import food and other basic consumer items, as the Allende government did in 1971–72, but in the long term, there must be a correspondence between the domestic productive structure and the structure of income distribution.

tion that favors white-collar workers would probably increase the demand for durable consumer goods. In fact, the changes brought about in the industrial sector in Chile during the period being considered were very much in line with changes in income distribution. As will be spelled out in more detail in Chapter Nine, industrial output increased most rapidly in consumer durables under Alessandri and Frei and in basic consumer goods under Allende. It is now necessary to look at how this related to the distributive policies under the three regimes.

Wages and Prices

There were several ways in which the remunerations policies of the three regimes differed. First was in the relationship between wage/salary increases and price increases. Second was the relationship between the increases for blue-collar workers as compared with white-collar workers. Third was the relationship between the increase in the *minimum* wage and salary and those of the higher-paid workers.

Before inspection of the data, some background information on the Chilean institutional situation is necessary. As was explained in Chapter Two, the Chilean working class was divided into two subclasses: white-collar workers *(empleados)* and blue-collar workers *(obreros)*. The two had different legal status, different social status, different benefits and privileges, and different remunerations. The bourgeoisie had taken advantage of the differentiation of the labor force (between physical and intellectual tasks), arising from development of the productive forces, in order to divide the working class and so increase their capacity to control the workers. Thus, they created the legal distinction between white- and blue-collar workers, gave the former special privileges, and tried to co-opt them by convincing them that they were not part of the working class but of some heterogeneous grouping called the "middle class." The legal distinction, in turn, led to two sets of remunerations— wages *(salarios)* and salaries *(sueldos)*.

In addition, a second set of divisions existed between workers who received minimum-level remunerations and higher-paid workers. The minimums were again divided into blue- and white-collar categories: the minimum industrial wage (the *salario mínimo industrial*—SMI) and the minimum salary (the *sueldo vital*—SV). The remunerations level of the higher-paid workers can be measured by looking at the Wage and Salary Index (Indice de Sueldos y Salarios—

ISS). This index is based on a survey conducted four times a year by the National Institute of Statistics, covering firms with 20 or more workers. In Chile, these factories were defined as medium and large industry and included slightly over 30 percent of all firms. The important point for this discussion is that remunerations in medium and large-size factories were much higher than in small industries. According to the 1967 industrial census, for example, factories employing between five and 19 workers paid an average of E°3,077 per year, while factories employing 20 or more workers paid an average of E°7,159.[16] That is, the larger factories paid almost two and a half times the per capita wages of the smaller firms, and these figures do not include those industries employing fewer than five workers, which paid even lower rates. Since unions were illegal in plants with fewer than 25 workers, this generally meant that the workers in small firms at best received increases corresponding to the minimum. Therefore, the ISS can be seen as an indication of actual wage increases in medium and large factories, but the minimums are a better indicator of increases in the small factories.

In Chile, the President had the power to set the minimum wage and salary; in addition, he determined the level of the general cost-of-living increase, which was legally mandatory for the public sector and a recommendation for private firms. In practice, however, this recommendation served only as a starting point for both public and private sector bargaining. On the other hand, the President could also set prices for a large number of goods, especially essential consumer items.

Wage and price policies were key elements of the stabilization programs, which were an explicit or implicit aspect of every administration's program, owing to Chile's chronic inflation problem. The main difference in these programs concerned who would pay. The Alessandri regime thought that wage increases were the main cause of inflation, and therefore the basis of its stabilization measures was wage increases that were less than the cost-of-living increases for the previous year. Alessandri considered that, in the long run, the workers would benefit because their wages would be worth more— even though they might suffer in the short run. Frei, in line with his "communitarian" ideology, believed that labor and capital should share the burden of stabilization. Wages would be raised exactly 100 percent of the previous year's inflation but no more, and prices would increase only in accordance with costs. The Allende position was that wages should go up *at least* the same amount as the cost-of-living and that most of this increase should come out of profits. (For an elaboration, see Chapter Three.)

The percentage increases shown in Figure 7.5 are real increases, which means that wage and price changes are both incorporated. When the real variation is negative, price increases for that year were greater than the wage and salary increases, and vice-versa. The first two bars in each set show the real variations of the SMI and SV. During the Alessandri period, both fell slightly, whereas under Frei both increased slightly. Under Allende, the SMI increased dramatically at the same time that the SV declined. As will be seen below, this divergence came about because of the Allende policy of providing the largest wage increases for the poorest sections of the population, which—in the industrial sector—consisted of those earning the minimum wage.

In addition to the minimums, over which the government had control, it is also important to look at what happened to overall wages and salaries, where government control was much less effective; this can be seen through the ISS, (the third bar in each set). There were increases under each regime, 1.6 percent under Alessandri, 9.1 percent under Frei, and 14.3 percent during the first two years of the Allende regime. When the first eight months of 1973

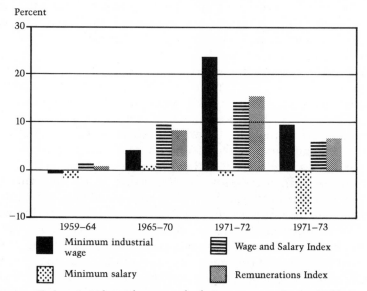

Fig. 7.5. Changes in industrial wages and salaries, 1959–73. Source: Table A.10.

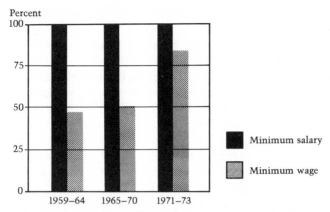

Fig. 7.6. Minimum wage for blue-collar workers as percentage of minimum salary for white-collar workers, 1959–73. Calculated from Banco Central, *Boletín Mensual*, various numbers.

are included, the average drops to 5.8 percent. As will be seen in Chapter Eight, all of the ISS increases were larger than the Executive branch had intended and had the effect of squeezing investment in the public sector. This was especially crucial in the Allende period. Finally, the fourth bar represents a combined index of industrial wages and salaries for all factories employing five or more workers. It consists of a weighted average of the increases in the SMI, SV, and ISS.* On the average, this combined index shows that real remunerations increased slightly under Alessandri (0.8 percent), rose significantly under Frei (8.3 percent), and increased even faster during Allende's first two years (15.5 percent). The 1971–73 average was lower, however, at 6.2 percent.

The other differences between the wage policies of the three regimes concerned the relationships between the increases in the remunerations received by various categories of workers. Figure 7.6 focuses on the relationship between white- and blue-collar workers. The minimum salary for white-collar workers had traditionally been about twice the minimum for blue-collar workers. The distinction in levels of minimums was maintained constant until late 1969, when the Frei government signed the first agreement on

* The weights come from the 1967 Industrial Census figures for number of workers employed in factories with 20 or more workers (covered by the ISS) and those with 5–19 workers, who are assumed to have received the minimum wage and salary. The percentages are SMI = 14.7, SV = 1.1, and ISS = 82.4 (70.8 percent blue-collar and 13.4 percent white-collar workers).

wages with the CUT. This agreement called for a 60 percent nominal increase in the SMI (which was twice the 1969 inflation rate) and the usual increase in the SV equal to the previous year's inflation. Under Allende, this trend was continued; the SV was raised by the amount of the cost-of-living increase, while the SMI was increased by a higher percentage. The effect of these changes in policy was that the SMI was 47 percent of the SV under Alessandri, 50 percent under Frei, and 83 percent under Allende. The remunerations of the better-paid workers, as measured by the ISS, followed a similar but less dramatic pattern.[17] Similar comparisons can also be made between the workers receiving the two minimums and those receiving higher remunerations, as measured by the ISS. In this case, the SMI as a percentage of the ISS dropped steadily each year, from an average of 41 percent under Alessandri to 28 percent under Frei. Under Allende, the gap narrowed during the first two years of the period but increased again in 1973.[18]

Unemployment

A second distributive policy focused on unemployment. In line with the generally laissez-faire policies of his regime, Alessandri thought that no special measures needed to be taken with respect to unemployment because the problem would automatically be resolved as production increased. Therefore, his emphasis was on increasing investment and production. Frei saw the matter differently and believed that unemployment must be attacked directly; his basic tool was an increase in education, both higher enrollments in the regular school system (especially the university) and special training programs for workers. Allende also thought that unemployment must be tackled directly. Although he, too, was in favor of increased access to educational facilities for workers, he saw a decrease in unemployment as a goal in itself and therefore put heavy emphasis on labor-intensive projects, which would provide employment, and increased employment in the state-controlled factories.[19]

Table 7.3 shows the effects of these differing approaches to the unemployment problem. Open unemployment among the industrial work force in Greater Santiago was over 8 percent when Alessandri took office in 1958.* This figure rose to 9 percent in 1959 and then gradually decreased to 5.4 percent in 1964. The average

* The problem of open unemployment was only the tip of the iceberg in Chile; underneath was the situation of disguised unemployment. The figures from the survey for open unemployment may also be underestimates, since new arrivals living

TABLE 7.3
Unemployment Rates in Industry, Greater Santiago,
1959–73
(Percent)

Period	Average unemployment rate	Average change in unemployment rate
1959–64	6.6%	−0.5%
1965–70	5.2	0.15
1971–73ᵃ	3.9	−1.2

SOURCE: Table A.11.
ᵃFor 1973, first half of year only.

annual decrease during the 1958–64 period was 0.5 percent. Unemployment decreased during Frei's first two years and then began to increase again till the average for 1970 was 6.3 percent; this meant that the unemployment rate actually increased slightly (0.15 percent) on an average basis. The average rate of unemployment for 1970 underestimated the problem that Allende faced, however, because production cutbacks by the bourgeoisie after the 1970 presidential election left industrial unemployment above 8 percent in December 1970. The reduction was quite spectacular, getting down to an average of 3.5 percent in 1972. By June of 1973, unemployment, at 2.7 percent of the industrial work force, was at its lowest rate since statistics began to be collected in 1956. The annual average drop in unemployment under Allende was 1.2 percent (see Table A.11).

The Alessandri policy was effective in reducing unemployment, although it left over 5 percent of the industrial work force out of work. The Frei policy, however, was much less successful. The essential problem, in addition to the economic stagnation during the latter part of his term, was that his education policies for decreasing unemployment were mostly long-term. Even the gains from the more short-range worker training programs, however, were more than offset by the Frei emphasis on capital-intensive technology. Although such technology might increase output, by its very nature it eliminated actual and potential jobs. The impressive increase in employment under Allende was, in practice, bought at the price of decreasing productivity.

in the shantytowns around Santiago were not usually included in the survey sample, and these groups were likely to have a high unemployment rate.

In addition to differences in the quantitative problem of lowering the unemployment rate, there were also qualitative differences in the employment policies followed by the three regimes. Under Alessandri and Frei, most of the new jobs created had been in commerce and the service sector. This was especially true under Frei, when only about one-quarter of the new jobs were in sectors producing goods (agriculture, mining, industry, and construction). Over two-thirds were in commerce and services, with the remainder in transportation, electricity, gas, and water. Under Allende, on the other hand, 52 percent of new jobs were in the production of goods and only 28 percent in services.[20]

Collective Consumption

The focus on monetary income tends to underestimate the differences between the three sets of distributive policies. To get a complete picture, it would be necessary to add at least two elements. First is government expenditure on collective consumption, such as education, public health, housing, recreational facilities, and day-care centers. As was implied in the discussion on the public sector budget, this type of expenditure was not a major priority of the Alessandri regime, became more important during the Frei administration, and was advanced to top priority under Allende. There was also a major qualitative change after 1970 in the attempt to increase the availability of such services to the low-income sectors of the population. Thus, there was emphasis on putting clinics in rural areas and in the shantytowns in cities, the program of school lunches for low-income students was stepped up, and so on. Probably the best-known of the Allende programs along these lines was that of providing a half-liter of milk a day for all children; this was obviously of greater benefit to the children of the working class than the bourgeoisie.

A second aspect of nonmonetary distribution under Allende involved physical distribution mechanisms for essential consumer goods. Beginning in 1972, many basic consumer items became difficult to find in grocery stores; in part this was due to increasing problems in production, but mostly to hoarding and black-market activities by groups opposed to the government. Scarcities were aggravated, of course, by the government's refusal to set prices high enough so that supply equaled demand (i.e. to squeeze the poor out of the market). The government's answer to the problem of shortages was to establish a distribution system whereby essential consumer goods were available at official (subsidized) prices in workers' neighborhoods and usually not in the upper-income suburbs. In the latter areas, goods often had to be purchased on the black market, at many times their official price. The black market also operated in the working-class areas, of course, but to a lesser extent. In other words, the purchasing power of a given income varied, and the working class tended to be the beneficiary of such differentials.[21]

RELATIONS WITH THE FOREIGN SECTOR

Foreign Investment

Probably the most publicized differences among the three regimes occurred in the area of foreign relations, and specifically with regard to the copper mines. Copper was of vital importance to the Chilean economy, since it provided about 80 percent of export revenues. Under Alessandri, the large copper mines (Gran Minería) were totally owned by two U.S. companies, Anaconda and Kennecott; Chile's only participation was through the taxes paid by the companies. Frei introduced the policy of "chileanization" of copper, whereby the government acquired 51 percent ownership of some of the mines. The highly unfavorable terms to which Frei's negotiators agreed have already been described in Chapter Two. Allende's policy was to nationalize the mines without payment, because of the excess profits the companies had received and the back taxes they owed. These three diverging policies with regard to copper established the general climate for relations with foreign capital. Within this framework, specific policies were set for the industrial sector, which was closely tied to foreign sources for capital equipment, raw materials, and technology.

Foreign finance designed especially for industry came from two main sources: loans obtained by CORFO and direct foreign investment. Foreign industrial investment entered Chile via two legal channels during the Alessandri and Frei periods: DFL 258 (promulgated in March 1960 to supersede DFL 437 of 1954) and Article 16 of Decree 1272 (promulgated in November 1961). The former was administered by CORFO and the latter by the Central Bank. Both were initiated by Alessandri (and maintained by Frei) in order to attract foreign investment; both gave foreign investors major incentives. DFL 258 allowed free convertibility into dollars for repatriation of capital, profits, and interest; exemptions from customs duties for importing machinery; and tax exemptions (guarantees that taxes would not be raised). Article 16 also allowed free convertibility and repatriation after four years and in annual quotas of not more than 20 percent.[22] The result was that industry became the most dynamic of the foreign investment sectors, but profit outflows were also high.

Allende changed the legal situation for foreign investment in June 1971, when Chile adopted the foreign investment rules of the Andean Pact (Decree 482). This put much tighter rules on foreign investment, such that profit remissions could not be more than 14 percent per year; the government would not guarantee foreign credits unless a joint venture was involved; foreign firms would have access only to short-term domestic credit; no new foreign investment would be allowed in public services, banking, insurance, or communications; and foreign investors had to sell their stock to nationals within a period of 15 years.[23]

The implementation of these policies had obvious effects on the flow of foreign investment into the industrial sector. The response, however, was slower than expected during the Alessandri period. The two laws were promulgated in 1960 and 1961, but large flows of capital did not actually come into the country until 1964. Thus, it was mainly the Frei government that witnessed large amounts of foreign investment in industry. In part, these flows were the materialization of arrangements made by the Alessandri government, but the Frei regime itself did even more than its predecessor to encourage foreign investment. Thus, referring back to Table 7.2, it can be seen that the average flow of foreign investment into industry via DFL 258 was about 50 percent higher under Frei than under Alessandri; under Article 16 the former was almost three times the latter.

There was, however, another face to this process—every dollar of foreign investment that entered Chile implied a flow of profits going in the other direction. Table 7.2 shows that a total of $29 million of industrial investment entered Chile via DFL 258 between 1959 and 1964; $45 million came in during the 1965–70 period. The division of profit flows, however, was quite different. Investment that came in at the end of the Alessandri period had not yet begun to earn large amounts of profits, so the total amount of profit repatriation under Alessandri was only slightly over $1 million; under Frei, on the other hand, $30 million of profits was repatriated. The *net* flows, then, were $28 million versus only $15 million, respectively.[24]

Under Allende, direct foreign investment from Western countries ceased entirely, although some negotiations were being carried out at the time of the coup with Citröen, Peugeot, and Pegaso. Many long-term lines of credit for industrial equipment had also been opened up by the socialist countries, but very few were used because appropriate projects had not yet been formulated. According to a CORFO report of June 1972, only 5 percent of the credits from the socialist countries had been utilized, in comparison with 74 percent of credits from the West.[25] Long-term prospects were more favorable, however, for using these credits as well as for developing technical assistance arrangements with East and West Europe.

Balance of Payments

Industry was also affected by the more general state of foreign economic relations, since industrial production was closely attuned to the state of the balance of payments. There were a number of reasons for this. First, like most Third World countries, Chile had only a very small capital goods sector; about 80 percent of all capital equipment was imported.[26] This, in turn, meant that a continual flow of spare parts had to be imported to keep the machinery in working order. Payments also had to be made for royalties and patents on the technology that was imported, and large amounts of raw materials were required from abroad. All of these factors meant that when there was a balance-of-payments squeeze, industry quickly found itself in trouble.

Balance-of-payments problems were certainly related to the government policies described at the beginning of this section, but they were also influenced by "external" factors, especially the price of copper. When copper prices were high, foreign exchange posed no constraint to development; this was the case in the late 1960's. When prices were low, industry suffered, as happened during some of the Alessandri years and all of the Allende period. Nevertheless, although crucial, copper prices were only one aspect of the balance-of-payments situation. In addition, export revenues could be offset by imports, and this was especially the case when import prices rose at the same time that copper prices fell (as happened in 1971 and 1972). Also, even if import expenditures were lower than export revenues, other items, such as shipping, insurance, profits, and in-

TABLE 7.4

Balance of Payments, 1959–73

(Millions of dollars)

Year	Current account	Capital account[a]	Errors, omissions	Balance of payments
1959	−24.8	20.8	28.6	24.6
1960	−144.3	64.7	40.6	−39.0
1961	−253.4	177.0	−63.9	−140.3
1962	−191.3	169.6	−50.6	−72.3
1963	−159.5	145.6	−14.9	−28.8
1964	−130.5	185.4	−32.2	22.7
1965	−57.1	138.8	−22.0	59.7
1966	−75.8	184.2	13.3	121.7
1967	−123.8	116.4	−17.5	−24.9
1968	−135.3	303.7	−41.4	127.0
1969	−5.6	263.1	−42.4	215.1
1970	−79.5	249.4	−18.2	151.7
1971	−188.8	−49.9	−84.5	−323.2
1972	−386.6	228.8	−169.8	−327.6
1973	−379.8	150.5	−19.5	−248.8

SOURCE: Banco Central, Boletin Mensual, various numbers.
[a] Autonomous capital flows only.

terest payments, combined to produce a negative balance on the current account. This was the case in every year of the period studied. In general, however, the entrance of foreign investment and loans of various kinds offset the current account deficit. These flows were most affected by the government policies discussed above.

Table 7.4 shows a summary of Chile's balance-of-payments situation, where there were deficits during four years of the Alessandri period, only one during the Frei years, and every year under Allende. A key point to notice, however, is that 1971 was the only year where the capital account (loans and foreign investment) was negative. This was the result of the "invisible blockade"—the cutoff of private investment, export credits, and loans from private banks, foreign governments, and international organizations—described in Chapter Six. By 1972, credits from Western Europe and the socialist countries had replaced those from the United States. In the short run, however, they were not of much use to industry, which still needed spare parts and raw materials from the United States, the supplier of almost all of Chile's industrial equipment over the years. This was another reason for the fall in industrial investment, since almost every investment project had a foreign currency component.

SUMMARY

As this chapter has shown, there were numerous differences between the three regimes with respect to policies influencing industrial development. All of the differences followed more or less directly from the class base and development ideologies associated with the three. The first difference related to control of resources. The Alessandri period showed a strong dominance of property ownership by the private national sector, the Frei period marked a trend toward greater participation by both foreign capital and the state, and the Allende period witnessed a shift from the entire private sector—foreign and domestic—in favor of greater state ownership. Similar trends toward greater state participation were found in the control of financial resources through the public sector budget and bank credit.

A second difference related to investment trends. On the one hand, there were differences in investment rates, with the highest rate during the Frei regime, the second highest under Alessandri, and the lowest under Allende. On the other hand, there were also differences in sectoral distribution of investment. In terms of sectoral distribution, there was no coordinated policy under the Alessandri regime; state investment was concentrated in oil and fish products, foreign investment in paper, and private national investment in basic consumer goods. Under Frei, there was an attempt to coordinate public and foreign investment—in part through the promotion of joint ventures—in the chemical and paper industries and in durable consumer goods. Finally, under Allende, almost all investment was done by the state, which put major emphasis on sectors providing for the food (agro-industry and fishing) and housing (construction materials) needs of the population and on the basic intermediate industries.

In terms of distribution, differences could be seen in policies relating to wages and employment. Under Alessandri, wages and prices rose by about the same amount, meaning that *real* wages were stagnant during the six years. Under Frei, real wages increased, and under Allende the increase was even faster. Within the working class, there were also differences, as the white-collar/blue-collar remunerations gap stayed constant under Alessandri, diminished somewhat at the end of the Frei period, and diminished more under Allende. The gap between workers receiving minimum wages and those receiving higher pay followed the same pattern, at least among blue-collar workers. Different policies for resolving the unemployment problem meant that unemployment was highest under Alessandri, next highest under Frei, and lowest under Allende.

A final important difference was in the area of relations with foreign capital. Both the Alessandri and Frei regimes supported laws giving many special privileges to foreign capitalists in order to induce them to invest in Chilean industry, although Frei was more successful than Alessandri in this respect. Allende's adoption of the foreign investment code of the Andean Pact, together with his support for the nationalization of the copper mines and some industries, produced a halt in foreign investment and an open battle with foreign capital. These policies, in turn, affected the balance of payments, which indirectly affected industrial activity.

As might be expected, these policies had major effects on the economic development pattern that resulted in the three periods; that is, on the rate of growth of industrial output, the sectoral composition of this growth, and the trends in income distribution as well. These effects will be discussed in detail in Chapter Nine.

CHAPTER EIGHT

Economic Policies: Similarities Among Regimes

Dᴀᴛᴀ ʜᴀᴠᴇ ʙᴇᴇɴ presented on a number of areas where the economic policies of the Alessandri, Frei, and Allende regimes varied considerably. In general, these variations were in line with the differences in the class base and development ideologies of the three. Perhaps even more interesting is an examination of the similarities among the three. How could a government that advocated laissez-faire carry out policies similar to those of another government that proposed major reforms of the capitalist system, as well as those of a regime that announced it was preparing the way for socialism? The easiest answer is to say that development ideologies are mere rhetoric and that all social classes act in more or less the same way. The hypothesis here is different—it will be assumed that the three administrations were serious in advocating different development ideologies, which reflected the interests of the classes they represented.

Governments, however, do not operate in isolation; the state has certain powers, but it is not all-powerful. There are a set of political, social, and economic constraints, resulting from the historical development over time of a given country, that limit the actions of *any* kind of government, whatever its inclinations and determination. The most important of these constraints for the Chilean case were outlined in Chapter Two. Here they will be briefly summarized, and then an examination will be made of how they affected the attempts to implement the Alessandri, Frei, and Allende development models.

One of the characteristics discussed was the nature of the Chilean state itself. The state had traditionally had a strong role in the economy in terms of credit, investment, setting of wages and prices, control of foreign trade, and so forth. On the other hand, it was divided into relatively autonomous branches—the Executive, Legislature, Judiciary, Comptroller. If these branches were controlled by parties representing different class interests, then they could stalemate each other. The second characteristic involved different social classes that were struggling for control of the Chilean state—the most powerful being different fractions of the bourgeoisie and the urban working class. All of these classes were well organized, in terms of both class organizations and political parties, and were thus capable of putting up a strong fight to defend their own interests. The third characteristic concerned the international context in which Chile was situated, i.e. the fact that Chile was a dependent capitalist country. This meant that through a series of mechanisms —the foreign debt, the need for various kinds of imports, the close connections between certain domestic groups and their foreign counterparts—capitalists and governments of the advanced countries could limit the possible actions of the Chilean government. The extreme version of these "limits" was seen in the U.S. role in the overthrow of the Allende government. Finally, the economic performance of the Chilean economy in the postwar period was discussed. Here the dominant characteristics were the slow rate of growth, the tendency for growth to be centered in sectors producing for the high-income minority, the unequal distribution of income, the lack of employment opportunities, and the high rate of inflation. The performance problems largely resulted from the other three characteristics of the society.

In an attempt to relate these structural and performance characteristics to the economic policies of the three governments, two types of data will be examined. First, the cyclical pattern of growth in the industrial sector will be analyzed—the pattern of high growth rates at the beginning of a presidential period, followed by a slump at the end. The second part of the chapter will consist of several case studies of attempts by the three governments to make changes, which were frustrated by the nature of the socioeconomic structure or the groups operating within it.

RECURRING CYCLICAL PATTERNS

Cycles in Output

From the growth data presented in Chapter Nine, it is readily apparent that a cyclical pattern was repeated during each of the three administrations. The main difference was in the amplitude and duration of the cycles, as can be seen in Figure 8.1. The peak of the cycle during 1959–64 was reached in the first year of the Alessandri period, when output increased by 14 percent. Although falling off somewhat from this peak, a high growth rate was maintained through the first four years of the Alessandri period (with the exception of a severe drop in 1960 owing to a major earthquake in the south of Chile, which is estimated to have destroyed 10 percent of the physical capital of the country). Under Frei, the peak was in the second year, when growth exceeded 8 percent; this high growth rate lasted only two years and was followed by a four-year recession. Finally, the peak in the Allende period was in the first year, when production increased by 13 percent; this time, rapid growth lasted only a single year and then dropped off rapidly. The immediate cause of this pattern seems to have been variations in demand, brought about by manipulation of public sector expenditures and wage and credit policies. When the rate of growth of demand in-

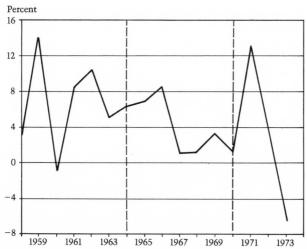

Fig. 8.1. Variations in industrial output, 1958–73. Averages of CORFO, INE, and SOFOFA data. For 1973, figures cover January–August only. Source: Table A.13.

183

creased, that of industrial output increased; when the rate of growth of demand fell, that of output fell as well. Why did the pattern keep recurring?* For the answer, it is necessary first to examine the various sources of demand.

Cycles in Demand

As was mentioned in the previous chapter, the public sector budget was composed of three parts—the fiscal sector, the decentralized sector, and the nationalized industries. Since there are no complete public sector data available for the years 1958–59, this analysis will focus on the fiscal sector. Either fiscal or public sector data will suffice, however, since both moved in the same direction, as can be seen in Figure 8.2.

Even though the Alessandri regime strongly believed that the private sector should be the dominant force in the economy, it was thought that an expansion of the private sector would exacerbate the inflation problem. Therefore, the Alessandri regime decided to increase fiscal investment in public works in order to promote a secondary expansion of "healthier" private investment. This policy led fiscal expenditure to increase considerably during the 1959–62 period, in comparison with 1956–58. During 1963–64, however, expenditures were cut back sharply. If an examination of the internal composition of the fiscal budget and the corresponding variations is made, it is found that the main increases were in fiscal investment rather than current expenditures (composed mainly of remunerations, family allowances, and social security payments). This emphasis was especially true in 1959.[1]

---

* It will be noted that the role of demand management policies is the reverse of the classical Keynesian model; that is, these policies are seen to *cause* rather than *mitigate* cycles. The difference arises from the particular structure of the Chilean economy. In an advanced capitalist country, the most important cyclical element comes from increases or decreases in private investment, which in turn sets off further changes through the multiplier. The government tries to counteract cycles begun by the private sector through adjustments in its own expenditures. In Chile, there are two structural differences which alter this pattern. First, the state rather than the private sector is the dominant investor; even before the Allende period, the state accounted for around 70 percent of all investment. Second, an increase in investment produces more of a multiplier effect in the advanced countries which supply Chile's imported capital goods than in Chile itself. (Investment in construction is more similar to the normal Keynesian pattern.) Thus, the main source of stimulus for increased output is not private sector investment but public sector expenditure and consumer demand (represented by remunerations); likewise the main cause for downturns is a fall in government or consumer demand.

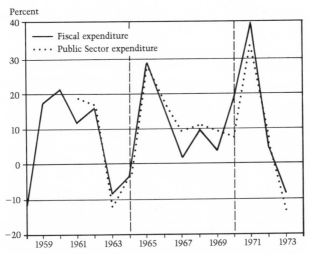

Fig. 8.2. Variations in fiscal and public sector expenditures, 1958–73. For 1973, figures cover January–August only. Source: Table A.12.

During the 1964–70 period, the Frei regime also planned a large increase in the fiscal budget. Frei, however, wanted to increase expenditures for both remunerations and investment. In practice, large increases did occur in 1965 and 1966. By 1967, however, the rate of growth of fiscal expenditures was cut back, in both current expenditures and investment, although the latter suffered more than the former. Spending increases continued to be modest until 1970, when the agreement signed with the CUT—discussed in Chapter Five—produced a large increase in remunerations. Over the course of the period, current expenditures increased slightly more than investment; this difference, however, was due only to the 1970 wage increase.

Like his predecessors, Allende included large increases in fiscal expenditure as a basic part of his program of reactivation and redistribution. In 1971, there was an increase in real terms of 41 percent, far larger than any other year in this study. Increases in remunerations, family allowances, and social security payments were slightly larger than funds for investment. The high inflation rates in 1972 and 1973, however, meant that the growth rate of fiscal expenditures in *real* terms dropped sharply in spite of *nominal* increases. The brunt of the decline was borne by investment while remunerations continued to increase. Figure 8.2 shows these variations in

185

fiscal expenditure and also the comparable data for public sector expenditure after 1960.

To fully understand the expansionary effects that these expenditures had on the economy, it is necessary to know how the budget increases were financed. If the expenditure increases were completely financed by tax increases, they would have a certain expansionary effect through the balanced budget multiplier. If, on the other hand, the state spends more than it collects in taxes, a deficit results that has a much larger expansionary effect. This additional amount (above taxes) can be financed in various ways: the two main ones are external loans and internal loans. In advanced countries, the latter are often financed by selling bonds to the public or commercial banks, again decreasing the money supply in the private sector. Since Chile, like most Third World countries, had no effective capital market, internal loans mainly meant printing money. This was the maximum expansionary strategy—a deficit financed by emissions.

The three regimes had different views on the preferable way to finance fiscal expenditures. The Alessandri economists did not want to increase tax rates; they thought this would discourage private initiative. Nor did they want to resort to printing money; they thought this would be inflationary. Therefore, they looked to foreign loans as the best means of finance. The Frei economists preferred a combination of internal and external sources; they would raise tax revenues, try to attract foreign loans, but, in addition, they would use some internal loans to provide a "planned deficit." The Allende economic team decided to rely heavily on internal loans, precisely because this would increase the expansionary effects of the deficit.[2] However, they were forced to adopt this strategy to a greater extent than was originally envisioned because Congress refused to approve tax increases and little foreign finance was available.

The second major tool that could be used to increase demand and thus stimulate the economy was wage and salary increases. As was mentioned previously, the Chilean state had the power to set minimum wages: the minimum salary for white-collar workers (SV), the minimum wage for blue-collar workers in industry and commerce (SMI), and the minimum wage for blue-collar workers in agriculture (SMA). The state also established the amount for the general wage readjustment; the latter (which was usually the same percentage as the minimums) was supposed to serve as the legal

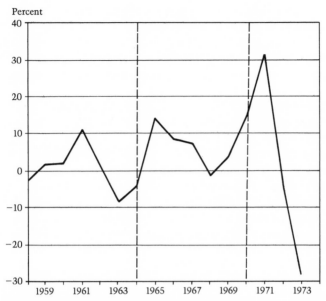

Fig. 8.3. Variations in remunerations index, 1958–73. For 1973, figures cover January–August only. Source: Table A.9.

readjustment for the public sector and the recommended readjustment for the private sector. In practice, both sectors often obtained increases well above the government recommendations.

Figure 8.3 shows the real variations of a remunerations index for all sectors of the economy; the index is composed of weighted changes in the SV, SMI, SMA, and ISS.* Again, the same pattern as occurred with fiscal expenditure reappears. Real wages and salaries increased during the first four years of the Alessandri period and decreased during the last two. In the Frei period, remunerations increases were fairly high during the first three years, then fell off, and rose again in 1970. Under Allende, there were large increases in 1971 and decreases during 1972 and 1973. This combined index,

* The difference between this index and the one used in Figure 7.3 is that this one includes all sectors of the economy, while the other one was only for the industrial sector. The weights used for this index are from a survey carried out in 1967 by the Centro de Estudios Estadísticos-Matemáticos of the University of Chile. The weights are SV=3.0%, SMI=26.0%, SMA=17.3%, and ISS=53.7%. (Calculated from ODEPLAN, *Antecedentes sobre el desarrollo chileno, 1960–70* [1971], pp. xxxii–xxxv.)

187

of course, hides differences in the trends of individual components of the index. The most important divergences from the index pattern involved the minimum wage and salary. For example, the minimums fell in real terms during 1959 and 1960 while the index increased. The SV also fell every year between 1967 and 1970, although the SMI and SMA rose in 1970 because of the agreement the government signed with the CUT. Under Allende, the SMI and SMA kept ahead of the inflation rate, through 1972, even though the index did not.

A third tool that could be used to regulate demand was credit to the private sector. Private sector credit came from two main sources: the commercial (private) banks and the State Bank (Banco del Estado). Trends in credit were generally similar to those of government expenditure and remunerations, as can be seen in Figure 8.4.* Comparing variations in credit among the three administrations, it is obvious that Alessandri was much more generous with credit to the private sector than was Frei. Thus, for example, during the first four years of the Alessandri regime, increases in credit averaged over 20 percent per year, although credit, like remunerations and fiscal expenditure, was cut back in 1963–64. Under Frei, on the other hand, credit was tight; there was only one year when credit expanded at a rate higher than 10 percent. In the case of the Allende regime, it might seem anomalous for private sector credit to have been as high as it was. The explanation lies in the failure to change accounting practices; therefore, factories under state control were still listed as private firms.†

* It is not possible to calculate the exact contribution of each of the components of demand that have been discussed because of overlaps between them. For example, about 30 percent of public expenditures consisted of remunerations, and, conversely, about 35 percent of all remunerations were paid out by the public sector. Indirect linkages were also present. In addition, much of the private sector credit in the Allende period went to pay wages. To give an approximate idea of the magnitudes involved, however, the 1970 figures can be taken as representative: public sector expenditures equaled E°41,966 million (of which fiscal expenditures were E°21,165), remunerations equaled E°33,889, and private sector credit equaled E°7,667. That is, public expenditures were the largest item, remunerations were 81 percent of public expenditures, and private sector credit was 18 percent.

† The problem was really more serious than indicated here. The social area firms were not only listed as private firms; they were also treated as private firms in the sense that the resources of each were maintained separately, rather than being pooled so that high profits could be made on luxury items and a deficit run on basic consumer items, which would be subsidized. On the other hand, the profit motive, which dominates the operation of private firms, was not followed in the state sector.

188

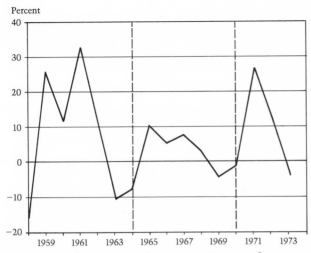

Fig. 8.4. Variations in private sector credit, 1958–73. For 1973, figures cover January–
August only. Source: Table A.12.

Inflation: The Explanatory Factor

Having seen that demand management policies followed similar
cyclical patterns, and that these same patterns were reflected in industrial production cycles, it is now time to return to the basic question: how can these similarities be explained? The immediate cause
was Chile's perennial enemy—inflation. Inflation had been a serious
economic problem in Chile since the end of the nineteenth century,
and the country had often had the highest price increases in the
world. In the mid-1950's, inflation reached 80 percent per year, and
the government responded by calling in the Klein-Saks Mission, an
American advisory team, which recommended the traditional orthodox remedies—cutting the fiscal budget, squeezing credit, cutting wages, limiting the welfare system. These policy recommendations were followed only in part, but this was sufficient to cause a
serious recesson. GDP increased by only 1.6 percent between 1955
and 1958; per capita GDP actually fell by 5.5 percent. Industrial
production in 1958 was only 7 percent above the 1953 level. The

State-owned firms were often ordered to sell at prices below cost to try to slow inflation as well as to provide subsidies. The resulting lack of profits was often used by
the opposition as evidence of the incompetence of the new management, time spent
on political activities, and so on. Although some of the latter problems certainly
occurred, they were not the principal cause of deficits in social area firms.

minimum wage fell by more than 25 percent in real terms, owing to the repeal of the law by which remunerations were automatically readjusted in line with the previous year's inflation. Unemployment rose to over 8 percent, and industry had idle capacity of over 25 percent.[3] These events constituted an important part of recent political history, with the result that control of inflation became a sine qua non for judging the success of a Chilean President. Stabilization was an explicit goal of every regime, although the priority attached to the goal varied. Alessandri considered it one of his top two priorities. Frei insisted that other goals should not be sacrificed to the control of inflation, although in practice this was done. Some of Allende's advisers recommended that stabilization should not be included as a specific goal, but the UP apparently felt that the matter was crucial, and it appeared prominently in the Basic Program.

For a variety of reasons, each regime was successful in lowering the rate of inflation at the beginning of its term in office. On the one hand, each enjoyed the cooperation implicit in a new administration's "honeymoon" period. On the other, each had special advantages that helped in the initial fight against inflation. Alessandri, for example, had the support of the bourgeoisie, who were anxious to show that their government could solve Chile's economic problems. SOFOFA's leaders urged their members to end their traditional habit of trying to increase prices as much as possible and to cooperate with the stabilization program. Frei's election as the first majority President in many years put him in an especially strong position. He was aided by the fact that his economic advisers were technically superior to those who had worked in previous administrations, and they endeavored to relate inflation control to an integral program for economic development. Allende theoretically could have used his influence with labor to press for wage constraint, but he chose not to do so. Nevertheless, the bourgeoisie's initial fear of his regime led them to heed price controls. This tendency was reinforced by the nationalization in 1971 of several small firms that were caught raising prices above the legal limit.

Sooner or later, however, in each case, inflation began to increase again, as can be seen in Figure 8.5. The Alessandri and Frei response was to cut back on fiscal expenditure, especially for investment, and to limit credit to the private sector. At the same time, real wages were allowed to fall as increases in the cost of living exceeded the government-decreed increase in the minimum wage and salary. Those workers who were members of strong unions, however, were

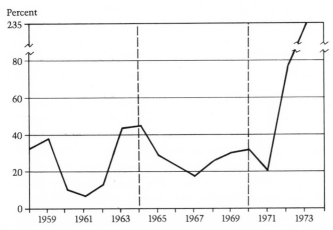

Fig. 8.5. Variations in consumer price index, annual average, 1958–73. For 1973, figures cover January–August only. Source: Table A.6.

sometimes able to protect themselves. The Allende phenomenon was different in intention although similar in result. For example, the cutback in the rate of expansion of fiscal expenditure in 1972 was certainly not planned as a counteraction to inflation; rather, it occurred because inflation was higher than expected and ate up most of the 82 percent nominal increase in the fiscal budget. Bank credit increased at a rate sufficient to far outrun inflation, and much of this credit was used to increase remunerations in the state-controlled factories, thus partially making up for the slow increase in the fiscal budget. Some of the remunerations were allowed to fall, but it should be noted that, in contrast to previous periods, those least able to defend themselves (i.e. those receiving the minimum blue-collar industrial and agricultural wage) were protected by the government. The wages that dropped were the white-collar minimum and the remuneration index of the better-paid workers in the medium and large factories. Nevertheless, the overall result was a fall in demand. In 1973, the tendency was the same, although in a more exaggerated form.

These policies led to a rather clear situation: a recession (or semi-recession) in the latter part of each presidential period, which led to unused capacity and high levels of unemployment. It was then possible for a new government, without much new investment, to greatly increase the rate of growth merely by increasing demand. This came from increasing the fiscal budget, credit to the private sector, and remunerations. When inflation began to return, all three were cut; the result was a return to recession, and the process began again.

But it is necessary to go one step further—inflation does not just happen. There have been many theories put forward to explain inflation in Chile. The two most prominent theories are those of the monetarists, who find the cause in the "uncontrolled" expansion of the money supply, and the structuralists, who insist that the roots lie in bottlenecks due to shortages of food and foreign exchange.[4] Here it will be argued that there are two basic causes, and both can be traced to the structural characteristics of the Chilean economy reviewed at the beginning of this chapter.

The first reason for the *perpetuation* of the high rates of inflation —the concern here is not with the origins—is the fact that both the bourgeoisie and the working class have been powerful and well organized since the end of the last century. Each group was ready, willing, and able to defend its own interests in the struggle over the distribution of income. In some cases, this struggle was carried out at the level of the individual factory in the collective bargaining process between capital and labor. Traditionally this struggle had been limited to the distribution of the surplus, but during the end of the Frei period and especially during the Allende years, workers extended their fight to include control of the means of production themselves, i.e. the takeovers of factories and farms. In other cases, the fight was raised from the local level to bargaining between the CUT and the government, especially over the percentage increase of the minimum wage and salary and the general cost-of-living increase. It was at this level that general strikes were used by the working class. At this same level, the bourgeoisie were putting pressure on the government to obtain price increases and, of course, to hold down wage and salary increases as much as possible. When there were bourgeois governments in power, the bourgeoisie made their demands through behind-the-scenes negotiations and the workers went into the streets. Under the workers' government in 1971–73, just the opposite occurred. Finally, the struggle between capital and labor was carried on at the level of the political parties, each of which had a definite class orientation, as discussed in Chapter Three. This electoral manifestation of the class struggle centered on the attempt to capture control of the presidency and the Congress, given the importance of the Chilean state in economic decision making.

The fact that neither side was able to completely dominate the other meant that inflation was the inevitable result. Thus, the bourgeoisie tried to increase their profits by raising prices, and the workers tried to at least keep up with the resulting increase in the cost of living by demanding higher wages. If wage increases were granted to the workers and the government could not simultaneously decrease the profits of the bourgeoisie, and assuming that productivity increases were not sufficient to cover the increases, then inflation had to be the result. Thus, inflation historically had served as a safety valve, so that neither the bourgeoisie nor the working class had to sacrifice short-term aims; who gained or lost in the long run was another question. As an American economist once observed, inflation was the alternative to civil war in Chile.[5]

In the Alessandri case, the government did not want to cut back on profits; it preferred to cut wages, but the strength of the working class prevented a cut sufficient to keep inflation down. In the Frei and Allende cases, profits were decreased, but not sufficiently to offset the wage increases. In the latter period, the problem was exacerbated because the opposition-controlled Congress deliberately refused to raise taxes to finance government wage increases and other parts of the fiscal budget, as part of their battle against the UP. This led to a very rapid increase in the money supply. In addition, production was sabotaged, an investment boycott was imposed, and goods were hoarded and diverted to the black market, all of which contributed to a decline in the supply of goods available to satisfy the increased demand. Thus, after 1970, other aspects of the class struggle were added to the battle over wages and profits as a spur to inflation.

The other major cause of inflation came from another structural characteristic—Chile's situation as a small, dependent country. The production structure of Chile had changed significantly since the industrialization process really got under way in the 1930's. With the development of import-substituting industries, mainly in the consumer goods sector, imports dropped from 24 to 12 percent of national income, although they doubled in absolute terms. At the same time, there was also a dramatic change in the import structure. Basic consumer-goods imports fell by over 50 percent, while intermediate and capital/durable consumer goods increased by about one-third.[6]

Thus imports continued to play an important quantitative role in the Chilean economy, and their qualitative importance may even have increased. Before the import-substitution process began, when a foreign exchange crisis occurred, the result was a drop in the import of consumer goods. This may have aroused political animosities, but there were no further ramifications in the domestic economy. After import substitution, however, a cut was more likely to fall on intermediate or capital goods necessary for the functioning of domestic industry. This implied a drop in industrial production and increased unemployment, as well as a drop in the investment rate, which led to long-term as well as short-term problems. Through this dependence on imports, inflation was easily imported via increases in international prices for the goods that had to be brought in from the outside.

The whole international side of inflation was made worse in the Chilean case because of the continual decline in the value of the escudo. Insofar as the escudo was devalued, Chile had to pay more (in terms of escudos) for its imports. Pressures for devaluation were essentially generated by the inflationary process discussed above. As the internal rate of inflation increased, there was pressure to lower the value of the escudo because imports became cheap in comparison with domestic products, exporters' profits fell, and balance-of-payments problems resulted. In addition, there was often pressure from the International Monetary Fund, the U.S. government, and others to eliminate an "overvalued" exchange rate as the price for receiving loans. Such was the case under Alessandri in 1961 and Allende at various times in the 1971–73 period. Frei's policy of minidevaluations on a fairly continual basis eliminated this bone of contention. The result was that the exchange rate was devalued and imports became more expensive in escudo terms.*
The increased price of imports then fueled the inflation process, increasing the price of finished-good imports directly and many others indirectly. The latter consisted of domestically produced goods that used imported inputs as well as goods with no import content, whose producers took advantage of a general tendency

---

*The offsetting advantage usually posited is that a devaluation will improve the balance of payments because export revenues (in foreign exchange terms) will increase. Under certain assumptions, this will be true in countries whose exports are primarily manufactured goods; this is because the foreign exchange price of exports can be lowered so as to capture a larger share of the market. In countries exporting primary products, however, the latter aspect of devaluation does not work, since prices are set on the international market, not by their individual producers. The OPEC (Organization of Petroleum Exporting Countries) cartel is an exception with respect to price-setting, but this does not affect the devaluation argument.

toward price rises to increase their own prices. These price increases then set off another round of wage demands, and the cycle was off again.

Thus, it is possible to understand how the inflationary process—maintained by the political stalemate between workers and bourgeoisie and by the increasing price of imports—led to similar policies of demand management by the three regimes. These demand management policies, in turn, produced similar cycles in industrial production.

FRUSTRATED ATTEMPTS AT CHANGE

All three regimes were similar in still another respect: each was frustrated when it attempted to implement economic policies in line with its development ideology. Sometimes the frustration resulted from specific pressures being applied by groups (domestic or foreign) who saw their interests being threatened. Other times it derived merely from the nature of the historical-structural situation in which Chile found itself. In order to see the form these pressures and problems took and the effects they had, three types of policy will be examined—investment, wages, and taxation. In each case, at least one regime tried to change policy but could not; the result was that the pattern of the three sets of policies showed much greater similarities than would have been predicted on the basis of the framework presented in Chapter One.

Investment

Investment policy posed problems for all three regimes. Alessandri was counting on the private sector—both domestic and foreign—to carry the burden of investment during his administration. Tax rates were lowered to stimulate domestic investment, and special laws were passed to encourage foreign investment. As it turned out, however, neither was forthcoming. The amount of investment by domestic capitalists declined continually during the Alessandri period (even when investment financed by the state is included). The Chilean bourgeoisie's traditional failure to sacrifice, innovate, and take risks could not be overcome even through the existence of a government headed by a leading industrialist.[7] Foreign investment began to increase in the last year of the Alessandri term, but previously the attempt to attract it had been unsuccessful, regardless of government policy. The reasons had to do with factors beyond the government's control: the international economic situation (the

"Eisenhower recession" in the United States, which only began to yield to Kennedy's Keynesian policies in mid-1962); the case of jitters that events in Cuba gave to companies thinking of investing in Latin America; the lack of a tradition of foreign *industrial* investment in Chile (almost all foreign investment had been in copper). These factors meant that, in spite of his laissez-faire ideology, Alessandri was forced to increase the share of investment by the state, which rose from 14 percent in 1961 to 40 percent in 1964. It will be remembered that there was a similar increase in the proportion of credit going to the public sector. Nevertheless, Alessandri was not willing to increase the state role sufficiently to overcome the problems in the private sphere; the result was that the regime did not succeed in significantly increasing the investment rate in spite of its avowed intention to do so.

Although it might seem ironic, Frei—who appeared to challenge U.S. capital by demanding 51 percent ownership in the copper mines —was more successful in attracting foreign investment than his predecessor, who was content with U.S. ownership. In reality, of course, the nature of the copper deal convinced foreign investors that the new government was not against them. More important, Frei's joint ventures in industry as well as copper offered foreign companies the opportunity to get substantial profits while investing relatively small amounts of their own money. Their association with the government lowered their political risk as well. Frei was also concerned about domestic investment, however, and thought the solution lay in raising the savings rate. When voluntary incentives did not have much effect during the first three years of the administration, an attempt was made in late 1967 to introduce a forced savings scheme. The wrath of the workers—part of whose wage readjustments were to go to this project—forced the government to cancel the scheme. Strikes and demonstrations were held, which eventually led to a cabinet reshuffle and the dismissal of the Finance Minister, who had sponsored the project. Nevertheless, in spite of this setback, Frei understood the nature of the accumulation process in Chile better than Alessandri did. His economic advisers realized that the state would have to provide the main portion of domestic investment, and they knew how to bring in foreign investment as a complement. Acting on these principles led to a better investment performance during the 1964–70 period than during 1958–64, as was seen in Figure 7.4. (More detailed statistics are included in Table A.7.)

The nature of the Allende ideology, and the actions taken to implement it, indicated that the investment rate might be expected to fall in comparison with previous years. In fact, foreign investment fell to practically nil, and private domestic investment continued its downward spiral. The fall was even more severe than UP economists had expected. They greatly underestimated the force with which foreign capitalists and foreign governments (particularly the United States) would attack; nor did they anticipate the extent of the investment boycott at home. On the one hand, the Allende strategy called for owners of small and medium firms to keep on investing, and greater amounts of credit were scheduled in order to stimulate this process. On the other hand, the government planned to take over certain large firms and use the profits to increase investment. Neither aspect worked out in practice because the government had misjudged the intensity of the class struggle, which it itself had unleashed. Owners of large firms managed to convince their counterparts in small and medium firms that they, too, were in line for expropriation, thus eliminating any possibility of the latter's cooperation with the government in either economic or political matters. In addition, before the government could nationalize the large firms, many of the owners managed to remove the bulk of their assets, leaving only empty bank accounts and rundown machinery. The government's own wage and price policies also helped turn potential profits into deficits in the state-controlled industries, further limiting investment possibilities. The overall result was that gross industrial investment as a percent of industrial output fell from an average of 10.3 percent under Frei to 5.0 percent under Allende, with net investment almost zero.

Wages

The previous chapter showed the trends in real wages. Although these trends, which reflected both wage policies and price increases, were quite different during the three administrations, there were, nevertheless, some underlying similarities with respect to the implementation of wage policies themselves. It is the latter that are of interest here. The basic similarity was very simple: every year, the workers in the medium and large factories managed to win wage increases that were well above the government's target increase. It happened under Alessandri, under Frei, and under Allende. This was even true in the public sector, which was supposed to be legally bound to the government target. Although the situation varied from

TABLE 8.1

Comparison of Government Wage
Targets and Actual Wage Increases
in Industry, 1960–73
(Percent)

Year	Government recommendation[a]	ISS increase
1960	10.0%	11.2%
1961	8.6[b]	15.9
1962	15.0	19.3
1963	21.7	34.8
1964	45.5	50.4
1965	38.4	40.1
1966	25.9	42.5
1967	20.0	32.1
1968	21.9	30.4
1969	27.9	38.3
1970	29.3	40.8
1971	34.9	50.3
1972	52.5[c]	83.9
1973	120.0[d]	170.0

SOURCE: Government recommendations: 1960–70, Ricardo Ffrench-Davis, *Politicas económicas de Chile, 1952–70* (Santiago, 1973); 1971–73, *Diario Oficial*. ISS increases: Banco Central, *Boletin Mensual*, various numbers.

[a] Highest recommendation for private sector, i.e. above certain limit, recommendation might be for *lower* increase.

[b] One-sixth of a *sueldo vital* applied to the average salary of a white-collar industrial employee.

[c] Public sector readjustment; no recommendation for private sector.

[d] Weighted average of recommendations.

year to year, the private sector was generally left free to negotiate, based on a government-recommended target. Only with respect to the minimum wage and salary did the government have real control, which meant, of course, that the gap between the minimums and the wages of the higher-paid workers tended to increase. Table 8.1 shows the government target increase for the private sector for each year, compared with the increase in the industrial Wage and Salary Index (measure of remunerations for workers in medium and large factories).

The situation under Alessandri was complicated because of the greater latitude the President had at that time in setting wage increases and the enormous delays in dispatching the wage bills. In 1961 and 1962, for example, the readjustments were not announced until almost the end of the year (retroactive), which makes comparisons with wage increases obtained during those years rather meaningless. Turning to the table, it can be seen that the actual increase was always above the government recommendation. Leaving out 1961 and 1962 for the reason just mentioned, the "drift" averaged about 28 percent. A more important setback for the Alessandri wage policy, however, concerned the law that automatically readjusted certain wages and salaries in line with the previous year's inflation rate. As pointed out above, one of the main results of the Klein-Saks recommendations was the elimination of this law, which provided Alessandri with some degree of autonomy in setting wage increases during the first half of his administration. In other words, he could recommend increases less than the increase in the cost of living during the previous year, in keeping with his view that this was the proper way to cut down the inflation rate. At the beginning of 1963, however, the automatic clause was reinstated over Alessandri's objections. This situation shows some of the limits of the power of the Executive in the face of various types of political pressures. One type of pressure came from the workers themselves and their federation, the CUT. The strikes and demonstrations that labor carried out in these years were important, though not decisive. In fact, the most successful labor activity actually came after the readjustment clause was reinstated. More important as a cause were the actions of the opposition parties in Congress. The Communists and Socialists, representing the blue-collar workers and some white-collar sectors, continually opposed Alessandri's wage policies. More crucial, however, was the opposition of the Radical Party, which had long dominated the Public Sector Employees' Union (Associación Nacional de Empleados Fiscales). The Radicals demanded a return to the automatic readjustment as a way of maintaining the standard of living of the government functionaries, and Alessandri ultimately had to accept this because he needed Radical support in order to maintain control of Congress.

The remunerations policy of the Frei government was designed to give the workers annual increases equal to 100 percent of the previous year's inflation rate. Since this had long been the chief demand of the CUT with respect to wages, Frei thus expected to gain the workers' support. Relations between the Frei government and the CUT were continually bad, however, since the former not only refused the latter's demand for official recognition but also tried to form rival confederations. The result was that even the Christian

Democratic labor leaders refused to heed the government's wage policies; this was especially the case after the government's 1967 attempt to institute a forced savings plan, described in the previous section. The unions were becoming more radicalized and increasingly tended to see the employers as class enemies; they were thus determined to capture as large a percentage as possible of the companies' profits. This pursuit was carried out through a great increase in unionization and in the number of strikes at the factory level. In addition, labor pressed its demands at the national level through general strikes and congressional maneuvers by the Communist and Socialist deputies and senators. More significant from the point of view of the government was the help the workers received from the left wing of the Christian Democratic Party itself. The result was that wage increases completely escaped the government's control, with settlements averaging more than 40 percent above government recommendations. The Frei government obviously felt betrayed by the workers' refusal to cooperate. Finance Minister Sergio Molina, for example, complained bitterly about the "paradoxical situation" whereby many workers supported the Christian Democrats in political rallies and the voting booths, but elected members of the opposition parties as union leaders. He explained this phenomenon by saying that the workers voted for those who could obtain the greatest economic benefits for them; this was the opposition that was not inhibited by the effects of its actions on the government's overall economic strategy.[8]

Allende encountered obstacles to the implementation of his remunerations policy that were, in some ways, analogous to the problems of Frei. In 1971, for example, the general wage readjustment was set for about 35 percent in nominal terms, which was the inflation rate for 1970; certain groups with low incomes were to receive more. The average increase, however, turned out to be around 50 percent, as workers took advantage of their new power, deriving from a government that would not send in the police or the army to break up strikes and that appointed pro-labor representatives to the wage arbitration boards. The situation in 1972 was much more extreme in terms of wage increases which exceeded government recommendations. In part, the 1972 situation was the result of the government having set goals that were unrealistic in the light of inflation trends. The union leaders of the government's own parties responded by encouraging wage demands that would be more likely to protect their members. In addition, however, the Christian Democrats engaged in the same type of activity of which the Frei government had accused the Socialists and Communists previously. That is, they encouraged the workers to demand very high wage increases, since this would obviously cause political and economic problems for the government. This strategy was complemented by the opposition-controlled Congress's refusal to authorize taxes that would finance wage increases, as will be discussed below. The culmination of the strategy was the miners' strike in May 1973. The Christian Democrats took advantage of a technical flaw in the September 1972 wage bill to convince the copper miners, who already received wages far in excess of the national average, that they deserved a 150 percent wage increase, instead of the 100 percent that all other workers received. Thus, the miners, including the UP members, went on strike. The government quickly convinced the latter to return to work, leaving only the Christian Democratic miners on strike. Great propaganda value was made out of the situation, as the Christian Democrats and the National Party announced to the world that the workers were striking against their own government. Although the miners eventually settled for the government's original offer, other wage increases again exceeded government recommendations; the average wage drift during 1971–73 was 49 percent, the highest of the three administrations.

The effect of the wage drift in all three periods was to squeeze investment. This became much more serious under Frei, who tried to compensate through his forced savings scheme, and under Allende. During the latter period, no solution was forthcoming before the coup.

Taxation

A third area of difficulty, especially for the Allende regime, was taxation. The Alessandri position on taxes was quite consistent with his general ideology. Long before taking office, Alessandri had expressed the opinion that "high" taxes had decapitalized private sector enterprises and that no further burden should be placed on the private sector. This philosophy was followed up in the various changes to the tax laws included in the 1959 economic package. Numerous new exemptions were introduced to induce the private sector to invest. At the same time, one of the few exemptions open to low-income groups was eliminated. The result was an increase in the percentage of tax revenue coming from sales tax and income tax on wages and salaries and a fall in corporation taxes and the *global complementaria* (a tax on retained profits and income above a certain amount). The main thrust of the 1964 tax reform was to rationalize and simplify the system, not to change it in any significant way.[9]

In spite of these measures, however, taxes increased as a percent of gross national product throughout the four years of the Alessandri administration, going from 11.4 percent in 1958 to 14.6 percent in 1962.[10] The main increases were accounted for by taxes on copper and by customs duties which were inflated by the large quantity of imports entering the country. The yield from property tax and corporate income tax also increased, however, in those years when inflation was falling (since taxes were paid with a year's delay).

Frei was very successful with respect to tax policy. He made proposals in line with his belief that taxes should be increased, and the burden shifted more toward the wealthy, and his congressional majority enabled him to put these proposals into practice. As a result, taxes as a percentage of GNP rose from 12.8 percent in 1964 to 21.2 percent in 1970. Most of this increase, however, was concentrated between 1965 and 1967, when tax rates were significantly increased and income taxes were made readjustable in accord with the Consumer Price Index. The latter move was important because taxes were paid at the end of the year, by which time inflation had consumed much of their value. A highly progressive tax on net wealth was introduced which affected some 80,000 people. In addition, the property tax reassessment, begun under Alessandri, was finished and promulgated with a threefold average effective increase.[11] By 1968, the government slowed down its attempt to increase taxes. Many public officials believed that the expansion of taxes had gone too far and that no more sacrifices should be demanded of the private sector. Pressure to raise taxes continued to come from the Christian Democratic Party, as opposed to the government. This was done in some cases, including an increase in the corporate income tax at the end of 1969. Nevertheless, many exemptions remained that benefited the bourgeoisie.

Allende tried on various occasions to raise tax rates as well as to reform the entire tax system. Power over taxes, however, was one of the main prerogatives of the Congress and, since this body was controlled by the opposition, few of Allende's proposals were accepted.* As a result, taxes fell from over 20 percent to less than 15 percent of GNP.[12] Control over finances became a major tool in the bourgeois battle against the UP; by refusing to provide financing for wage increases and social programs, the opposition-controlled Congress forced the government to print money, thus raising the inflation rate and eating up much of the wage increases that had been granted. The nature of this increasing problem can be seen in the fact that the financing approved for the January 1972 wage increase was 57 percent of the President's request; in September 1972, it was down to 49 percent; and it fell drastically to 12 percent in May 1973. As would be expected, those taxes that were cut out were mainly new taxes on property and high incomes; those approved tended to be sales taxes on cigarettes, beer, gasoline, and similar items. The extreme case occurred again in May 1973, when Allende's proposal called for 52 percent of the financing for the wage increase to come from income and property taxes, whereas what financing the Congress finally did approve consisted of only 5 percent taxes of this variety.[13]

The components of the tax structure are shown in Table 8.2. Comparing the Frei and Alessandri periods shows that the relative weight of direct taxes increased, with emphasis on personal income tax and taxes on the large copper mines. Sales taxes also increased, with a significant drop in the relative weight of customs duties as the quantity of imports fell from their unusual high in the early 1960's. The Allende tax structure is difficult to compare with the other two because of the huge fall in copper taxes. Focusing on changes in absolute amounts, however, indicates that income tax almost maintained its 1970 weight; sales and production taxes increased in importance; and all other categories fell.[14]

A clear-cut interpretation of these data is difficult. Generally it is assumed that the sales tax is the most regressive tax and income tax is the most progressive. In Chile, this was not true, since sales tax fell largely on luxury items, with basic consumer items exempt. In general, however, it seems clear that Alessandri was fairly successful in his attempt to avoid "burdening" the business sector with

---

* The only major tax reform that was passed under Allende was the Unified Tax for blue- and white-collar workers. This reform was very progressive in theory, but in practice it meant higher taxes for only 1 or 2 percent of the population covered. The significant point is that only the working class was included; the bourgeoisie and petty bourgeoisie were not touched. (See *El Mercurio*, International Edition, Nov. 27–Dec. 3, 1972.)

TABLE 8.2

Composition of Tax Revenue, 1959–73

(Percent)

Revenue	1959–64	1965–70	1971–73
Direct taxes			
Personal income	7.8	12.4[a]	25.3
Corporate income	10.1	10.1[a]	
Mining	13.2	15.9	0.8
Property	6.7	4.9	4.7
TOTAL	37.8%	43.3%	30.8%
Indirect taxes			
Sales	21.5	25.9	36.8
Production	8.9	7.2	10.9
Customs	18.6	11.5	8.8
Other	13.2	12.1	12.7
TOTAL	62.2%	56.7%	69.2%

SOURCE: 1959, Universidad de Chile, Instituto de Economía, *La economía chilena en el periodo 1950–63*, Tomo II (1963), p. 155; 1960–70, ODEPLAN, *Antecedentes sobre el desarrollo chileno, 1960–70* (1971), p. 389; 1971–73, Ministerio de Hacienda, *Balance consolidado del sector público, 1971–73*, p. 173.

[a] Separation between personal and corporate income taxes for 1965–69 only. 1970 figure allocated on basis of 1965–69 ratio.

more taxes; that Frei succeeded in making the tax system much more progressive; but that political and institutional forces were such that Allende was unable to use taxes as a complement to his wage policy in the battle to increase the equality of income distribution.

SUMMARY

This chapter has shown how certain structural characteristics of the Chilean economy could bring about the apparent anomaly of similar policies from governments with different bases of class support and different development ideologies. Two types of similarities were examined. First were the policies of demand management (government expenditure, remunerations, credit), which led to cycles in the industrial sector. All three of these policies followed a pattern whereby demand was increased at the beginning of a presidential administration and then cut back later as inflation recurred. This cutback could be intentional, as was the case with the Alessandri and Frei regimes, or unintentional, as when Allende's large nominal increases were canceled by the high inflation rates. The effect of the cutbacks was to cause a drop in the rate of growth of output and an increase in unemployment at the end of an administration, such that a new President could increase demand, and therefore production, without new investment. This was the pattern in each of the three periods studied. It came about because of the recurring inflation problem, which, in turn, derived from structural characteristics of the economy—the high level of organization of both workers and bourgeoisie and the effects of the balance of trade and long-term capital flows.

The second type of similarity involved attempts at change by one or more of the three regimes and the frustration of these attempts because of the structural characteristics. Three examples were given. First was investment policy, where Alessandri tried but failed to stimulate private investment, Frei tried but failed to institute a forced savings scheme, and Allende tried to increase public investment but failed to do so sufficiently to offset a private investment boycott. The second example concerned wage policies, where workers managed to obtain increases that went beyond the government recommendations in each of the three regimes. A final example dealt with taxes. Allende was unable to increase taxes because the opposition-controlled Congress refused to approve his proposals. Again the obstacles were closely related to the structural characteristics of the economy.

Outcomes: Economic Growth and Income Distribution

THE FINAL COMPONENT of the framework consists of the economic development outcomes—growth and distribution. According to the framework being used, the policies that have been analyzed in Chapters Seven and Eight should have been translated into differences in outcomes. This was indeed the case, and the differences in aggregate and sectoral growth of industrial output and in between-class and within-class distribution of income in the industrial sector will be shown.

AGGREGATE OUTPUT

Several sets of indicators of industrial production in Chile are available. They include (1) changes in the industrial production index of the National Institute of Statistics (INE); (2) changes in value added as compiled by the State Development Corporation (CORFO); and (3) changes in the physical production index calculated by the National Industrial Society (SOFOFA). It will be noted that these three sets of data differ in two basic ways. First, they are calculated by different groups: two government offices and the private association of industrialists. Second, they are composed of slightly different measures of industrial production: value of production (INE and CORFO) and physical volume of production (SOFOFA). In spite of these differences, the trends are quite similar, as can be seen in Table A.13.

Table 9.1 shows the average rate of growth of industrial output

TABLE 9.1
Changes in Industrial Output and
Productivity, 1959–73
(Percent)

Average for period	Output[a]	Productivity[b]
1959–64	7.4%	3.6%
1959–61	7.3	2.5
1965–70	3.6	1.2
1965–67	5.5	2.2
1971–73[c]	3.1	−1.3

SOURCE: Tables A.13 and A.16.
 [a] Average of INE, SOFOFA, and CORFO growth statistics.
 [b] CORFO statistics.
 [c] 1973 figures for January–August only.

during each presidential period according to the average of the three indicators. They show that growth was highest under Alessandri (1958–64), with an average rate of 7.4 percent. The second highest growth rate came during the Frei period (1964–70), where output increased at an average of 3.6 percent per year. Finally, the lowest rate was found under Allende (1970–73), when the average growth rate was 3.1 percent. This pattern is reinforced if the sets of three-year growth averages are examined. These were added as an attempt to compensate for the problem that, since growth was highest at the beginning of a presidential period, comparing three years of the Allende period with six years for Alessandri and Frei might bias the results. These three-year averages show the same pattern: Alessandri highest, Frei second, and Allende third. Table 9.1 also shows data for changes in productivity (output per worker) during each period. The trends are the same as those for output, with the average increase in productivity under Alessandri 3.6 percent, under Frei 1.2 percent, and under Allende, a decline of −1.3 percent.

In addition to the *average* growth rate during presidential periods, it is also important to look at the year-by-year fluctuations. As was discussed in some detail in Chapter Eight, a pattern prevailed within each period, with growth highest at the beginning of the period and then tapering off at the end. The decline in production in 1960 (due primarily to the serious earthquake in May of that year) was the only major deviation from this pattern. The relative peaks for each period were 14.2 percent growth in 1959 (Alessandri's first year),

8.4 percent in 1966 (Frei's second year), and 13.0 percent in 1971 (Allende's first year). In comparison with these peak years, the later years of each administration were much less dynamic. What should be noticed, however, is that the length of time that growth stayed relatively high differed in the three administrations. In the Alessandri case, there was a four-year dynamic period (with the exception of 1960, as already mentioned), followed by two years of lower growth. The Frei high-growth period lasted two years, whereas, under the Allende regime, it was only one year.

These growth rates, both the averages by presidential periods and the yearly fluctuations, can be traced back to some of the policies discussed in the previous chapters. There are two aspects involved in growth of output: the increase in capacity and the utilization of capacity. Increase in capacity is mainly determined by investment rates, which must be analyzed taking lags into account. That is, if large investment projects take two or three years to mature, then it is necessary to look at investment during the end of the Ibáñez period and the beginning of the Alessandri period, in order to determine the change in capacity, which affected growth during the Alessandri period as a whole. Similar adjustments, of course, must be made for the Frei and Allende periods. When these lags are taken into account, it can be seen that increases in capacity are generally in line with growth during the three periods. High investment rates during the 1956–58 period, as well as high investment at the beginning of the Alessandri administration, left the Alessandri regime as a whole with a substantial increase in capacity. The low investment rates at the end of the Alessandri period and the early Frei years produced a squeeze on capacity for the Frei regime. Finally, the high investment rates during 1968–70 did not benefit the Frei administration, but began to be effective during the Allende administration. The quality of this investment is also important; that is, the type of technology embodied. Capital-intensive investment—implying less employment per unit of investment—was most common under Frei. Investment under Alessandri was probably slightly less capital-intensive than under Frei and a good deal less under Allende.

The existence of capacity, however, did not necessarily mean that it would be utilized. Utilization was determined by the state of aggregate demand in the economy as a whole. Policies affecting demand—public sector expenditure, credit, and wages—were analyzed in the discussion on cycles. When expenditure in these areas kept demand high, output increased rapidly; when the rate of growth of demand fell, the rate of growth of output fell also. To understand the *average* growth rates over the presidential periods, it is necessary to look at the amplitude and duration of the growth cycles. The amplitude depended primarily on what could be called the initial conditions of the economy. That is, the more idle capacity and unemployment that existed, the greater were the possibilities for rapid growth based on that capacity. The duration of the cycle in the Chilean case depended on the behavior of inflation, which, in turn, depended on the behavior of wages, profits, import prices, and productivity changes, as explained earlier. When inflation rose, it could cut demand in two ways. Either the government could consciously cut demand in an attempt to combat inflation, or the inflation rate could simply exceed the nominal increase. Thus, the Alessandri regime had the highest *average* growth rate because (1) the output peak was higher (owing to more idle capacity and unemployment in 1958), and (2) the boom part of the cycle lasted longer (because inflation was held down longer). The Frei cycle had a lower peak and shorter boom period, which led to an average growth rate that was much lower than under the previous administration. The Allende peak was almost as high as that during the Alessandri administration, but it lasted for only a single year; thus the average growth rate was even lower than under Frei.

Productivity changes combine the growth in output just analyzed with changes in the size of the work force; that is, productivity measures output per worker. To account for changes in productivity, it is therefore necessary to refer back to the discussion on the employment policies of the three administrations. The Alessandri administration made no special effort to increase employment, being content to rely on increases in production to create jobs as more capacity was put to work. This policy, combined with the relatively capital-intensive type of investment strategy pursued, meant that employment increased less rapidly than output, leading to a fairly large increase in productivity. Productivity also increased under Frei, because the rise in output outdistanced that in employment, as Frei's capital-intensive strategy undermined his attempts to solve unemployment problems through education. Allende, however, considered full employment per se as a major goal and so created jobs at a rate that outdistanced increases in output. This accounted for part of the fall in productivity between 1971 and 1973.

SECTORAL GROWTH

For the sectoral growth analysis, the 20 industrial categories of the U.N. Standard Industrial Classification System were grouped into three sectors: basic consumer goods, intermediate goods, and durable consumer and capital goods. Basic consumer goods consist of food, beverages, tobacco, textiles, clothes and shoes, furniture, printing, and miscellaneous industries. Intermediate goods include wood, paper, leather, rubber products, chemicals, petroleum, non-metallic minerals, and basic metals. Durable consumer and capital goods are metal products, nonelectrical machinery, electrical equipment, and transportation equipment. Most of these categories are quite straightforward and are the divisions commonly used.[1] A few words are necessary, however, about the durable consumer and capital goods sector. In Chile, like most Third World countries, the production of capital goods is very underdeveloped; therefore, this sector consists almost entirely of durable consumer goods, especially household appliances like stoves, refrigerators, washing machines, radios, and televisions but also automobiles. Only the category "nonelectrical machinery" represents a significant quantity of capital goods.

Figures 9.1 and 9.2 present data on the average growth rates of each sector according to the CORFO value-added indicator. As can

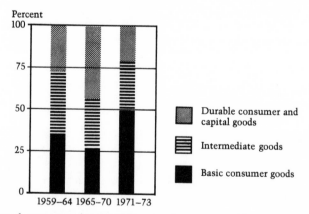

Fig. 9.1. Growth structure of industrial production, 1959–73 (the average growth rate of a sector multiplied by its percentage of total value added and divided by the total change in value added for the industrial sector). For 1973, figures cover January–August only. Source: Table A.14.

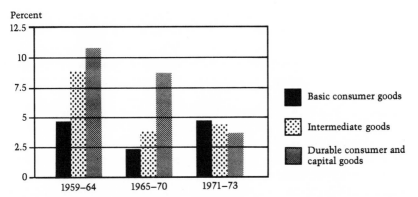

Fig. 9.2. Growth rates by industrial sectors, 1959–73. For 1973, figures cover January–August only. Source: Table A.14.

be seen, the industrial growth patterns were quite different during the three regimes. This is especially true of changes in growth structure (the growth rate for each sector weighted by its percentage of total value added). By use of this measure, it can be seen that the intermediate goods sector was dominant under Alessandri (accounting for 39 percent of total growth), the consumer durable and capital goods sector under Frei (43 percent of growth), and the basic consumer goods sector under Allende (50 percent). Examining growth rates, on the other hand, we see that the picture changes slightly. The consumer durable sector continues to be the pacesetter under Frei (8.7 percent growth as compared to 4.0 percent for industry as a whole), as does the basic consumer sector under Allende (4.8 percent over 4.3 percent for the total). The Alessandri pattern, however, comes to resemble the Frei pattern more closely. The durable consumer and capital goods sector grows at 10.8 percent, above intermediate goods at 8.8 percent and the total of 7.0 percent. It is clear, however, that consumer durables were much more significant in total growth under Frei than Alessandri. The growth in the durable consumer and capital goods sector between 1958 and 1964 was only about 50 percent above growth in industry as a whole, whereas this ratio was almost 120 percent between 1964 and 1970. Looking at the situation this way, and seeing that it has been the durable consumer goods sector that has been the fastest growing during the entire decade of the 1960's, the change that the Allende regime was able to make becomes quite dramatic.

A final level of disaggregation leads us to look at those individual industries that were growing fastest under each administration. Three of the five fastest under Alessandri were intermediate sector industries (basic metals, rubber, and petroleum), whereas the other two were durable consumer industries (metal products and transportation equipment). A substantial interrelationship can be seen within this group, as growth in the basic metals industry provides inputs for the metal products industry, as do petroleum and rubber for the transportation sector.* Under the Frei administration, the two fastest growing industries were paper and chemicals, followed by three durable consumer industries (transportation, electrical machinery, and metal products). Although the latter group would be expected to grow rapidly under Frei, it might seem strange to find two intermediate industries leading the list. The reason is that these two sectors were the two main industrial export products that the Frei regime was trying to promote. The Allende period saw a completely different list of industries as pacesetters. First came nonelectrical machinery, followed by four basic consumer goods industries (miscellaneous industries, beverages, furniture, and tobacco). As was mentioned above, nonelectrical machinery was the only industry within the consumer durable and capital goods sector that produced a significant amount of capital goods (and that incidentally was one of the slowest growing industries all during the 1960's, when emphasis was on importing capital goods instead of producing them at home). Given the foreign exchange shortage under Allende and the general economic ideology of the regime, more emphasis was placed on producing capital goods at home.

Several of the policies discussed previously are relevant to explaining sectoral growth, but first it should be pointed out that the class alliances behind each regime already implied a certain emphasis in terms of sectoral output. Family budget data show that the lower the income level, the larger the percentage of family income is spent on basic consumer goods, as opposed to consumer durables. Therefore, the assumption is that emphasis on the production of basic consumer goods is most directly beneficial to blue-collar workers and the lower-income sectors of the petty bourgeoisie, whereas consumer durables are mainly purchased by white-collar

---

* The even stronger relationship that would be expected on the basis of U.S. experience, between metal and transportation industries, does not hold in Chile because the automobile industry is composed of assembly plants, not automobile manufacture. Some of the smaller parts did come to be made in Chile during the Frei years.

workers and the higher-income petty bourgeoisie. As is obvious, no consumer group as such buys substantial amounts of intermediate goods, but rather these are purchased by the industrialists in order to produce finished goods. Since intermediate goods have usually been sold at subsidized prices in Chile, the capitalist class could thus increase its profits and was the main beneficiary of a strategy emphasizing intermediate goods. The emphases on intermediate goods under Alessandri, consumer durables under Frei, and basic consumer goods under Allende, are, therefore, those that would be predicted from the class alliances behind each regime.

The specific policies connecting these general preferences with sectoral growth included investment and income distribution (i.e. capacity and demand or utilization). From a look back to the discussion on the sectoral distribution of investment, it will be remembered that state investment under Alessandri was mainly directed toward intermediate goods, as was foreign investment, though the latter, coming in 1964, did not have time to affect growth during the Alessandri administration. State and foreign investment under Frei was concentrated in the two main export sectors—paper and chemicals, which were the fastest growing industries during this period—and in durable consumer goods. Main state investment under Allende was in agro-industry. The different rates at which investment projects matured in different sectors, and the variations in capital-output ratios,* cause difficulty in making direct connections between investment and output by sector; certain relationships, however, are obvious.

The relationship between income distribution and sectoral growth is closer. The demand structure can be conceptualized in two different ways. The first is in terms of low income vs. high incomes within the working class as a whole. Here it would be expected that the lower-paid workers would spend the vast majority of their incomes on basic consumer goods and the higher-paid workers

---

* Capital-output ratios by sector for the year 1960 were basic consumer goods 1.14, intermediate goods 2.88, and durable consumer and capital goods 1.58. For the total industrial sector, the capital-output ratio was 1.73. There ratios were calculated from Table A.14 and ODEPLAN, *Capital a valor de reemplazo en la industria* (1962). This ODEPLAN study is one of the few that can be used for this purpose, since it values capital at replacement cost rather than historical cost. In an economy characterized by rapid inflation, the latter method undervalues capital, such that artificially low capital-output ratios are obtained. This appears to be the case, for example, with the 1967 Industrial Census, which yields an overall capital-output ratio for industry of only 0.81.

would spend more on durable consumer goods. To test this hypothesis, it is necessary to compare the relative growth rates of basic consumer goods and consumer durables with the relative increases in the real incomes of lower-paid workers (those earning the *minimum* wage or salary) and those earning more (as seen in the wage and salary index, which represents incomes in the larger factories). During the Alessandri years, on the average, the index rose faster than the minimums, and consumer durables grew faster than the basic consumer goods sector. The same was true under Frei and the opposite under Allende. In addition, this same pattern—durable consumer goods growing faster when the index exceeded the minimums and vice-versa—was present in each separate year, with only three exceptions (1961, 1970, and 1972). Obviously, this relationship is one of correlation, not causation, but the pattern is striking.

Inspection of the figures given later in this chapter on changes in income distribution between and within classes yields similar conclusions on the correlation between demand structure and sectoral growth in industry. For example, during the Alessandri period, the share of national income going to the bourgeoisie increased, as did the concentration of income within the class. The share of income to the petty bourgeoisie decreased, but concentration also increased such that this group, as well as the best-paid white-collar workers, could purchase the durable consumer goods that were beginning to be produced in Chile. These included televisions and radios, as well as automobiles, which began to be assembled in quantity in Chile in the 1960's. By 1964, however, it was obvious that this small group alone could not consume a sufficient amount to maintain the dynamism of the durable consumer goods market. Under the Frei regime, two changes occurred. First, the share of income going to labor increased substantially as wages and salaries increased in real terms. This enabled a new stratum of people to enter the durable consumer goods market. At the same time, however, concentration *within* the working class increased, thus giving even more income to the best-paid workers. The pattern of concentration was quite significant. The top half of the blue-collar workers increased their share of the income at the expense of the bottom half, such that the former, for the first time, became significant purchasers of consumer durables. Among the white-collar workers, however, only the top 20 percent increased its share of the income. The effect was to add this 20 percent of white-collar workers to the bourgeoisie and some members of the petty bourgeoisie who formed the market for automobiles.*

BETWEEN-CLASS INCOME DISTRIBUTION

The next two sections will present data on distribution of income between and within social classes. Class is defined in the Marxist sense and is made operational in terms of the census categories of capital (the bourgeoisie, *empleadores*, and petty bourgeoisie, *trabajadores por cuenta propia*) and labor (white-collar workers, *empleados*, and blue-collar workers, *obreros*). It would, of course, be desirable to have a more detailed disaggregation of these classes and subclasses. Since the focus is on the industrial sector, however, this problem is not as serious as it would be for the entire economy because there is less diversity within classes in industry. Nevertheless, it would be of interest to be able to separate workers by industrial sector, by size of factory, by type of technology employed, as well as by other less important divisions.

Between-class distribution is measured by what economists call functional distribution of income. Functional distribution shows the division of national (or domestic) income between capital and labor. Labor's share is composed of wages and salaries received by blue- and white-collar workers, whereas capital's share is composed of returns to capital—rent, interest, dividends, and income to proprietors. In the Chilean case, statistics are calculated such that income to capital is divided between income to the petty bourgeoisie and the rest (mainly income of various types to the bourgeoisie). The functional distribution data presented here were calculated by the National Planning Office (ODEPLAN).[2]

In order to use functional distribution as a measure of interclass distribution, a major assumption is necessary: that all income received by workers comes from wages and salaries and that all income to petty bourgeoisie and bourgeoisie comes as returns to capital. This assumption is probably not far off in Chile. The basic

---

*Family budget studies in Chile have shown that a family enters the market for automobiles only after its income reaches at least eight sueldos vitales. The average personal income of the top 20 percent of the white-collar industrial workers was only 5.0 SV in 1964, but 9.5 in 1970; family incomes were generally about 1.7 times personal income in Santiago. (Figures calculated from unpublished data in the data bank of the Joint Program between the Facultad Latinoamericana de Ciencias Sociales and the Programa Regional de Empleo para América Latina y el Caribe on size distribution of income and unemployment in Greater Santiago, 1959–72.)

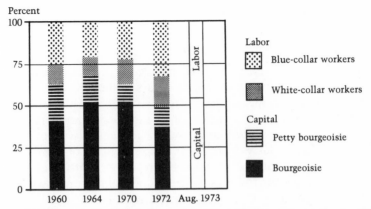

Fig. 9.3. Distribution of income between classes in industry, 1960–73. Source: Table A.19 (eliminating social security payments because it was not possible to break them down into percentages going to white- as opposed to blue-collar workers; also because this does not compose part of the current income available to workers).

argument against it in the United States would be that many workers (especially white-collar workers) own stocks, bonds, savings accounts, and so forth, thus supplementing their salaries with income from capital. This is not very common in Chile because of lack of available cash, on the one hand, and lack of opportunities, on the other. That is, Chile has no effective stock or bond market and the chronic inflation generally served to discourage savings.*

Figure 9.3 shows the percentage of national income going to each class at the beginning and end of each presidential period. The major trends are quite obvious: by combination of the bourgeoisie and petty bourgeoisie, it can be seen that there was an increasing share of income to capital during the Alessandri period, a decreasing share during the Frei years, and a much sharper decrease under Allende. Thus, capital had 63 percent of total income in 1960, which increased to 68 percent by 1964. By 1970, it had returned to 63 percent, and took a sharp drop to 48 percent in 1972. The share to labor, of course, followed the opposite trend.

The trends within these two categories, however, are equally important. The income share of blue-collar workers declined under

---

* The main exception was probably savings accounts in savings and loan associations or buying houses or apartments through social security retirement-fund mortgages on the part of certain elements of the petty bourgeoisie and white-collar workers. These types of saving probably changed little during the 15-year period, so would not alter the *trends* described.

Alessandri (from 25 to 21 percent), and, although it increased under Frei, it still remained lower than the 1960 percentage. Under Allende, the blue-collar workers' share increased to 32 percent in 1972. The white-collar workers' share, on the other hand, declined only slightly under Alessandri (12 to 11 percent) and then more than regained this loss under Frei (increasing to 15 percent). White-collar workers also increased their share under Allende (to 19 percent), though this gain was less than that for blue-collar workers. Within the capitalist sector, the share of the petty bourgeoisie declined sharply (from 22 to 15 percent) under Alessandri and continued in the same direction under Frei (to 10 percent). This trend was only slightly altered under Allende (12 percent). Finally, the bourgeoisie gained rapidly under Alessandri, going from 41 to 53 percent, and then stayed at this same level under Frei. It was only during the Allende regime that the bourgeoisie began to lose their lion's share of industrial income, declining from 53 to 37 percent. The Allende comparisons just discussed cover only the period 1970–72 because the breakdown by subclasses is complete only through this point. Some additional calculations, however, have been made (for labor and capital only) to take the trends up through August 1973. During the first eight months of heavy inflation in 1973, the workers were losing their share of income until they had only 45 percent compared to 55 for capital. Even with this decline in 1973, however, the share to labor was still well above the 1970 percentage.

In addition to these trends, three major items should be pointed out about Figure 9.3. First, it is possible to see which class or subclass was the most favored during each regime. Under Alessandri, it was obviously the bourgeoisie; under Frei, the white- and blue-collar workers gained about evenly, with a slight emphasis on the former; whereas under Allende, the main gainers were the blue-collar workers. The second item of importance is that the petty bourgeoisie were continually losing throughout the entire period (with a slight respite during the Allende years). This factor is significant for at least two reasons. First it means that, in Chile, it is not necessarily the case that, as labor increases its share of the income, the bourgeoisie must lose. This was very clear during the Frei period, when labor increased its share from 32 to 37 percent, while the bourgeoisie stayed at the same level. This was possible because there was a third group (i.e. petty bourgeoisie) that could be squeezed. As should be clear from Chapter Two, such a squeeze was politically possible because the petty bourgeoisie were not well organized, while both the workers and the bourgeoisie were. The decline in income to the petty bourgeoisie was also important because the objective worsening of conditions among this class convinced many leaders of the UP that this group would be open to an alliance with the workers. As was shown in Chapter Six, however, the petty bourgeoisie's view of their long-term interests made them rebuff this alliance and side with the bourgeoisie.

The final point to be made about Figure 9.3 is the changing meaning of income to capital over the period being considered. This change arises because income to capital includes profits going to state-owned as well as privately owned industries. Before 1964, the number of state-owned industries was minute; this number increased under Frei. After 1970, however, the state came to control a significant percentage of the industrial sector, and the decline in profits represented not only a lower income to private capital but also increasing budget deficits. (Data on percentages of industry owned by the state, foreign capital, and private national capital can be found in Figure 7.1, p. 157.) There was also a change with regard to income to foreign capital, which is included in Figure 9.3, since it is domestic income that is being considered.* This percentage increased under Frei and declined under Allende.

So far, this discussion has omitted any mention of per capita shares of income that might have changed as a result of shifts in the structure of the industrial work force. The most important shifts were from the status of blue-collar to white-collar workers;† the former declined from 60.7 percent of the industrial work force in 1960 to 58.7 percent in 1972, while the latter increased from 14.3 to 16.8 percent during the same period (see Table A.18). These changes, however, did not alter the trends of income distribution between classes, which have been described above. That is, in per capita terms, the bourgeoisie were still the main gainers under Alessandri—at the expense of all other groups; workers (especially

---

* Gross domestic product is the output produced within a given country; gross national product is that part of the product accruing to nationals of the country. That is, GNP is GDP minus payments on foreign capital, plus payments received by nationals with assets abroad. In advanced countries, the two measures are approximately equal; in less-developed countries GDP is almost always larger.

† For the most part, these shifts did not involve changes in jobs performed, but were merely attempts to co-opt "trouble-making" blue-collar workers by removing them to the higher-status white-collar classification, while they continued performing the same tasks. To the extent that this was true, it creates some definitional problems in equating *empleados* with white-collar workers.

white-collar workers) gained most under Frei—primarily at the expense of the petty bourgeoisie; and workers also gained most under Allende (especially blue-collar workers)—this time at the expense of the bourgeoisie.

The policies that contributed to these results included those on wages and prices, employment and credit. Figure 7.5 (p. 170) presented data on real wages, showing that they remained more or less constant under Alessandri (an average annual increase of 0.8 percent), increased significantly under Frei (8.3 percent), and increased even more under Allende (15.5 percent for 1971–72, falling to 6.5 for 1971–73). This means that wage and price policies were such that the two increased at about the same rate under Alessandri, whereas wages far outdistanced prices under Frei and Allende. These facts alone would account for the changes in between-class distribution between 1964 and 1973, but another factor needs to be brought into the Alessandri case. Other things being equal, constant real wages would imply an unchanging distribution between capital and labor, but if there are constant real wages *and* rising productivity (as was the case under Alessandri), then this means that the bourgeoisie receives all the additional income deriving from productivity increases. Under Frei and Allende, wages increased far more quickly than productivity.

Employment policy reinforced some of these trends. The effect of employment on between-class distribution will vary, depending on the behavior of input and output prices, wages rates, productivity, and so on. Other things being equal, however, if productivity is rising faster than wages, additional workers will increase the share of income to capital and vice-versa. Therefore, the increasing employment under Alessandri (with productivity increasing faster than wages) reinforced the trend toward an increased share of income to capital. In the opposite direction, increasing employment under Allende (with wages outstripping productivity) reinforced the rising share to labor. The situation during the Frei regime—increasing unemployment, with wages rising more quickly than productivity—meant that the employment policy counteracted the income distribution trend toward a higher share for labor.

A third type of policy that contributed to explaining the between-class income distribution trends was credit policy—both the distribution of credit and the interest rate. Credit was highly concentrated in favor of the large bourgeoisie under both Alessandri and

Frei; under Allende, over four-fifths of all credit went to the state, which, in turn, spent a large percentage of it on increasing remunerations in public administration and the state-controlled industries. Interest rate policy entered the picture, since most loans under Alessandri were made at negative interest rates; thus the bourgeois borrowers were being subsidized at the expense of small savers. Under Frei, various taxes were added to the interest rate, so that obtaining credit involved low positive costs. The negative cost returned under Allende, but this subsidy was going to labor, as just explained.*

WITHIN-CLASS INCOME DISTRIBUTION

Distribution of income within classes (and subclasses) is measured here by the so-called personal distribution of income. Personal income distribution shows the level of concentration of income within any group. Usually the group selected is the entire society (as represented by a sample), but it might be any other group as well. In this case, data are presented for the entire industrial work force, but, of equal importance, they are then broken down to show concentration within the bourgeoisie, petty bourgeoisie, white-collar workers, and blue-collar workers. The basic summary measure used is the Gini index, a relatively simple index that varies from o (perfect equality) to 1 (perfect inequality).†

The data come from an annual survey carried out by the Institute of Economics at the University of Chile in June of each year. Questions were asked about monthly income (after taxes) for the previous month. The sample is stratified by *comuna* (geographical division), with a random sample taken within each comuna. The sample size is approximately 15,000, although this represents only about 5,000 households, since data are collected for each member of the household. The data presented are personal (as opposed to family) income for each person whose main employment was in the industrial sector. This industrial subsample consisted of about 1,500 persons (or about 25 percent of the income recipients in the total sample).[3]

---

*Tax policy would also reinforce the Alessandri and Frei trends but go against the Allende redistribution. In terms of the comparisons in Figure 9.3, however, tax policy is irrelevant, since the data are compiled before taxes.

†Although the Gini index is probably the best summary measure of income concentration, it has one major flaw. Different *kinds* of inequality can be represented by the same Gini index. To correct for this problem, it is necessary to look at the figures from which the index was constructed. In this case, these were deciles that are found in Table A.17.

TABLE 9.2
Within-Class Income Distribution in Industry, Greater Santiago, 1959–72
(Gini indexes)

Class	1959	1964	1970	1972
Blue-collar workers	.311	.326	.373	.314
White-collar workers	.411	.400	.505	.398
Petty bourgeoisie	.445	.519	.535	.530
Bourgeoisie	.353	.475	.395	.307
TOTAL	.450	.493	.552	.471

SOURCE: Calculated from data in Table A.17.

The major problem with these data, from the point of view of this study, is that the survey covered only the Greater Santiago area. Therefore, a brief comment is necessary about how Santiago compared to the rest of the country. First, approximately 57 percent of all industrial workers were located in Santiago.[4] Second, although incomes in Santiago tend to be higher on the average than elsewhere in the country, the shape of the distributions are very similar, and this is what is of interest here.[5]

Table 9.2 shows the Gini indexes for the entire industrial sector and separately for the bourgeoisie, petty bourgeoisie, white-collar workers, and blue-collar workers. Beginning with the sector as a whole, it can be seen that concentration of income increased during the Alessandri period (going from .450 to .493), increased more rapidly under Frei (.493 to .552), and decreased under Allende (.552 to .471). In spite of the strong decrease during Allende years, however, the index of concentration still remained above that in 1959.

Even though overall concentration increased under both Alessandri and Frei, there were different patterns *within* the various classes. During the Alessandri years, concentration did not increase significantly within the working class. In fact, it decreased slightly among white-collar workers while rising slightly among blue-collar workers. Concentration increased sharply, however, among the petty bourgeoisie and even more among the bourgeoisie. During the Frei period, the process was exactly the opposite. That is, concentration decreased among the bourgeoisie, stayed about the same among the petty bourgeoisie, but increased sharply within both the blue-and white-collar sectors of the working class. Under Allende, concentration decreased within all groups except for the petty bourgeoisie, where it remained constant. This change returned the workers to more or less the same position they were in in 1959,

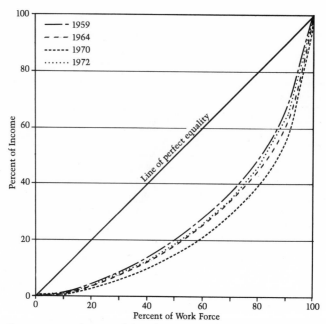

Fig. 9.4. Lorenz curve of personal distribution of income for the industrial sector, 1959–72. Source: Table A.17.

whereas concentration among the bourgeoisie in 1972 dropped to a much lower level than in 1959. Concentration among the petty bourgeoisie, on the other hand, remained well above the 1959 level.

As was mentioned above, the Gini index should be presented in conjunction with a detailed breakdown of the population. Deciles are given in Table A.17 for each group for each of the four years. Here only the decile breakdown for the total industrial sector (in the form of a Lorenz curve) is shown. From Figure 9.4 and the accompanying Table A.17, the following patterns emerge. During the Alessandri years, the top and bottom levels of the population gained at the expense of the middle. Thus, the first and tenth deciles increased their share while two through nine lost. Obviously, the gain by the top decile far outweighed that of the bottom, thereby producing the overall increase in concentration shown by the Gini index. Under Frei, the pattern of concentration was such that the wealthiest part of the population gained at the expense of all the rest. Thus, deciles nine and ten increased their share and the others decreased. Those losing most were the bottom half of the population (unlike the 1959–64 situation), and the only real gainer was the tenth decile. The Allende pattern was more or less the opposite—all gained at the expense of the tenth decile.

The same general patterns followed within each class and subclass, with the following exceptions: first, under Alessandri, concentration among white-collar workers *decreased*, while concentration as a whole *increased* during the 1958–64 period. Second, concentration among the bourgeoisie *decreased* under Frei, while concentration as a whole *increased.* * In addition, three groups—blue-collar workers under Alessandri, petty bourgeoisie under Frei, and petty bourgeoisie under Allende—varied in the same direction as the total sample but less strongly.

Several of the policies that have been discussed can help to explain the trends in concentration of income. Wage policies once again played a crucial role, with policies on employment and technology also involved. The important aspect of wage policy with respect to income concentration was the difference between the rate of increase of the *minimum* wage and salary and the remunerations of the better-paid workers (measured by the wage and salary *index*). Under both Alessandri and Frei, the index increased much faster than the minimums, meaning that the gap between them increased, which would, in turn, lead to a higher Gini index of concentration. This was the case for both blue- and white-collar workers between 1959 and 1970. Under Allende, the pattern was mixed. For white-collar workers, the better-paid again increased their remunerations faster than those receiving the minimums. Among blue-collar workers, however, the trend was reversed during 1971–72. The minimum wage increased almost four times as fast as the index for blue-collar workers, pointing to a decrease in income concentration. In 1973, however, this pattern reverted to the pre-1971 situation. Therefore, although no data are available for 1973, it would not be surprising if concentration increased.

Employment policies are also related to trends in income concentration. That is, the more unemployed persons there are at any given

* This finding would appear to contradict other information at the level of firms, which shows that concentration among industrial firms *increased* during the Frei period. The explanation is that those sectors of the bourgeoisie included in the sample survey were only small and medium bourgeois elements. Thus only 11 percent of the bourgeois sample had incomes above 10 SV (1964). Among the strata captured by the sample, concentration fell as (1) a growing share of profits accrued to the very top group of industrialists and (2) the smallest firms went bankrupt.

time, the higher the level of concentration will be, all other things being equal, because more people will have very low or zero incomes. Since almost all the *un*employed (as opposed to the *under-*employed) are found among white- and blue-collar workers, the effects of changes in unemployment would primarily affect these classes. Alessandri's relative success in lowering unemployment between 1958 and 1964 would therefore tend to cancel out some of the effects of wage policy described in the previous paragraph and help explain why concentration *within the working class* did not change much during his administration. Overall concentration, of course, did increase. The rising unemployment under Frei, on the other hand, tended to reinforce the wage effects leading to higher concentration. Likewise, the rapid decline in unemployment under Allende would reinforce the wage effects among blue-collar workers and counteract those among white-collar workers.

A final policy discussion in Chapters Seven and Eight that is relevant to income concentration is technology. In general, capital-intensive technology increases concentration by tending to divide workers into two sectors: a labor aristocracy working in large modern plants, receiving relatively high wages; and the mass of workers in smaller factories with older equipment, where the level of remuneration is much lower. Thus, the more capital-intensive investment under Frei would tend to increase concentration, and the less capital-intensive investment under Alessandri and especially under Allende would have the opposite effect. The existence of different types of industry—modern and traditional—also tends to increase concentration within the bourgeois class, since the owners of modern plants tend to make much higher profits than their more traditional competitors.

Neither this discussion on policies relating to concentration nor the previous discussions on policies affecting growth and between-class distribution pretend to be complete explanations of the trends discovered in the growth and distribution data.[6] Nevertheless, the policies described in the earlier chapters are, in general, consistent with the outcome data and surely represent the most important determinants of the trends.

OVERALL PATTERNS

After a separate look at data on aggregate growth, sectoral growth, between-class distribution, and within-class distribution in the industrial sector during the three regimes, it is now possible to combine the data to see what kinds of patterns are formed. As it happens, the growth/distribution trends form three distinct patterns that are quite consistent with the nature of the regimes themselves.

Under Alessandri, the highest growth rates were found, with growth concentrated in intermediate industries. There was both an increasing share of income to capital and an increasing concentration of income. Under Frei, the second highest growth rates were encountered, with highest growth in consumer durables. A decreasing share of income to capital was combined with increasing concentration. Under Allende, the lowest growth rates accompanied a growth emphasis on basic consumer items. It was only during this administration that both a decreasing share of income to capital *and* decreasing concentration were found.

At first glance, it would appear that the patterns provide support for the orthodox view of a contradiction between growth and distribution. There was indeed a contradiction, but the mechanisms involved were not the same as those posited by neoclassical economists. The neoclassical theory states that an unequal distribution of income (sometimes interpreted as a high share for the top 5 or 10 percent and at other times as a high share to the capitalist class) is necessary in order for rapid growth to occur. This is because only the wealthy and/or capitalists save and invest, and investment is necessary for growth. There are two reasons for believing that this mechanism would not hold in Chile. First is the fact that the wealthy in Chile used a significant portion of their money for luxury consumption or sent it abroad. The second reason is that the state accounted for a very large percentage of investment in Chile, and therefore a new factor is introduced that neoclassical theory does not consider.

The view taken here, unlike that of neoclassical economics, is that there is no necessary direct connection between growth and distribution. Both can, however, be explained by the same set of structural factors—those that have underlain all the analysis in this book. Distribution trends are relatively straightforward. They clearly derive from the economistic interests of the hegemonic and allied classes and class fractions of the alliance in control of the state apparatus at a given time. Growth trends, on the other hand, are much more complex. The problem of time lags, for example, means that a regime in power for six years is as much affected by others' investment decisions as by its own. Perhaps the most important aspect of investment in determining growth over a fairly short period is the type of investment—whether construction (which stimulates various domestic industries) or the accumulation of machinery (which relies primarily on imports). The most immediate way in which government policies affect growth, however, is through demand management. When demand is high, growth is high (though *how* high depends on another complicating factor, i.e. the economic conditions that a regime encounters when it takes office). But insofar as demand is affected by inflation in the ways described in Chapter Eight, and inflation is determined by class struggle and the ramifications of Chile's insertion in the international capitalist system, then the focus is again on the class structure, the state, and the foreign sector as causal elements in growth as well as distribution.

CHAPTER TEN

Conclusions

TODAY—ALMOST five years after the Allende government was overthrown—policy makers, political activists, and intellectuals are still debating the lessons of the Chilean experience. This is true in Latin America, in Western Europe, and even in Africa and Asia, where the relevance of the Chilean example is much less obvious. Most of the attention has focused on the Allende period and its failure as evidenced by the coup of September 1973.[1] Probably the most often discussed issue has been that of elections versus armed struggle as the way to achieve socialism. This is unfortunate because as important as the UP years were, and as important as the question of strategy is, the Chilean experience is much richer than such a narrow focus would indicate. This final chapter, then, will take a broader view. It will draw on the entire 15-year period from 1958 to 1973 to suggest some of the varied types of political and economic lessons that the Alessandri, Frei, and Allende development models and processes, when looked at in comparative perspective, may offer.*

* Before the most important of these lessons are studied, it is necessary to indicate two rather serious shortcomings with the data base from which this study, and the Chilean experience itself, suffer. First is the focus of this study on the industrial sector. Although the dominant sector of the economy, Chilean industry does not necessarily reflect political or economic trends in each specific sector, especially agriculture. On the other hand, with respect to growth and distribution trends, the industrial sector does appear to be representative of the economy as a whole, even if sometimes in exaggerated form. (It should be noted that this opinion is not shared

To evaluate the 1958–73 period necessitates going back to the question that began to be posed in the early 1950's: What could be done to replace the import-substitution economic model and the Radical-Left political alliance that dynamized Chilean development during the 1938–50 period? All three strategies that were put forth in 1958, and tried in succession, have failed. The Junta model has failed even more miserably, but that is the subject of another book.

The political alliances all failed by definition. That is, all three governments were thrown out of office—Alessandri and Frei by elections and Allende by armed force.* Why did all three prove non-viable? The answer would seem to center on their heterogeneous nature. This answer must be divided into two parts: what was happening with the mass base of the alliances and what was happening at the leadership level.

The base for the Alessandri alliance in 1958 was mainly unorganized sectors in urban areas (petty bourgeoisie and non-unionized workers) and rural population under the control of large landowners. This was an old-style coalition, based on response to a paternalistic image by unorganized masses, on the one hand, and fear and intimidation, on the other. Its future was doomed in the sophisticated context of Chilean politics, where political consciousness and organization were already at a high level and spreading rapidly. In addition, the Alessandri supporters saw that they were getting no material benefits from backing the alliance. In terms of purchasing power, the real wages of the workers were stagnant during the Alessandri period, while the incomes of the petty bourgeoisie declined rapidly.

At the leadership level, there was first the problem of disagreement on policies and then a crisis of confidence. Alessandri had been elected as the candidate of the Liberal and Conservative parties, but the electoral support of these parties fell off significantly by the March 1961 parliamentary election for the reasons described above. Therefore it became necessary to incorporate the Radical Party into the alliance. The Radicals, who had a strong base among

---

by all Chilean economists.) The second problem is the short time period during which each regime held power. Six years is a very short amount of time (and the three years of the UP even shorter) to observe the effects of different development strategies. Nevertheless, certain patterns emerge clearly in spite of the problems mentioned.

*Alessandri and Frei were not personally thrown out of office, since Chilean presidents are not allowed to stand for reelection in the immediately succeeding period. It was the parties they represented that were defeated.

white-collar workers in the state sector, demanded policies that contradicted the Alessandri economic strategy. Specifically, their demands were among the factors that broke the stabilization program. As the strategy disintegrated and electoral support fell, a crisis of confidence began to appear among the bourgeoisie themselves, which, in turn, only intensified the political and economic problems of the alliance. The switch to Frei followed swiftly.

The Frei alliance, even leaving aside the support from the Liberal and Conservative parties, which evaporated soon after the 1964 election, had much more serious problems in terms of heterogeneity than the Alessandri alliance. The Christian Democratic Party itself, in contrast to Chilean tradition, was self-consciously a multiclass party. Its mass base drew on many of the same elements as that of Alessandri but with an important difference. The Christian Democrats were not content to rely on "spontaneous" support, but rather set out to organize the so-called marginal sectors. These included tenants and small farmers in the countryside and shantytown dwellers and petty bourgeoisie in the urban areas. White-collar organizations were also strengthened. A highly sophisticated ideology was fashioned which gave coherence to these diverse groups, as well as to the bourgeois elements of the alliance. The ideology stressed change and modernization; even the word "revolution" was used— but with the clear indication that this was a revolution within a capitalist framework, not one meant to overthrow capitalism as the Marxist parties advocated.

Within the leadership of the alliance, the petty bourgeoisie spoke for the marginal sectors, stressing the need to make major structural changes in Chile's capitalist system. The bourgeois wing agreed with these ideas at the highest level of abstraction. They even agreed on concrete measures that had the ultimate effect of transferring resources from the better-paid white-collar workers and professionals to the marginals and from the landowners to the industrial bourgeoisie. When it came to taking resources and power from the industrialists themselves, however, then the bourgeois and petty bourgeois wings of the Christian Democratic leadership parted company.

These divisions were manifested in struggles over party leadership. In 1967, the petty bourgeois faction won control, but it was ousted by Frei early in 1968. The result was the division of the party into *oficialista, tercerista,* and *rebelde* factions. The oficialistas were the hard-line bourgeois group which wanted to slow down (if not stop) the pace of change and to ally with the conservative National Party. The rebeldes represented the petty bourgeois faction which wanted to speed up reforms and make an alliance with the Marxists. The terceristas tried to mediate between the two. In 1969, the divisions became irreconcilable and the rebeldes left the Party to form the MAPU and become part of the UP alliance. The terceristas stayed in the party since their leader, Radomiro Tomic, was the presidential nominee. Tomic's nomination, however, caused many of the oficialistas to leave the coalition to back the National Party and Jorge Alessandri. As a result of these defections, the Christian Democrats came in third in the 1970 presidential race, with 28 percent of the vote compared with the Party's all-time high of 42 percent in April 1965. The nonviability of this multiclass alliance was demonstrated as well, and it was confirmed in 1971 when the majority of the terceristas finally left the Party to form the Christian Left and join the UP.

The UP was proclaimed an alliance between the workers and the petty bourgeoisie. Whether this was a concrete reality—rather than the statement of a goal—must be regarded with serious doubt. At the mass level, the UP did indeed have a share of the petty bourgeois vote, but a smaller share than either the PN or the PDC, only 23 percent. The petty bourgeoisie made up only 16 percent of the UP alliance, compared with 49 percent blue-collar workers and 30 percent white-collar workers. But it was only among the blue-collar workers that the UP captured a larger percentage than its opponents; this was the hard core of the alliance. In terms of parties, the Radicals were supposed to represent the petty bourgeoisie, but their contribution was minimal. In 1971, the PR provided 8 percent of the UP votes. In 1972, however, the Party split and the UP share fell to 3.5 percent.

The nonviability of the UP coalition, then, also centered on the problem of a multiclass alliance, but with a slightly different twist than in the previous cases. Here the problem was the implementation of policies *to try to win* the support of the petty bourgeoisie and small and medium bourgeoisie and to solidify the support of the white-collar workers. Thus resources were devoted to maintaining the purchasing power and the preferred basket of goods of those target groups that the UP wanted to win over. On the other hand, certain steps were taken against the perceived interests of these target groups (e.g. the government's refusal to send in the police to evict leftist groups that occupied small farms), which made the political alliance more difficult.

The ambiguity in UP policy resulted from another type of division. Among the parties representing the working class, there were at the very least tactical differences, and perhaps strategical differences as well, with regard to the Chilean road to socialism. One faction wanted a gradual route, placing heavy emphasis on the need for an alliance with the petty bourgeoisie. The other wanted a much faster pace, leaving aside the petty bourgeoisie, because they did not believe such an alliance was possible (and most did not think it was desirable either). Thus *intra*class divisions came to exacerbate the *inter*class problems. Whether the desired alliance could have come into existence under the most favorable of circumstances is open to doubt; the bourgeoisie made sure that it would not by mounting an extremely effective ideological campaign oriented around the theme of the "middle class." As had happened in the past, petty bourgeoisie and white-collar workers were told that they were members of a separate middle class and, furthermore, that the latter was much closer in terms of its long-term interests to the bourgeoisie than to the workers. The UP lost some support to this campaign, but probably more than regained it through the adherence of blue-collar workers who had previously supported the PN and PDC. (In the April 1972 CUT election, the UP and its allies received almost 85 percent of blue-collar workers' votes, but less than 60 percent of white-collar workers'.) Thus the alliance became more solidly blue-collar in its mass base, but the ambiguity remained at the leadership level, which left the alliance open to assault by the Right.

From this brief review, it can be seen that the main lesson to be be drawn from Chile's recent political history is the extreme difficulty in constructing a multiclass alliance with sufficient internal coherence to enable it to implement its development model. Such an alliance may be possible in a society with abundant and increasing resources, and where class conflict is muted, but these conditions did not prevail in Chile—nor do they in most other Third World countries. All three regimes succeeded in implementing their models for a short period of time, but then the internal contradictions of the alliances reached such a stage that "caretaker" governments were all that were possible. This situation, of course, lost even more support.

If all three alliances were nonviable in political terms, they were equally nonviable in economic terms. That is, none was able to impose a satisfactory solution to the problems of capital formation and demand management that had plagued the Chilean economy since the Radicals' import-substitution model exhausted itself in the early 1950's. The interrelationship between political and economic viability is obvious: the failure to have strong political support means the inability to impose an economic model, while the failure to solve economic problems erodes political support.

Capital formation has been a chronic problem in Chile. The country has had one of the lowest investment rates in Latin America in the postwar period, not to mention comparisons with fast-growing economies in Asia, Western Europe, and the socialist countries. This is one problem that any successful economic model must solve. There are three possibilities in terms of sources of investment: private national investors, foreign investors, and the state. The Alessandri laissez-faire model determined to rely on the first two sources. In spite of various types of incentives, however, neither foreigners nor the private national sector responded adequately. State investment was forced to increase, but this was seen as a stopgap measure and the long-term problem remained unresolved.

Frei's model of capital formation was not dissimilar from Alessandri's in the sense that both tried to induce private investors to take the lead. Frei, however, saw a more positive role for the state in joint ventures with the private sector. In reality, this was merely a new kind of incentive which guaranteed private companies access to state funds and eliminated potential political problems. The solution attracted large amounts of foreign investment in the early years of the regime, but domestic investors did not respond, and foreign investment later fell off as well. The state, meanwhile, was running short of investment funds because of the larger than expected amounts devoted to current expenditure (especially remunerations).

Allende's model of capital formation called for the state to take over investment in all crucial sectors of the economy; private investment would be restricted to nonessential areas. This strategy failed for several reasons. The profits of state enterprises rapidly disappeared because prices were frozen in order to subsidize consumption and to keep the inflation rate down. Also the emphasis on consumption and increased money incomes led to a situation in which resources for investment simply were not available. Finally, the need for greater skills in planning and project implementation

232

implicit in the Allende model proved beyond the capacity of the UP in the short run. The situation was made worse because the private sector (domestic and foreign) cut its investment to still lower levels than in previous regimes.

Several lessons can be drawn from this series of experiences. First, the private domestic bourgeoisie simply cannot be relied on to provide the main source of investment. They have neither the tradition nor the resources (although they have many more resources than those they devote to investment). In the crucial industrial sector, private investment in Chile fell in absolute terms from E°317 million in 1961 to E°260 million in 1970 (1965 escudos). In relative terms, this was a drop from 86 to 43 percent of total investment. Under Allende, of course, the drop was far more precipitous.

Second, foreign investors, who do have adequate resources, cannot be relied upon as the major investment source because they are pursuing an overall international investment scheme that does not take into account the needs of individual countries and especially small Third World countries. Foreign corporations invest in those sectors that are most profitable to them but that may not match the priorities of host countries. Their exports and imports are based on the needs of the corporations, not the balance of payments of the host country. Third, given these facts, the state *has no choice* but to take the lead in the accumulation process if investment is to meet the country's needs in terms of amount of investment, timing, and sectoral priorities. This decision, of course, has further implications. It means getting hold of necessary resources. It means establishing a reliable system of planning and project implementation. Most of all it means enforcing certain power relationships between the state and the private sector.

The second set of problems that none of the three regimes was able to solve concerned demand management. Whether the existing capacity will actually be used depends on the state of demand in the economy; likewise demand will influence decisions on new investments. In theoretical terms, demand can come from four sources: investment, consumption, government expenditures, and exports. As has been pointed out previously, however, investment in Chile (except for construction) did not provide a significant source of demand, since four-fifths of all equipment was imported. This was true for state or private investment. External demand certainly existed for some Chilean products—primarily copper—though at prices that fluctuated greatly. Certain agricultural and fish products were also export possibilities, but industrial exports were much more dubious, since high tariff barriers had made Chilean industry highly inefficient. Demand, then, was primarily a function of consumption and government current expenditure. This gave special weight to the Keynesian policies that all three governments followed in attempts to stimulate the economy.

Within these Keynesian policies, there were both quantitative and qualitative differences among the three regimes. In the first year of their administrations (traditionally the year of the biggest jump in real fiscal expenditure for Chilean governments), Alessandri increased fiscal expenditures by 17 percent, Frei by 29 percent, and Allende by 41 percent. In qualitative terms, there were differences with respect to the nature of government expenditure. Alessandri's economists saw the initial increase as a one-shot action to escape from the existing slump. Beyond that, it was hoped (and expected) that private initiative and the market would take care of the matter automatically. Frei's economic team, on the other hand, saw the need for continual and substantial state intervention in the economy, although within a capitalist framework. Allende, in line with his declared intention to move from a capitalist to a socialist mode of production, foresaw state expenditure becoming the dominant force in the economy. By the end of each administration, however, public expenditure was falling in real terms or growing very slowly. Under Alessandri and Frei, this resulted from a deliberate policy decision in response to increasing inflationary pressures; under Allende prices simply increased so fast that the public sector was unable to maintain expenditures in real terms.

Trends in consumption were similar. All three regimes increased real wages for at least some groups of the population at the beginning of their administrations. Again there were important quantitative differences: on the average across the economy, remunerations increased in real terms in Alessandri's first year by 2 percent, by 14 percent in Frei's first year, and by 31 percent in Allende's first year. By the end of each administration, on the other hand, real wages were falling or growing slowly as inflation rose, and the governments could not, or would not, allow remunerations to rise with or faster than prices.

The failure of these policies—as indicated by their exacerbating rather than mitigating cycles—provides two other lessons. The first is the difficulty in using Keynesian-type policies in the presence of serious inflation, when both capitalists and workers are able to raise their incomes in line with inflationary expectations. Many other capitalist countries have been experiencing this problem in the 1970's; Chile was merely a forerunner, although this was not recognized at the time. Keynes's own formulation of his theory occurred in the midst of the depression of the 1930's; prices were falling rather than rising. When the opposite occurs, and the government is trying to slow down inflation and increase growth at the same time, then the classical Keynesian formulas are no longer directly applicable. In the postwar period, there came into vogue the idea of a trade-off between inflation and employment (the latter closely correlated with movement in output), but even this relationship, if it ever existed, has evaporated as inflation and stagnation occur at the same time. Nevertheless, policy makers act as if there were a trade-off between growth and inflation, cutting down on government spending in an attempt to cut inflation. This is what happened under both Alessandri and Frei. They increased demand when they came into office, and the result was growth without inflation because of the existence of excess capacity. When full capacity was reached, inflation began to recur, and demand was cut back. Growth fell but inflation increased. In the Allende case, demand was not cut back, but prices increased so rapidly that demand fell in real terms.

The second lesson follows directly from the first. Keynesian-type policies cannot resolve structural problems. Keynesian demand management implies that the supply (production) side of the economy is in good shape; only demand is missing to put workers and machines to work. The diagnosis of structural problems, on the other hand, means that slow growth has much deeper causes, deriving from the supply side rather than the demand side. Examples include the land tenure system in agriculture, the structure of industry, the lack of foreign exchange, and problems of technology.

Alessandri essentially ignored this aspect of the stagnation problem. Frei saw it, but his solutions were insufficient because of the contradictions of capitalist development in Third World countries. The Allende government, on the other hand, saw this problem clearly and believed that the only solution was for the state to take control of the economy and to move from a capitalist to a socialist mode of production. Thus it was made clear that reactivation policies must be accompanied by structural change—a Keynesian and

235

structural solution at the same time. The nature of Allende social-ism, however, along with the problems that have been analyzed earlier, prevented the solution the government was seeking.

The failure to resolve the problems of capital formation and de-mand management led to the two characteristics of the growth pat-tern in Chilean industry: a slow overall rate of growth and a cyclical pattern with growth rates high at the beginning of a period but rela-tively stagnant at the end. In this sense, none of the economic models provided viable successors to the import-substitution model of the 1930's and 1940's. They could not have continued in the same way, even if the respective governments had not been thrown out of office.

The problem of consumption must be dealt with at some length, for disturbing trends—albeit different ones—developed in each ad-ministration. Under Alessandri, real wages were stagnant. Mean-time, a process had been under way whereby a growing portion of national income was concentrated in the hands of a small percent-age of the population. Income to the 3 percent of the population de-fined as employers, for example, increased from 25 to 35 percent between 1960 and 1964. Under Frei, the process was different. On the average, real wages tended to rise, but for the poorest groups (those receiving the minimum wage) they declined after the first two years. Thus, differentials within the working class increased, while income to the bourgeoisie remained constant in percentage terms. Under Allende as well, distribution trends reversed them-selves at the end of the period. Not only did the share to labor de-cline between 1972 and 1973 (although still remaining well above 1970 level), but better paid and better organized workers lost less than those who had to rely on the government-decreed minimums.

These distribution/consumption trends had both economic and political implications. In economic terms, they affected both capital formation and demand management. The Alessandri trends fore-shadowed a serious contraction of the domestic market. Where was domestic industry going to sell its expanding output if the workers' income did not rise, given the lack of demand for investment goods and the inability of Chilean industry to break into the export mar-ket? The upper-income groups could only absorb a certain number of cars, television sets, refrigerators, and so forth, in addition to which they had a high propensity to import these items. The Frei situation was quite different. The increasing share of income to labor (especially in agriculture) expanded the domestic market, although skewing it in favor of the higher-income groups and thus skewing production toward consumer durables. But wage increases together with price freezes also had the effect of limiting investment funds—thus the desperate attempt to impose a forced savings scheme in 1967. Under Allende, the situation was similar to that under Frei. The market was greatly expanded, although this time with a bias toward lower-income groups, but again (and more drastically) the result was a squeeze on investment.

In political terms, the consumption pattern leads back to the disintegration of the alliances. The Alessandri base was increasingly cut out of the benefits of what economic expansion there was, leading to a drop in electoral support. A similar phenomenon occurred under Frei when the "marginal" groups, both in the cities and the countryside, increasingly lost out. The cut in government expenditure for construction eliminated public works jobs; the fall in the minimum wage hurt low-paid workers of all kinds. Electoral support dropped as well. Under Allende, the political effect of falling wages was not absolutely clear. The March 1973 election indicated that the workers were still supporting the government in spite of the declining material conditions; the explanation would seem to be the heightened level of political consciousness that developed during the UP years. On the other hand, the fall in real income of those opposing the government probably increased their determination to bring about its overthrow.

If all three economic models represented failures, what alternatives are left? By process of elimination, the Chilean case points to a socialist model but of a different type than that practiced by the UP: a socialist model with greater emphasis on investment—and therefore on planning and project implementation—and less on the rapid increase of money income. This could be accompanied by an increase in collective consumption which would partially offset the slower rise in private consumption. The question, of course, is whether an alliance could be constructed to support this kind of model—even if it were potentially viable in economic terms. The UP's answer to this question seemed to be no. Their actions implied that they thought it necessary to buy support through increasing incomes, but the election trends call this conclusion into doubt. It is true that support fell between the April 1971 municipal elections, when the UP gained 50 percent of the vote, and the March 1973 parliamentary election, when the alliance dropped to 44 percent. But it must be remembered that this was 44 percent in the midst of the most severe economic and social problems imaginable—and it was 8 percent above the 1970 presidential totals, when Allende received only 36 percent of the vote. With more attention to political education and a chance for the planning and distribution (rationing) mechanisms to actually begin to operate, it would not seem farfetched for an alliance to be built around a more solid socialist model. Living through the experience of the Junta, with its huge costs in economic and social terms, may increase the chances for such an alliance in the future.

Thus far nothing has been said about the role of the foreign sector in the implementation of a socialist model. The Chilean experience certainly has something to offer on this subject. Most of the attention in this area has focused on the role of the United States government and corporations, with the extreme view being that the United States was *the* cause of the 1973 coup. This is a misreading of the facts. There is no doubt that the U.S. government, and corporations with investments in Chile, strongly disliked the Allende government and wanted it out of the way. In fact, these same agents had spent large amounts of money in previous years to keep Allende from being elected, and had provided significant quantities of resources to Alessandri and especially to Frei to build up their regimes as attractive alternatives to a socialist model. The various U.S. actors stood to lose much if Allende were to provide a successful model for other Third World countries to follow, but those who stood to lose most were the Chilean bourgeoisie. The United States has shown that it can coexist (and do business) with socialist countries, but the Chilean bourgeoisie would lose all—their political power, their economic wealth, their social standing—if socialism were to come to their country. They, then, were the prime movers in the propaganda campaigns, the owners' strikes, the hoarding and sabotage, the arrangements with the military. The United States certainly provided aid and assistance wherever and whenever possible, but this was primarily a supplement to the activities of the Chilean bourgeoisie.

If lessons are to be drawn on this subject, two might be considered. First, it is necessary to carefully examine the nature of the links that exist between Third World economies and the United States. Thus it would be possible to predict the kind of weapons that could be used and to make preparations for defending against them (e.g. hoarding foreign exchange for vital imports, renegotiating debt burdens immediately, establishing links with countries likely to be more sympathetic than the United States). More knowledge of advanced capitalist countries and how they operate would also provide more opportunities to exploit contradictions within the capitalist system. Second, it is necessary to understand the complementary nature of the relationship between the activities of the U.S. governmental agencies and corporations and the Chilean Right. Mistakenly assigning sole blame to the external actors is as dangerous as ignoring them entirely.

Lessons on external actors, however, cannot be limited to the Western powers; important lessons also emerged with respect to the socialist countries. It now seems clear that the Soviet Union is not willing to become as involved with another Latin American country as it has with Cuba. The drain on resources in a far-away region is considered too great—especially when it might endanger the new relationship of détente. International arrangements between superpowers thus limit the bargaining capacity that Third World countries had in the 1960's. In addition, the specific kind of economic aid that the Soviet Union and Eastern European countries can or will provide is limited by the rigidities of the Five-Year Plans and their lack of foreign exchange. The aid offered Chile was mostly for long-term development projects using Soviet equipment; it could not be used to resolve short-term difficulties. All of these limitations must be taken into account *from the beginning* if a rational strategy to achieve socialism—whether by revolutionary or evolutionary means—is to be planned.

Whether these "lessons" are transferable to other countries is certainly open to question. The Chilean experience shows the pitfalls of trying to transfer models. The Junta has obviously failed to import the "Brazilian miracle." The close organic relationship between the different models in Chile itself also casts doubts on transferability. Nevertheless, many groups are looking to the Chilean experience in planning their own strategies. The Eurocommunists in Italy, France, and Spain have explicitly extracted lessons from the Chilean situation and modified their strategies accordingly. On the other hand, many of the guerrilla organizations in Latin America and elsewhere have had their own views reinforced through extracting very different conclusions from what happened in Chile.

The point here is not to enter into the debate on the parliamentary vs. revolutionary way to socialism. It is a more limited one: to insist that those trying to learn from Chile must look at a longer span of Chilean history than the three years of the UP. The failure of the other models must be taken into account as well. For example, the Italian Communists who are trying so desperately to form an alliance with the Christian Democrats should look with great care at the Frei period. Likewise, other Third World groups who have thus far rejected a socialist solution should study the alternative problems that Chile has faced. Difficult as comparisons between countries are, the fact remains that Chile is the only small Third World country that has had such a varied political and economic experience. The price that the Chileans have paid must not be lost.

STATISTICAL APPENDIX

TABLE A.I

Electoral Results by Party, 1957–73

Party	1957 Parliamentary	1958 Presidential	1960 Municipal	1961 Parliamentary	1963 Municipal	1964 Presidential
National						
Conservative	154,877 (17.6%)	⎱ 389,909 (31.2%)	173,875 (14.1%)	198,260 (14.3%)	226,717 (11.0%)	
Liberal	134,741 (15.4%)		188,314 (15.4%)	222,485 (16.1%)	260,197 (12.6%)	
Christian Democratic		255,769 (20.5%)	171,503 (13.9%)	213,468 (15.4%)	455,522 (22.0%)	1,409,012 (55.7%)
Falange	82,710 (9.4%)					
Agrarian Labor	68,602 (7.8%)					
Radical	188,526 (21.5%)	192,077 (15.2%)	245,911 (20.0%)	296,828 (21.4%)	431,470 (20.8%)	127,233 (4.9%)
Communist			112,251 (9.2%)	157,572 (11.4%)	255,776 (12.4%)	⎱ 977,902 (38.6%)
Socialist	38,783 (4.4%)	356,493 (28.6%)	119,506 (9.7%)	149,122 (10.7%)	229,229 (11.1%)	
Popular Socialist	55,044 (6.3%)					
Other	154,986 (17.6%)	41,304 (3.3%)	163,756 (13.3%)	102,161 (7.4%)	138,976 (6.7%)	
Blank/void	—	14,798 (1.2%)	54,387 (4.4%)	45,780 (3.3%)	70,576 (3.4%)	18,550 (0.8%)
Total	878,269 (100.0%)	1,250,350 (100.0%)	1,229,503 (100.0%)	1,385,676 (100.0%)	2,068,463 (100.0%)	2,532,697 (100.0%)
Abstention	407,930 (31.6%)	247,624 (16.5%)	540,178 (30.5%)	473,304 (25.5%)	501,946 (19.5%)	384,424 (13.2%)
Total registered voters	1,286,199	1,497,974	1,769,681	1,858,980	2,570,409	2,917,121

TABLE A.I *(continued)*

Party	1965 Parliamentary	1967 Municipal	1969 Parliamentary	1970 Presidential	1971 Municipal	1973 Parliamentary
National		334,656 (14.3%)	480,523 (20.0%)	1,031,159 (34.9%)	513,874 (18.1%)	776,190 (21.2%)
Conservative	121,882 (5.2%)					
Liberal	171,979 (7.3%)					
Christian Democratic	995,187 (42.3%)	834,810 (35.6%)	716,547 (29.8%)	821,801 (27.8%)	729,398 (25.7%)	1,043,815 (28.5%)
Falange						
Agrarian Labor						
Radical	312,912 (13.3%)	377,074 (16.1%)	313,559 (13.0%)	1,070,334 (36.2%)	228,426 (8.1%)	129,615 (3.5%)[a]
Communist	290,635 (12.4%)	346,105 (14.8%)	383,049 (15.9%)		477,862 (16.9%)	663,259 (18.1%)
Socialist	241,593 (10.3%)	324,965 (13.9%)	294,448 (12.2%)		633,367 (22.3%)	578,695 (15.8%)
Popular Socialist						
Other	148,255 (6.3%)	73,744 (3.1%)	119,386 (5.0%)		215,210 (7.6%)	383,541 (10.5%)[b]
Blank/void	70,680 (3.0%)	51,933 (2.2%)	98,617 (4.0%)	31,505 (1.1%)	37,265 (1.3%)	86,783 (2.4%)
Total	2,353,123 (100.1%)	2,343,287 (100.0%)	2,406,129 (99.9%)	2,954,799 (100.0%)	2,835,402 (100.0%)	3,661,898 (100.0%)
Abstention	567,492 (19.4%)	730,705 (23.7%)	838,763 (25.8%)	584,948 (16.5%)	957,280 (25.2%)	853,389 (18.9%)
Total registered voters	2,920,615	3,073,992	3,244,892	3,539,747	3,792,682	4,515,287

SOURCE: Unpublished data from Registro Electoral.

[a] In 1972, the Partido Radical divided into the Partido Radical (supporting the Unidad Popular) and the Partido de la Izquierda Radical (supporting the opposition). Votes here include only the former.

[b] The 1973 election was essentially fought between two electoral federations—the Unidad Popular (Partido Comunista, Partido Socialista, Partido Radical, Movimiento de Acción Popular Unitario, Izquierda Cristiana, Acción Popular Independiente, in loose association with the Union Socialista Popular) and the Confederación Democrática (Partido Nacional, Democracia Radical, and Partido de la Izquierda Radical). The "other" votes were divided in the following way: 181,544 for the Confederación Democrática and 201,997 for the Unidad Popular (including the Union Socialista Popular).

TABLE A.2

Party Preferences by Class, 1958–72

The first number in the group of three is absolute frequency, the second is row percent, and the third is column percent.

AUGUST 1958

Class	Liberal/ Conservative	Radical	Christian Democratic	Socialist/ Communist	Total
Bourgeoisie	35	6	10	4	55
	63.6%[a]	10.9%	18.2%	7.3%	100.0%
	18.2%[a]	5.7%	7.5%	3.7%	10.2%
Managers/ professionals	19	10	16	7	52
	36.5%[a]	19.2%	30.8%[a]	13.5%	100.0%
	9.8%[a]	9.5%	12.0%[a]	6.5%	9.7%
Petty bourgeoisie	55	32	31	17	135
	40.7%[a]	23.7%[a]	23.0%	12.6%	100.0%
	28.5%[a]	30.5%[a]	23.3%	15.9%	25.1%
White-collar workers	51	40	46	25	162
	31.5%	24.7%[a]	28.4%[a]	15.4%	100.0%
	26.4%	38.1%[a]	34.6%[a]	23.4%	30.1%
Blue-collar workers	33	17	30	54	134
	24.6%	12.7%	22.4%	40.3%[a]	100.0%
	17.1%	16.2%	22.6%	50.5%[a]	24.9%
TOTAL	193	105	133	107	538
	35.8%	19.5%	24.7%	20.0%	100.0%
	100.0%	100.0%	100.0%	100.0%	100.0%

AUGUST 1964

Class	Radical	Chr. Dem./ Lib./Cons.	Socialist/ Communist	Total
Bourgeoisie	3	13	4	20
	15.0%[a]	65.0%	20.0%	100.0%
	14.3%[a]	5.0%	3.5%	5.1%
Managers/ professionals	2	29	7	38
	5.3%	76.3%[a]	18.4%	100.0%
	9.5%	11.2%[a]	6.2%	9.6%
Petty bourgeoisie	3	63	24	90
	3.3%	70.0%	26.7%	100.0%
	14.3%	24.2%[a]	21.2%	22.8%
White-collar workers	9	72	25	106
	8.5%[a]	67.9%	23.6%	100.0%
	42.9%[a]	27.7%[a]	22.1%	26.9%
Blue-collar workers	4	83	53	140
	2.9%	59.3%	37.9%[a]	100.1%
	19.0%	31.9%	46.9%[a]	35.5%
TOTAL	21	260	113	394
	5.3%	70.0%	26.7%	100.0%
	100.0%	100.0%	99.9%	99.9%

TABLE A.2 *(continued)*

AUGUST 1970

Class	National	Christian Democratic	UP	Total
Bourgeoisie	6	1	0	7
	85.7%[a]	14.3%	—	100.0%
	5.0%[a]	1.1%	—	2.3%
Professionals	13	1	5	19
	68.4%[a]	5.3%	26.3%	100.0%
	10.9%[a]	1.1%	5.3%	6.3%
Petty bourgeoisie	32	18	15	65
	49.2%[a]	27.7%	23.1%	100.0%
	26.9%[a]	20.5%	16.0%	21.6%
White-collar workers	45	43	28	116
	38.8%	37.1%[a]	24.1%	100.0%
	37.8%	48.9%[a]	29.8%	38.5%
Blue-collar workers	23	25	46	94
	24.5%	26.6%	48.9%[a]	100.0%
	19.3%	28.4%	48.9%[a]	31.2%
TOTAL	119	88	94	301
	39.5%	29.2%	31.2%	99.9%
	99.9%	100.0%	100.0%	99.9%

JUNE 1972

Class	National	Christian Democratic	UP	Total
Bourgeoisie/ managers	6	6	4	16
	37.5%[a]	37.5%[a]	25.0%	100.0%
	9.2%[a]	3.0%[a]	1.2%	2.7%
Professionals/ técnicos	10	21	15	46
	21.7%[a]	45.7%[a]	32.6%	100.0%
	15.4%[a]	10.7%[a]	4.6%	7.8%
Petty bourgeoisie	13	43	54	110
	11.8%[a]	39.1%[a]	49.1%	100.0%
	20.0%[a]	21.8%[a]	16.6%	18.7%
White-collar workers	24	72	104	200
	12.0%[a]	36.0%[a]	52.0%	100.0%
	36.9%[a]	36.5%[a]	32.0%	34.1%
Blue-collar workers	12	55	148	215
	5.6%	25.6%	68.8%[a]	100.0%
	18.5%	27.9%	45.5%[a]	36.6%
TOTAL	65	197	325	587
	11.1%	33.6%	55.4%	100.1%
	100.0%	99.9%	99.9%	99.9%

SOURCE: Calculated from raw data gathered by Eduardo Hamuy in surveys of Greater Santiago, Chile, August 1958–June 1972.

[a] Cell percentage is larger than marginal percentage.

TABLE A.3

CUT Election Data by Party and Subclass, April 1972

Party	Blue-collar workers		White-collar workers		Total	
	Number	Percent	Number	Percent	Number	Percent
Unidad Popular:	236,500	81.3%	76,000	52.1%	312,500	71.5%
Communist Party	113,000	38.8	33,000	22.6	146,000	33.4
Socialist Party	95,900	33.0	29,000	19.9	124,900	28.6
MAPU	22,000	7.6	3,000	2.1	25,000	5.7
Radical Party	5,600	1.9	11,000	7.5	16,600	3.8
MIR	5,800	2.0	6,000	4.1	11,800	2.7
Christian Democrats	47,400	16.3	61,000	41.8	108,400	24.8
Other	1,300	0.4	3,000	2.1	4,300	1.0
TOTAL	291,000	100.0%	146,000	100.1%	437,000	100.0%

SOURCE: Pablo Lira, "The Crisis of Hegemony in the Chilean Left," in Philip O'Brien, ed., Allende's Chile (New York, 1976), p. 31.

TABLE A.4

Membership in Labor Unions, 1958–72

Year	Plant unions[a]	Craft unions[b]	Agricultural unions	Total
1958	154,650	119,666	2,030	276,346
1959	169,919	110,923	1,656	282,498
1960	172,306	108,687	1,424	282,417
1961	144,650	111,082	1,831	257,563
1962	134,478	110,669	1,860	247,007
1963	143,009	117,989	1,500	262,498
1964	142,958	125,926	1,658	270,542
1965	154,561	135,974	2,118	292,653
1966	179,506	161,363	10,647	351,516
1967	190,367	173,346	47,473	411,186
1968	191,987	224,302	83,472	499,761
1969	194,228	232,090	104,666	530,984
1970	197,651	239,323	114,112	551,086
1971	205,300	252,924	127,782	586,006
1972	213,183	282,181	136,527	631,891

SOURCE: III Mensaje del Presidente Salvador Allende ante el Congreso Nacional (1973), pp. 792–94.

[a] Plant unions (sindicatos industriales) have only blue-collar workers as members and are organized in units consisting of single factories.

[b] Craft unions (sindicatos profesionales) can have blue- or white-collar workers as members, although the latter predominate, and can be organized across plants or among self-employed workers. Craft unions are generally weaker than plant unions.

TABLE A.5

Numbers of Strikes and Strikers, 1958–72

Year	No. of strikes	Blue-collar workers	White-collar workers	Total workers
1958	120	64,450	164	64,614
1959	207	41,379	1,713	43,092
1960	257	83,259	5,200	88,459
1961	262	96,426	15,485	111,911
1962	401	79,201	4,491	83,692
1963	413	109,630	7,474	117,104
1964	564	128,359	10,115	138,474
1965	723	167,780	14,579	182,359
1966	1,073	168,287	27,140	195,427
1967	1,114	165,875	59,605	225,480
1968	1,124	a	a	292,794
1969	1,277	a	a	362,010
1970	1,819	a	a	656,170
1971	2,709	182,770	119,628	302,398
1972	3,289	232,373	164,769	397,142

SOURCE: 1958–67, Instituto Nacional de Estadisticas, *Sintesis estadistico*, various numbers. 1968–70, Organización de Estados Americanos, *América en cifras, situación social* (1972), pp. 164–65. 1971–72, *III Mensaje del Presidente Salvador Allende ante el Congreso Nacional* (1973), pp. 788–89.
a Not available.

TABLE A.6

Inflation Rates and Price Indexes, 1957–73

Year	Increase in inflation[a]	Consumer price index (1965 = 100)	Wholesale price index (1965 = 100)
1957	25.9%	15.5	16.2
1958	33.3	19.5	23.2
1959	38.6	27.0	30.1
1960	11.6	30.1	31.7
1961	7.7	32.4	32.0
1962	13.9	36.9	34.7
1963	44.3	53.2	53.4
1964	46.0	77.6	80.4
1965	28.8	100.0	100.0
1966	22.9	122.9	122.9
1967	18.1	145.2	146.6
1968	26.6	183.8	188.7
1969	30.7	240.2	257.6
1970	32.5	318.3	350.6
1971	20.1	382.3	413.4
1972	77.8	679.7	702.8
1973 [b]	235.2	2,278.4	2,024.8

SOURCE: Banco Central, *Boletin Mensual*, various numbers.
a Annual average increases in consumer prices.
b January–August only.

TABLE A.7

Investment in Fixed Capital in Industry, 1961–73

(Millions of 1965 escudos and percent)

Year	Total investment (4) + (7) (1)	Public investment			Private investment		
		Direct (2)	Indirect (3)	Total (2) + (3) (4)	National (5)	Foreign (6)	Total (5) + (6) (7)
	MILLIONS OF 1965 ESCUDOS						
1961	367	32	18	50	312	5	317
1962	341	20	22	42	280	19	299
1963	357	60	19	79	269	9	278
1964	407	128	33	161	182	64	246
1965	472	156	28	184	205	83	288
1966	561	185	31	216	294	51	345
1967	450	98	111	209	92	149	241
1968	450	60	111	171	160	119	279
1969	577	145	170	315	160[a]	102	262
1970	610	188	162	350	160[a]	100[a]	260
1971	466			373			93[a]
1972	258			219			39[a]
1973[b]	213			192			21[a]
	PERCENT						
1961	100.0%	8.7%	4.9%	13.6%	85.0%	1.4%	86.4%
1962	100.0	5.9	6.4	12.3	82.1	5.6	87.7
1963	100.0	16.8	5.3	22.1	75.3	2.5	77.9
1964	100.0	31.5	8.1	39.6	44.7	15.7	60.4
1965	100.0	33.1	5.9	39.0	43.4	17.6	61.0
1966	100.0	33.0	5.5	38.5	52.4	9.1	61.5
1967	100.0	21.8	24.7	46.5	20.4	33.1	53.5
1968	100.0	13.3	24.7	38.0	35.6	26.4	62.0
1969	100.0	25.1	29.5	54.6	27.7	17.7	45.4
1970	100.0	30.8	26.6	57.4	26.2	16.4	42.6
1971	100			80			20
1972	100			85			15
1973[b]	100			90			10

SOURCE: Col. 1, 1961–68, ODEPLAN, *Antecedentes sobre el desarrollo chileno, 1960–70* (1971), p. 155. 1969–73, total of cols. 4 and 7.

Cols. 2–4. 1961–69, ODEPLAN, *La inversión pública en el periodo 1961–70* (1971), cuadros 1, 14, 24. 1970–73, extrapolation based on data in Ministerio de Hacienda, *Balance consolidado del sector público, 1971–73*, p. 181.

Col. 5. 1961–68, col. 7 minus col. 6. 1969–70, estimate based on figures in CORFO, Gerencia de Industrias, División de Planificación Industrial, *Datos básicos sector industria manufacturero, periódo 1960–70* (1971), p. 17.

Col. 6. 1961–69, Luis Pacheco, "Inversión extranjera en la industria chilena" (Memoria de Prueba, Facultad de Ciencias Físicas y Matemáticas, Universidad de Chile, 1970). 1970, estimate based on interviews with government economists.

Col. 7. 1961–68, col. 1 minus col. 4. 1969–73, estimate based on interviews with government economists.
  [a] Estimate.   [b] January–August, on annualized basis.

TABLE A.8

State Investment in Industry by Sector, 1961–70

(Percent)

Sector	1961	1962	1963	1964	1965	1966	1967	1968	1969	1970
Food	3.7%	0.7%	5.0%	2.2%	0.6%	3.1%	0.8%	5.1%	1.5%	1.6%
Sugar	3.1	—	—	1.8	4.2	22.1	8.5	4.8	6.8	22.0
Fish products	34.0	43.5	20.7	22.4	3.3	3.7	7.6	5.5	1.2	—
Textiles	—	—	—	—	0.4	1.1	7.7	—	—	0.6
Wood and paper	5.6	5.8	2.4	1.6	4.7	7.1	11.2	12.1	18.5	24.2
Chemicals	4.9	—	—	—	1.5	3.1	2.4	13.7	19.5	13.9
Oil	34.6	29.0	51.5	61.4	70.2	47.8	32.2	11.6	25.2	21.6
Construction	—	0.7	—	0.2	1.0	0.4	0.3	0.1	0.1	0.4
Metals	0.6	—	—	2.5	4.4	5.5	19.8	15.6	5.5	5.1
FAMAE/ASMAR[a]	8.6	12.3	7.8	2.9	2.0	1.7	1.8	3.1	2.8	1.0
Other	4.9	8.0	6.4	0.5	0.5	2.4	3.4	3.5	5.4	9.0
Technology[b]	—	—	6.2	4.5	7.0	2.1	4.3	24.7	13.6	0.6
TOTAL	100.0	100.0	100.0	100.0	99.8	100.1	100.0	99.8	100.1	100.0

SOURCE: The basic source is ODEPLAN, *Antecedentes sobre el desarrollo chileno, 1960–70* (1971), cuadros 119–20. In addition, investments corresponding to CORFO were further broken down, with information obtained from the following sources: CORFO, *Memoria* (1961–64); CORFO, *Labor realizado noviembre 1964–septiembre 1967* (1965–67); CORFO, *Boletín Estadístico* (1968–70). (The method used was to take the absolute investment figures calculated by ODEPLAN and apply the percentages calculated from the CORFO data.)

[a] Army and Navy metal works.
[b] Includes feasibility studies and money for the Technical Cooperation Service (Servicio de Cooperación Técnica, SERCOTEC), the National Training Institute (Instituto Nacional de Capacitación, INACAP) and the Technological Research Committee.

TABLE A.9

Real Variations in Remunerations Indexes for the Total Economy, 1958–73
(Percent)

Year	SV	SMI	SMA	ISS	Remunerations Index
1958	−4.6%	−2.2%	−1.7%	−3.7%	−3.0%
1959	−1.3	−0.7	8.6	0.3%	1.4
1960	−10.3	−10.3	8.9	3.1	2.2
1961	15.7	19.0	10.3	6.9	10.9
1962	2.2	2.2	1.4	0.0	0.9
1963	−14.2	−14.2	−9.1	−5.5	−8.6
1964	−0.3	−0.4	2.1	−8.5	−4.3
1965	7.4	7.3	22.2	14.8	13.9
1966	2.4	2.3	10.9	12.6	9.3
1967	−1.0	−1.0	4.3	15.1	8.6
1968	−3.7	−3.7	−3.7	0.6	−1.4
1969	−2.1	−2.1	−2.1	8.3	3.5
1970	−2.4	21.0	21.0	10.2	14.5
1971	12.2	38.7	38.7	25.8	31.0
1972	−14.2	8.0	8.0	−6.2	−2.9
1973 [a]	−34.2	−32.1	−32.1	−24.2	−27.9

SOURCE: For SV (minimum salary), SMI (minimum industrial wage), and SMA (minimum agricultural wage), Banco Central, *Boletín Mensual*, various numbers. For ISS (Wage and Salary Index, calculated by the Instituto Nacional de Estadísticas for firms with 20 workers or more), Banco Central, *Boletín Mensual*, average of four yearly surveys for all years except 1958–59, which were taken from Ricardo Ffrench-Davis, *Políticas económicas en Chile, 1952–70* (Santiago, 1973), p. 344 (*remuneraciones imponibles sector privado*). The Remunerations Index, an index for all workers, is a weighted average of the other four columns. The weights, from a survey carried out in 1967 by the Centro de Estudios Estadísticos-Matemáticos of the University of Chile, are SV 3.0%, SMI 26.0%, SMA 17.3%, and ISS 53.7%. Calculated from tables in ODEPLAN, *Antecedentes sobre el desarrollo chileno, 1960–70* (1971), pp. xxxii–xxxv.

[a] January–August only.

TABLE A.10

Real Variations in Remunerations Indexes in Industry, 1958–73
(Percent)

Year	SMI	SV	ISS (industry)	Remunerations Index (industry)
1958	−2.2%	−4.6%	—	−3.4%
1959	−0.7	−1.3	—	−1.0
1960	−10.3	−10.3	−0.4	−2.0
1961	19.0	15.7	7.2	9.0
1962	2.2	2.2	4.8	4.4
1963	−14.2	−14.2	−6.7	−7.9
1964	−0.4	−0.3	3.1	2.5
1965	7.3	7.4	11.6	10.9
1966	2.3	2.4	16.1	13.9
1967	−1.0	−1.0	11.9	9.9
1968	−3.7	−3.7	3.0	1.9
1969	−2.1	−2.1	5.8	4.6
1970	21.0	−2.4	6.3	8.4
1971	38.7	12.2	25.1	27.0
1972	8.0	−14.2	3.4	3.9
1973 [a]	−32.1	−34.2	−19.5	−21.5

SOURCE: For SMI (minimum industrial wage) and SV (minimum salary), Banco Central, *Boletin Mensual*, various numbers. For ISS, industry (Wage and Salary Index for industry, calculated by Instituto Nacional de Estadisticas for firms with 20 workers or more); 1960–64, unpublished data from Instituto Nacional de Estadisticas; 1965–73, Banco Central, *Boletin Mensual*, various numbers. The Remunerations Index, an index for all workers, is a weighted average of the other three columns. The weights, from the 1967 Industrial Census figures for workers in factories with 20 or more workers (covered by the ISS) and those with 5–19 workers (assumed to receive the minimum wage and salary), are SMI 14.7%, SV 1.1%, and ISS 84.2% (70.8% blue-collar and 13.4% white-collar workers). 1958 and 1959 are averages of SMI and SV only.

[a] January–August only.

TABLE A.II

Unemployment Rates in Industry, Greater Santiago,
1958–73
(Percent)

Year	Unemployment rate	Year	Unemployment rate
1958	8.2%	1965	4.6%
1959	9.0	1966	4.6
1960	7.1	1967	5.8
1961	6.9	1968	5.3
1962	5.7	1969	4.7
1963	5.5	1970	6.3
1964	5.4	1971	4.8
		1972	3.5
		1973	2.9

SOURCE: Universidad de Chile, Instituto de Economía y Planificación, *Ocupación y desocupación en Gran Santiago,* various numbers.
NOTE: Figures are averages of March, June, September, and December unemployment rates, except for 1973, which is March and June average only.

TABLE A.I2

State Expenditure and Private Sector Credit, 1957–73
(Millions of 1965 escudos[a])

Year	Fiscal expenditure	Public sector expenditure Total incl. municipalities	Public sector expenditure Total excl. municipalities	Credit to private sector
1957	2,193.8			1,185.2
1958	1,940.9			1,025.8
1959	2,269.1			1,295.7
1960	2,747.6	5,126.5		1,454.3
1961	3,065.6	6,095.6		1,934.4
1962	3,538.9	7,088.8		2,121.0
1963	3,221.0	6,286.1		1,904.4
1964	3,105.7	6,063.1		1,772.4
1965	4,002.0	7,790.5		1,968.0
1966	4,619.2	9,137.9		2,074.9
1967	4,686.9	9,947.7		2,236.7
1968	5,130.9	10,974.8		2,311.6
1969	5,306.3	11,826.4	11,158.8	2,206.1
1970	6,241.3		11,969.8	2,186.8
1971	8,818.7		15,979.3	2,765.1
1972	9,241.7		17,273.4	3,095.0
1973 [b]	8,533.3		14,979.3	2,974.3

SOURCE: Fiscal expenditure: 1957–70, Ricardo Ffrench-Davis, *Políticas económicas en Chile, 1952–70* (Santiago, 1973), p. 328; 1971–73, Ministerio de Hacienda, *Balance consolidado del sector público, 1971–73.* Public sector expenditure: 1960–69, ODEPLAN, *Antecedentes sobre el desarrollo chileno, 1960–70* (1971), pp. 397–98; 1969–73, Ministerio de Hacienda, *Balance . . . , 1969–70* and *1971–73.* Credit to private sector: Banco Central, *Boletín Mensual,* various numbers.
[a] Escudos are deflated by the wholesale price index.
[b] January–August only, on annualized basis.

TABLE A.13

Aggregate Industrial Output According to Three Indicators, 1958–73

Year	INE (1968 = 100)	CORFO	SOFOFA (1969 = 100)
1958	61.6	2,910	50.1
1959	70.3	3,299	57.6
1960	68.6	3,249	58.2
1961	73.4	3,498	64.8
1962	80.4	3,874	72.1
1963	85.7	4,071	74.8
1964	89.9	4,351	80.0
1965	94.2	4,651	87.2
1966	100.8	5,053	95.6
1967	100.3	5,189	96.9
1968	100.0	5,318	98.3
1969	104.2	5,506	100.0
1970	104.0	5,509	103.5
1971	119.3	6,248	114.7
1972	122.6	6,485	117.6
1973 [a]	115.2	6,212	106.7

SOURCE: INE, Banco Central, *Boletin Mensual*, various numbers. CORFO, Table A.14; SOFOFA, unpublished data.

NOTE: Series represent the following: INE (Instituto Nacional de Estadisticas), index of value of industrial production; CORFO (State Development Corporation), value added in industry (millions of 1965 escudos); and SOFOFA (National Industrial Society), index of physical production in industry.

[a] January–August only, on annualized basis.

TABLE A.14

Industrial Output (Value Added) by Sector, 1958–73

(Millions of 1965 escudos)

Sector	1958	1959	1960	1961	1962	1963	1964	1965
Basic consumer goods:								
20. Food	357	386	399	416	446	449	469	532
21. Beverages	109	116	133	140	143	146	144	189
22. Tobacco	65	72	80	86	92	82	88	88
23. Textiles	348	401	359	380	403	454	462	501
24. Clothing, shoes	435	479	445	498	530	535	528	526
26. Furniture	123	139	152	162	190	189	202	164
28. Printing	104	97	112	122	122	126	121	131
39. Diverse	73	94	97	98	116	124	130	139
TOTAL	1,614	1,784	1,777	1,902	2,042	2,105	2,144	2,270
Intermediate goods:								
25. Wood	96	122	122	130	151	161	183	199
27. Paper	55	67	61	77	74	83	87	131
29. Leather	75	75	66	72	72	72	72	70
30. Rubber	41	55	60	64	69	81	101	111
31. Chemicals	167	166	173	181	186	193	194	296
32. Petroleum	46	48	57	62	81	83	89	80
33. Non-met. minerals	164	204	186	206	225	232	241	214
34. Basic metals	228	304	265	247	317	344	459	384
TOTAL	872	1,041	990	1,039	1,175	1,249	1,426	1,485
Durable consumer and capital goods:								
35. Metal products	102	123	128	155	176	210	227	256
36. Non-elec. mach.	83	79	75	84	104	111	114	142
37. Elec. equip.	93	105	113	127	136	139	175	200
38. Transp. equip.	146[b]	161[b]	166	191	241	258	265	298
TOTAL	424	468	482	557	657	718	781	896
GRAND TOTAL	2,910	3,293	3,249	3,498	3,874	4,072	4,351	4,651

TABLE A.14 *(continued)*

Sector	1966	1967	1968	1969	1970	1971	1972	1973[a]
Basic consumer goods:								
20. Food	594	611	676	674	681	734	722	698
21. Beverages	211	215	204	186	181	226	232	263
22. Tobacco	99	105	95	92	87	109	112	113
23. Textiles	533	558	547	569	525	602	618	554
24. Clothing, shoes	563	560	509	543	525	592	615	561
26. Furniture	183	158	154	151	178	177	252	253
28. Printing	130	131	132	139	138	220	160	137
39. Diverse	137	154	166	164	149	202	229	233
TOTAL	2,450	2,492	2,483	2,518	2,464	2,862	2,940	2,812
Intermediate goods:								
25. Wood	222	206	222	234	236	282	314	214
27. Paper	173	193	220	227	212	220	224	239
29. Leather	75	68	68	64	68	79	59	70
30. Rubber	122	111	114	118	126	153	152	154
31. Chemicals	340	336	340	380	409	485	506	501
32. Petroleum	95	113	119	128	126	153	165	147
33. Non-met. minerals	225	225	244	259	246	289	294	293
34. Basic metals	315	331	328	344	340	357	380	358
TOTAL	1,567	1,583	1,655	1,754	1,763	2,018	2,094	1,976
Durable consumer and capital goods:								
35. Metal products	284	320	332	339	327	365	394	413
36. Non-elec. mach.	151	152	161	175	152	213	256	287
37. Elec. equip.	222	248	282	291	290	332	305	258
38. Transp. equip.	379	394	405	427	513	458	496	466
TOTAL	1,036	1,114	1,180	1,232	1,282	1,368	1,451	1,424
GRAND TOTAL	5,053	5,189	5,318	5,504	5,509	6,248	6,485	6,212

SOURCE: 1958–59, extrapolation back from 1960 value added, based on changes in Instituto Nacional de Estadísticas industrial index. 1960–70, CORFO, *Datos básicos sector industrial manufacturero, periodo 1960–70*, p. 10. 1971, ODEPLAN, *Informe económico anual, 1971*, cuadro 60, p. 142. 1972–73, extrapolation forward from 1971 value added, based on change in INE index.

[a] January–August only, on annualized basis.

[b] Estimate based on total growth of sector.

TABLE A.15
Industrial Work Force by Sector, 1958–73
(Thousands of persons)

Sector	1958	1959	1960	1961	1962	1963	1964	1965
Basic consumer goods:								
20. Food	39.2	39.1	47.9	51.5	53.1	56.7	58.3	64.3
21. Beverages	8.4	8.7	9.0	9.2	9.4	11.1	13.4	16.7
22. Tobacco	1.1	1.1	1.2	1.3	1.3	1.4	1.4	1.4
23. Textiles	38.6	39.5	37.1	41.3	41.0	42.7	44.9	49.7
24. Clothes, shoes	107.5	106.7	103.1	108.5	107.6	105.9	102.3	102.3
26. Furniture	22.4	27.4	29.3	32.1	32.0	32.5	33.9	37.0
28. Printing	9.2	9.8	10.3	10.5	10.3	10.7	10.0	10.1
39. Diverse	*a*	*a*	14.0	12.3	14.9	16.7	17.2	12.7
TOTAL			251.9	266.7	269.6	277.7	281.4	294.2
Intermediate goods:								
25. Wood	18.8	23.0	24.0	23.3	23.0	24.2	25.3	28.2
27. Paper	5.0	5.2	5.0	5.3	5.0	4.6	5.3	5.3
29. Leather	5.1	4.6	5.4	6.2	5.9	6.0	6.2	7.7
30. Rubber prod.	2.5	2.6	2.9	3.1	3.1	3.3	3.4	3.5
31. Chemicals	13.1	13.4	13.6	15.0	15.3	15.8	16.2	17.2
32. Petroleum	*a*	*a*	2.5	2.6	2.7	2.8	2.9	3.4
33. Non-met. minerals	18.8	14.6	14.4	16.3	17.6	16.7	16.7	17.6
34. Basic metals	11.8	10.2	9.9	11.0	11.3	12.1	12.9	14.2
TOTAL			77.7	82.8	83.9	85.5	88.9	97.1
Durable consumer and capital goods:								
35. Metal products	*a*	23.5	24.8	26.8	32.0	34.8	36.3	32.9
36. Non-elec. mach.	15.8	15.5	15.7	16.3	15.8	17.2	18.2	20.2
37. Elec. equip.	10.3	10.5	11.1	12.8	13.1	14.9	15.8	18.7
38. Transp. equip.	31.9	32.3	31.4	34.3	36.0	34.4	37.3	43.6
TOTAL		81.8	83.0	90.2	96.9	101.3	107.6	115.4
GRAND TOTAL	391.9	398.6	412.6	439.7	450.4	464.5	477.9	506.7

TABLE A.15 *(continued)*

Sector	1966	1967	1968	1969	1970	1971	1972	1973[a]
Basic consumer goods:								
20. Food	66.5	69.2	70.2	69.1	70.0	[b]	[b]	[b]
21. Beverages	17.1	17.1	16.9	17.1	17.0			
22. Tobacco	1.3	1.6	1.6	1.5	1.6			
23. Textiles	51.5	51.9	51.8	52.8	53.0			
24. Clothes, shoes	105.3	105.3	105.1	107.2	111.4			
26. Furniture	37.5	34.8	33.8	32.3	34.0			
28. Printing	11.6	13.1	13.7	14.0	14.6			
39. Diverse	13.3	14.9	16.7	18.0	17.4			
TOTAL	304.1	307.9	309.8	312.0	319.0	350.0	382.1	401.5
Intermediate goods:								
25. Wood	29.2	29.6	30.5	31.4	32.6			
27. Paper	6.0	6.2	7.0	7.1	7.0			
29. Leather	8.0	7.9	7.9	7.5	7.7			
30. Rubber prod.	4.2	5.2	5.4	5.4	5.6			
31. Chemicals	19.5	20.5	20.9	21.1	22.5			
32. Petroleum	4.0	4.3	4.4	4.3	4.4			
33. Non-met. minerals	18.2	18.5	18.1	18.5	18.5			
34. Basic metals	15.5	16.7	17.7	18.6	18.3			
TOTAL	104.6	108.9	111.9	113.9	116.6	113.7	112.1	116.0
Durable consumer and capital goods:								
35. Metal products	34.7	35.3	37.3	39.5	41.4			
36. Non-elec. mach.	20.0	17.9	18.0	18.1	18.0			
37. Elec. equip.	19.5	19.7	21.2	20.5	19.8			
38. Transp. equip.	44.8	44.8	46.4	46.7	48.1			
TOTAL	119.0	117.7	122.9	124.8	127.3	136.6	142.1	146.5
GRAND TOTAL	527.7	534.5	544.6	550.7	562.9	600.3	636.3	664.0

SOURCE: 1958–59, extrapolation back, based on Dirección de Estadísticas y Censos employment index. 1960–70, ODEPLAN, *Balances económicos de Chile, 1960–70* (1973), pp. 101–11. 1971–73, ODEPLAN, unpublished data.

[a] First half of year only.
[b] Data not available.

TABLE A.16

Productivity in Industry by Sector, 1958–73

(Value added per worker, in 1965 escudos)

Sector	1958	1959	1960	1961	1962	1963	1964	1965
Basic consumer goods:								
20. Food	9,107	9,872	8,330	8,078	8,399	7,919	8,045	8,274
21. Beverages	12,976	13,333	14,778	15,217	15,213	13,153	10,746	11,317
22. Tobacco[b]	59,091	65,455	66,667	66,154	70,769	58,571	62,857	62,857
23. Textiles	9,016	10,152	9,677	9,201	9,829	10,632	10,290	10,080
24. Clothes, shoes	4,047	4,489	4,316	4,590	4,926	5,052	5,161	5,142
26. Furniture	5,491	5,073	5,183	5,047	5,938	5,815	5,959	4,432
28. Printing	11,304	9,898	10,874	11,619	11,845	11,776	12,100	12,970
39. Diverse	[a]	[a]	6,929	7,967	7,785	7,425	7,558	10,945
TOTAL			7,054	7,132	7,574	7,580	7,619	7,716
Intermediate goods:								
25. Wood	5,106	5,304	5,083	5,579	6,565	6,653	7,233	7,057
27. Paper	11,000	12,885	12,200	14,528	14,800	18,043	16,415	24,717
29. Leather	14,706	16,304	12,222	11,613	12,203	12,000	11,613	9,091
30. Rubber prod.	16,400	21,154	20,690	20,645	22,258	24,545	29,706	31,714
31. Chemicals	12,748	12,388	12,721	12,067	12,157	12,215	11,975	17,209
32. Petroleum	[a]	[a]	22,800	23,846	30,000	29,643	30,690	3,529
33. Non-met. minerals	8,723	13,973	12,917	12,638	12,784	13,892	14,431	12,159
34. Basic metals	19,322	29,804	26,768	22,455	28,053	28,430	35,581	27,042
TOTAL			12,741	12,548	14,005	14,596	16,040	15,294
Durable consumer and capital goods:								
35. Metal products	[a]	5,234	5,161	5,784	5,500	6,034	6,253	7,781
36. Non-elec. mach.	5,253	5,097	4,777	5,153	6,582	6,453	6,264	7,030
37. Elec. equip.	9,029	10,000	10,180	9,922	10,382	9,329	11,076	10,695
38. Trans. equip.	4,671	4,986	5,287	5,569	6,694	7,500	7,105	6,835
TOTAL		5,721	5,807	6,175	6,780	7,088	7,258	7,764
GRAND TOTAL	7,425	8,276	7,874	7,955	8,601	8,764	9,104	9,179

TABLE A.16 *(continued)*

Sector	1966	1967	1968	1969	1970	1971	1972	1973
Basic consumer goods:								
20. Food	8,932	8,829	9,630	9,754	9,729	*a*	*a*	*a*
21. Beverages	12,339	12,573	12,071	10,877	10,647			
22. Tobacco[b]	76,154	65,675	59,375	61,333	59,375			
23. Textiles	10,350	10,751	10,560	10,777	9,906			
24. Clothes, shoes	5,347	5,318	4,843	5,065	4,713			
26. Furniture	4,880	4,540	4,556	4,675	5,235			
28. Printing	11,207	10,000	9,635	9,929	9,452			
39. Diverse	10,301	10,336	9,940	9,111	8,563			
TOTAL	8,057	8,094	8,015	8,071	7,724	8,177	7,694	7,004
Intermediate goods:								
25. Wood	7,603	6,959	7,279	7,452	7,239			
27. Paper	28,833	31,129	31,429	31,972	30,086			
29. Leather	9,375	8,608	8,608	8,533	8,831			
30. Rubber prod.	29,048	21,346	21,111	21,852	22,500			
31. Chemicals	17,436	16,390	16,268	18,009	18,178			
32. Petroleum	23,750	26,279	27,045	29,767	28,636			
33. Non-met. minerals	12,363	12,162	13,481	14,000	13,297			
34. Basic metals	20,323	19,820	18,531	18,495	18,579			
TOTAL	14,981	14,536	14,790	15,399	14,889	17,748	18,680	17,034
Durable consumer and capital goods:								
35. Metal products	8,184	9,065	8,901	8,582	7,899			
36. Non-elec. mach.	7,550	8,492	8,944	9,669	8,444			
37. Elec. equip.	11,385	12,589	13,302	14,195	14,646			
38. Trans. equip.	8,460	8,795	8,728	9,143	10,665			
TOTAL	8,706	9,465	9,601	9,872	10,071	10,746	10,622	10,021
GRAND TOTAL	9,576	9,708	9,765	9,998	9,787	10,408	10,192	9,355

SOURCE: Tables A.14 and A.15.

a Data not available.

b Productivity figures for tobacco are artificially high because value added includes indirect taxes, and indirect taxes (sales tax) were much higher for tobacco than for other industries.

TABLE A.17

Within-Class Distribution of Income in Industry by Deciles, 1959–72

(Percent)

		Percent of income							
	Cumulative percent of population	1959		1964		1970		1972	
Decile		%	Cum. %	%	Cum. %	%	Cum. %	%	Cum. %
		TOTAL INDUSTRY							
1	10%	0.7%	0.7%	0.9%	0.9%	0.3%	0.3%	1.1%	1.1%
2	20	3.3	4.0	2.9	3.8	2.1	2.4	3.0	4.1
3	30	4.5	8.5	4.0	7.8	3.2	5.6	3.8	7.9
4	40	5.6	14.1	4.8	12.6	4.1	9.7	4.8	12.7
5	50	6.3	20.4	5.7	18.3	5.0	14.7	5.8	18.5
6	60	7.3	27.7	6.7	25.0	6.2	20.9	7.1	25.6
7	70	9.4	37.1	8.3	33.3	7.7	28.6	9.1	34.7
8	80	11.4	48.5	10.4	43.7	10.0	38.6	11.7	46.4
9	90	15.4	63.9	14.6	58.3	14.7	53.3	17.0	63.4
10	100	36.1	100.0	41.7	100.0	46.9	100.2	36.7	100.1
		BOURGEOISIE							
1	10	2.0	2.0	1.0	1.0	1.3	1.3	2.6	2.6
2	20	3.6	5.6	2.0	3.0	1.8	3.1	3.8	6.4
3	30	5.1	10.7	2.7	5.7	4.0	7.1	5.7	12.1
4	40	6.0	16.7	3.5	9.2	6.3	13.4	6.7	18.8
5	50	8.0	24.7	7.1	16.3	7.6	21.0	8.9	27.7
6	60	9.1	33.8	9.9	26.2	9.7	30.7	10.8	38.5
7	70	11.2	45.0	10.9	37.1	12.5	43.2	10.8	49.3
8	80	13.6	58.6	12.0	49.1	13.9	57.1	13.5	62.8
9	90	17.7	76.3	15.6	64.7	18.3	75.4	15.4	78.2
10	100	23.8	100.1	35.3	100.0	24.6	100.0	21.9	100.1
		PETTY BOURGEOISIE							
1	10	0.4	0.4	1.1	1.1	0.3	0.3	0.9	0.9
2	20	2.9	3.3	2.6	3.7	1.8	2.1	1.8	2.7
3	30	3.7	7.0	3.2	6.9	2.8	4.9	2.7	5.4
4	40	5.0	12.0	4.3	11.2	4.1	9.0	3.8	9.2
5	50	6.8	18.8	5.2	16.4	5.1	14.1	5.1	14.3
6	60	8.5	27.3	6.2	22.6	6.5	20.6	7.0	21.3
7	70	11.1	38.4	8.1	30.7	8.6	29.2	8.8	30.1
8	80	13.4	51.8	11.0	41.7	12.7	41.9	11.7	41.8
9	90	16.8	68.6	14.4	56.1	18.7	60.6	17.3	59.1
10	100	31.5	100.1	43.8	99.9	39.3	99.9	40.7	99.8
		WHITE-COLLAR WORKERS							
1	10	0.1	0.1	1.0	1.0	0.8	0.8	1.5	1.5
2	20	2.8	2.9	4.0	5.0	2.6	3.4	3.5	5.0
3	30	5.2	8.1	5.0	10.0	4.0	7.4	4.6	9.6
4	40	6.5	14.6	6.0	16.0	4.9	12.3	5.9	15.5
5	50	7.5	22.1	6.5	22.5	6.0	18.3	7.0	22.5
6	60	8.9	31.0	8.2	30.7	7.8	26.1	8.5	31.0
7	70	10.5	41.5	10.1	40.8	9.4	35.5	10.2	41.2
8	80	12.5	54.0	12.9	53.7	12.1	47.6	12.9	54.1
9	90	16.0	70.0	16.6	70.3	16.6	64.2	16.7	70.8
10	100	30.0	100.0	29.7	100.0	35.6	99.8	29.3	100.1

TABLE A.17 *(continued)*

	Cumulative percent of	Percent of income							
		1959		1964		1970		1972	
Decile	population	%	Cum. %	%	Cum. %	%	Cum. %	%	Cum. %
		BLUE-COLLAR WORKERS							
1	10%	1.0%	1.0%	1.2%	1.2%	0.3%	0.3%	2.0%	2.0%
2	20	4.9	5.9	4.4	5.6	3.7	4.0	4.9	6.9
3	30	6.5	12.4	6.1	11.7	5.2	9.2	6.2	13.1
4	40	7.5	19.9	7.6	19.3	6.7	15.9	7.0	20.1
5	50	8.6	28.5	8.2	27.5	8.2	24.1	8.2	28.3
6	60	9.5	38.0	9.5	37.0	9.3	33.4	9.0	37.3
7	70	11.3	49.3	11.0	48.0	11.0	44.4	10.7	48.0
8	80	13.1	62.4	12.7	60.7	13.3	57.7	12.9	60.9
9	90	14.9	77.3	15.4	76.1	16.7	74.4	15.7	76.6
10	100	22.6	99.9	23.9	100.0	25.6	100.0	23.5	100.1

SOURCE: Calculated from unpublished information in the data bank of the Joint Program between the Facultad Latinoamericana de Ciencias Sociales and the Programa Regional de Empleo para América Latina y el Caribe.

TABLE A.18
Industrial Work Force by Class, 1960–73
(Thousands of persons)

Year	Bourgeoisie	Petty bourgeoisie	White-collar workers	Blue-collar workers	Total
1960	8.3	94.1	58.5	248.2	409.1
1961	8.4	100.7	63.3	263.0	435.4
1962	8.5	103.0	66.0	268.0	445.5
1963	8.5	106.6	69.2	274.7	459.0
1964	8.5	109.5	72.3	281.4	471.7
1965	8.6	115.4	78.4	297.3	499.7
1966	8.9	116.3	83.7	310.7	519.6
1967	9.4	119.1	85.2	312.7	526.4
1968	9.3	129.6	85.0	309.8	533.7
1969	11.0	115.6	87.0	327.2	540.8
1970	10.7	128.3	94.6	329.3	562.9
1971	10.8	132.7	99.0	357.2	600.3
1972	11.5	144.4	106.9	373.5	636.3
1973 [a]	11.3	153.4	111.6	387.1	664.0

SOURCE: 1960–69, ODEPLAN, *Balances económicos de Chile, 1960–70*, pp. 100–110. 1970, total work force from ODEPLAN, "La ocupación," mimeo (1973), and individual classes from ODEPLAN, *Balances*, p. 111. 1971–73, total work force from ODEPLAN, "Ocupación," and individual classes from changes in class structure for overall work force, also from "Ocupación."
[a]First half of year only.

TABLE A.19

Between-Class Distribution of Income in Industry, 1960–73

(Millions of escudos)

Year	Labor				Capital			Total industrial income
	Blue-collar workers	White-collar workers	Social security[a]	Total	Petty bourgeoisie	Bour-geoisie	Total	
1960	181	89	61	331	160	294	454	785
1961	206	101	72	379	180	337	517	896
1962	245	126	82	453	207	496	703	1,156
1963	363	195	117	675	273	820	1,093	1,768
1964	543	290	186	1,019	407	1,382	1,789	2,808
1965	740	427	288	1,455	594	1,737	2,331	3,786
1966	1,022	621	429	2,072	753	2,361	3,114	5,186
1967	1,405	848	551	2,804	902	3,356	4,258	7,062
1968	2,169	1,339	730	4,238	1,198	5,098	6,296	10,534
1969	3,170	1,952	1,097	6,219	1,365	7,406	8,771	14,990
1970	4,529	2,940	1,637	9,106	1,990	10,773	12,763	21,869
1971	7,173	4,190	2,463	13,826	2,688	9,226	11,914	25,740
1972	13,941	8,221	4,560	26,722	4,939	15,844	20,783	47,505
1973 [b]	62,470		14,636	77,106			75,353	152,459

SOURCE: 1960–71, ODEPLAN, *Distribución del ingreso y cuentas de producción, 1960–71*, cuadro 15, and estimates by Helio Varela, ex-director of ODEPLAN Income Distribution Office. 1972–73, author's estimates based on the method suggested by Romilio Carrasco, director of ODEPLAN National Accounts Statistics, Oct. 1974.

NOTE: Carrasco's method is as follows: (1) The average annual increase in wages and salaries was calculated, based on the INE industrial index. These figures were 84.0 percent for 1972 and 170.0 percent for January–August 1973. (2) Increases in the industrial work force were added to the wage and salary increases (6.0 percent in 1972 and 4.4 percent in the first half of 1973). (3) Social security payments were assumed to be the same percentage of income as in 1971. (4) Total industrial income for 1972 was obtained by multiplying the 1971 figure by the Table A.14 estimates for 1972 growth (3.8 percent) and inflation (77.8 percent). The comparable figures for January–August 1973 were −4.2 percent and 235.2 percent.

[a] Employers' contributions only.   [b] January–August only, on annualized basis.

NOTES

CHAPTER ONE

1. For a discussion that tries to sort out the various uses of the term political economy, see Barbara Stallings, "Toward a Political Economy of Development" (unpub. paper, Cambridge Univ., 1976). The main distinction drawn is between Marxist and non-Marxist political economy. With respect to the former, authors discussed, in addition to Marx himself, include Lenin (*The Development of Capitalism in Russia*), Dobb (*Studies in the Development of Capitalism*), Baran (*The Political Economy of Growth*), Amin (*Accumulation of Capital on a World Scale* and *Unequal Development*), Wallerstein (*The Modern World-System*), and some members of the so-called Dependency School. The discussion of non-Marxist political economy focuses on the group of writers concerned with governmental choices, especially with respect to the economy. Examples include Ilchman and Uphoff (*The Political Economy of Change* and *The Political Economy of Development*), Anderson (*The Political Economy of Modern Spain*), and Chenery et al. (*Redistribution with Growth*). Albert Hirschman also works in this vein with his analysis of "reform-mongering" (*Journeys toward Progress*). Other approaches to non-Marxist political economy might include the group of historians trying to formulate a neoclassical model of the effect of institutions on the development process. North and Thomas (*Rise of the Western World*) and Davis and North (*Institutional Change and American Economic Growth*) are representatives of this group. The writings of the Structuralist School in Latin America, which tried to analyze the effects of sociopolitical phenomena such as land tenure systems and foreign relations on economic development, constitute yet another non-Marxist approach to the political economy of development.

2. For a discussion of this point, see Francis Bator, "The Simple Analytics of Welfare Economics," *American Economic Review*, 47, No. 1 (March 1957):22–59.

3. Probably the most comprehensive study about Latin America, based on a socioeconomic status approach to class, is the three-volume study of Venezuela by Frank Bonilla and José Silva Michelena. See especially José Silva Michelena, *The Illusion of Democracy in Dependent Nations* (Cambridge, Mass., 1971), chap. 4. For a useful discussion comparing the concepts of class and stratification, see Rodolfo Stavenhagen, *Social Classes in Agrarian Societies* (Garden City, N.Y., 1975), chap. 2.

4. Gerhard Lenski, *Power and Privilege: A Theory of Social Stratification* (New York, 1966), chap. 11. Examples of this kind of literature with special reference to Latin America can be found in John J. Johnson, ed., *Continuity and Change in Latin America* (Stanford, 1964), and S. M. Lipset and Aldo Solari, eds., *Elites in Latin America* (New York, 1967). In general, the class analysis of the U.N. Economic Commission for Latin America (ECLA) would also fit into the functionalist framework.

5. See, for example, John J. Johnson, *Political Change in Latin America: The Emergence of the Middle Sectors* (Stanford, 1958). A list of 14 characteristics of the "new middle class" is given in Victor Alba, "Latin American Style and the New Social Forces," in Albert Hirschman, ed., *Latin America Issues: Essays and Comments* (New York, 1961), pp. 50–51.

6. See Nicos Poulantzas, *Classes in Contemporary Capitalism* (London, 1975), Part 3.

7. See Erik Olin Wright, *Classes, Crisis, and the State* (London, 1978), chap. 1. See also Manuel Castells, "La teoría marxista de las clases sociales y la lucha de clases en América Latina," in Raúl Benítez Zenteno, ed., *Las clases sociales en América Latina* (Mexico, 1973), pp. 159–91.

8. One of the best analyses of the state from the point of view of neoclassical economics is William Baumol, *Welfare Economics and the Theory of the State* (London, 1965). Baumol's analysis focuses specifically on the problem of externalities.

9. A summary of ECLA's position on planning can be found in *El pensamiento de la CEPAL* (Santiago, 1969).

10. See, for example, Ronald I. McKinnon, *Money and Capital in Economic Development* (Washington, D.C., 1973), which stresses the need for creating capital markets in Third World countries.

11. Many of the issues in this debate were brought out in the discussion of the manual on project appraisal of the Organization for Economic Cooperation and Development. See, for example, the symposium in the *Bulletin of the Oxford University Institute of Economics and Statistics*, 34, No. 1 (Feb. 1972). For an analysis of the questions with which a full-scale planning apparatus must deal, see Maurice Dobb's classic book *An Essay on Economic Growth and Planning* (London, 1960).

12. The main elaboration of the concept of relative autonomy is found in the work of Nicos Poulantzas, *Political Power and Social Classes* (London, 1973), esp. Part 4. In addition to Poulantzas, the other person responsible for the resurgence of interest in the Marxist theory of the state is Ralph Miliband (*The State in Capitalist Society*; New York, 1969). See the debate between the two carried out in the following issues of *New Left Review*: Nos. 58, 59, 82, 95 (1969, 1970, 1973, 1976). Important commentaries on

the Poulantzas-Miliband debate include Ernesto Laclau, "The Specificity of the Political: Around the Poulantzas-Miliband Debate," *Economy and Society*, 5, No. 1 (Feb. 1975); David Gold et al., "Recent Development in Marxist Theories of the Capitalist State," *Monthly Review*, 25, Nos. 5 and 6 (1975); Gosta Esping-Andersen et al., "Modes of Class Struggle and the Capitalist State," *Kapitalistate*, Nos. 4–5, 1976; and Simon Clarke, "Marxism, Sociology and Poulantzas' Theory of the State," *Capital and Class*, No. 2, Summer 1977. A review of these and various other Marxist theories of the state is Bob Jessop, "Remarks on Some Recent Marxist Theories of the Capitalist State," *Cambridge Journal of Economics*, 1, No. 4 (Dec. 1977).

13. The model of maximization of welfare through international specialization is well described by Harry Johnson. See his article "The Efficiency and Welfare Implications of the International Corporation," in Charles Kindleberger, ed., *The International Corporation* (Cambridge, Mass., 1970), pp. 35–56.

14. The first, and best known, article expressing these views is Raúl Prebisch, *El desarrollo económico de América Latina y algunos de sus principales problemas* (U.N. document E/CN.12/89/Rev. 1, 1950).

15. The literature based on this point of view is extensive and, incidentally, formed the intellectual justification for the Alliance for Progress. For a collection of articles on the aid question, see Jagdish Bhagwati and Richard Eckaus, eds., *Foreign Aid* (Harmondsworth, Middlesex, Eng., 1970).

16. For recent reviews of the literature on dependency theory, plus bibliography, see Ronald H. Chilcote, "A Critical Synthesis of the Dependency Literature," *Latin American Perspectives*, 1, No. 1 (Spring 1974):4–29, and Richard Fagen, "Studying Latin American Politics: Some Implications of a Dependencia Approach," *Latin American Research Review*, 12, No. 2 (1977):3–26. A discussion of the origins and development of dependency theory is found in Fernando Henrique Cardoso, "The Consumption of Dependency Theory in the United States," *Latin American Research Review*, 12, No. 3 (1977):7–24.

17. The classical Marxist analysis of imperialism is Lenin's *Imperialism: The Highest Stage of Capitalism* (New York, 1939). Lenin, in turn, drew heavily on the work of Hobson and Hilferding. An annotated bibliography of recent writings on imperialism can be found in Roger Owen and Robert Sutcliffe, eds., *Studies in the Theory of Imperialism* (London, 1972).

18. For the most detailed compilation of information on multinationals, see *Multinational Corporations and United States Foreign Policy* (hearings before the Subcommittee on Multinational Corporations of the Committee on Foreign Relations, U.S. Senate, 93d Congress, 2d sess., 1974). Information on multilaterial agencies can be found in Teresa Hayter, *Aid as Imperialism* (Harmondsworth, Middlesex, Eng., 1971), and Cheryl Payer, *The Debt Trap* (Harmondsworth, Middlesex, Eng., 1974).

19. See *New York Times*, Jan. 20, 1972, p. 1.

20. This evidence has been spelled out in great detail in three documents of the U.S. Congress: *United States and Chile during the Allende Years, 1970–73* (hearings before the Subcommittee on Inter-American Affairs of

the Foreign Affairs Committee, U.S. House of Representatives, 93d Congress, 2d sess., 1974); *Covert Action, 1963–73* (Staff Report of the Select Committee to Study Governmental Operations with Respect to Intelligence Activities, 94th Congress, 1st sess., 1975); and *Alleged Assassination Plots Involving Foreign Leaders* (Interim Report of Select Committee to Study Governmental Operations with Respect to Intelligence Activities, 94th Congress, 1st sess., 1975).

21. See, for example, Luciano Martins, "The Politics of U.S. Multinational Corporations in Latin America," in Julio Cotler and Richard Fagen, eds., *Latin America and the United States: the Changing Political Realities* (Stanford, 1974), pp. 368–402.

22. A more rigorous attempt to explain the growth/distribution pattern is found in Barbara Stallings, "Economic Development and Class Conflict in Chile, 1958–73" (Ph.D. dissertation, Stanford University, 1975).

23. See *ibid.*, pp. 10–14, for a more detailed comparison of the industrial sector and the rest of the economy.

CHAPTER TWO

1. The most detailed political-economic history of nineteenth century Chile is Francisco Encina's *Historia de Chile, desde la prehistoria hasta 1891* (20 vols.; Santiago, 1940–52). A three-volume summary was prepared by Leopoldo Castedo, *Resumen de la historia chilena* (Santiago, 1961). A much more readable history is Ricardo Donoso, *Breve historia de Chile* (Buenos Aires, 1970). An important essay on the Chilean economy is Aníbal Pinto, *Chile, un caso de desarrollo frustrado* (Santiago, 1962). See also R. M. Will, "La política económica de Chile, 1810–1864," *El Trimestre Económico*, 27 (1960):238–57. For statistical data, see Markos Mamalakis, *The Growth and Structure of the Chilean Economy: From Independence to Allende* (New Haven, 1973). See also Mamalakis, "Historical Statistics of Chile" (Economic Growth Center, Yale University, 1967, mimeo.).

2. For a discussion of the various economic, social, and political ramifications of nitrate in Chile, see Carmen Cariola and Osvaldo Sunkel, "Expansión salitrera y transformaciones socioeconómicas en Chile: 1880–1930" (Institute of Development Studies, University of Sussex, 1976, mimeo). See also Enrique Reyes, *El desarrollo de la conciencia proletaria en Chile: el ciclo salitrero* (Santiago, n.d.).

3. Hernán Ramírez Necochea, *Historia del imperialismo en Chile* (Santiago, 1970), pp. 46–47. On this subject, see also Roger Burbach, "The Chilean Industrial Bourgeoisie and Foreign Capital, 1920–1970" (Ph.D. dissertation, University of Indiana, 1974), and Charles G. Pregger Román, "Dependent Development in Nineteenth Century Chile," (Ph.D. dissertation, Rutgers University, 1975).

4. For information on the formation of these organizations, see *Los gremios patronales* (Santiago, 1973).

5. On the social and political developments of Chile in the nineteenth century, see Encina; Alberto Edwards, *La fronda aristocrática en Chile* (Santiago, 1936); Julio César Jobet, *Ensayo crítico del desarrollo socioeconómico de Chile* (Santiago, 1955); Arnold Bauer, *Chilean Rural Society from the Spanish Conquest to 1930* (Cambridge, Eng., 1975); and Hernán

Godoy, ed., *Estructura social de Chile* (Santiago, 1971; includes an extensive bibliography).

6. On the early period of the labor movement, see Hernán Ramírez Necochea, *Historia del movimiento obrero en Chile, Siglo XIX* (Santiago, 1956); Julio César Jobet, *Recabarren y los orígenes del movimiento obrero y el socialismo* (Santiago, 1955); Jorge Barría, *El movimiento obrero en Chile* (Santiago, 1971); Manuel Barrera, "Perspectiva histórica de la huelga obrera en Chile," *Cuadernos de la Realidad Nacional*, No. 9, Sept. 1971, pp. 119–55; and Alan Angell, *Politics and the Labor Movement in Chile* (London, 1972).

7. Elías Lafertte, *Vida de un comunista* (Santiago, 1961), p. 101.

8. Mario Ballesteros and Tom Davis, "The Growth of Output and Employment in Basic Sectors of the Chilean Economy, 1908–57," *Economic Development and Cultural Change*, 11, No. 2, Part 1 (Jan. 1963):160.

9. For a sociopolitical perspective of the period 1920–64, written by a Chilean politician who was involved in many of the events he describes, see Arturo Olavarría Bravo, *Chile entre dos Alessandri* (4 vols; Santiago, 1962–65). A book by an American political scientist treating much the same period is James Petras, *Politics and Social Forces in Chilean Development* (Berkeley, Calif., 1970). Other books covering shorter time spans of this period are Enzo Faletto, Eduardo Ruíz, and Hugo Zemelman, *Génesis histórica del proceso político chileno* (Santiago, 1970), and Paul Drake, *Socialism and Populism in Chile, 1932–52* (Urbana, Ill., 1977).

10. The major history of the Communist Party is Hernán Ramírez Necochea, *Origen y formación del Partido Comunista de Chile* (Santiago, 1965). For more personal histories, see the works of two former general secretaries of the Party: Lafertte; and Eduardo Labarca, *Corvalán: 27 horas* (Santiago, 1972). A series of documents was issued on the Party's 50th anniversary: Partido Comunista de Chile, *Documentos del cincuentenario* (Santiago, 1972).

11. Major histories of the Socialist Party include Julio César Jobet, *Historia del Partido Socialista* (2 vols.; Santiago, 1971); Fernando Casanueva and Manuel Fernández, *El Parido Socialista y la lucha de clases en Chile* (Santiago, 1973); and Drake, *Socialism and Populism in Chile*. For a collection of PS documents, see Julio César Jobet and Alejandro Chelén, *Pensamiento teórico y político del Partido Socialista de Chile* (Santiago, 1972).

12. A useful, though anecdotal, history of the early years of the Christian Democratic Party is Ricardo Boizard, *La democracia cristiana en Chile* (Santiago, 1963). See also George Grayson, "The Chilean Christian Democratic Party: Genesis and Development" (Ph.D. dissertation, Johns Hopkins University, 1967). From the point of view of the Party itself, the ideas of the right wing are found in the works of Jaime Castillo; see, for example, *Fuentes de la democracia cristiana* (Santiago, 1963). The views of the former left wing (now outside the Party) are outlined in Julio Silva Solar and Jacques Chonchol, *Desarrollo de la nueva sociedad en América Latina* (Santiago, 1965).

13. John Reese Stevenson, *The Chilean Popular Front* (Philadelphia, 1942). See also Marcelo Cavarozzi, "The Government and the Industrial

Bourgeoisie in Chile, 1938–64" (Ph.D. dissertation, University of California, Berkeley, 1976).

14. For a detailed analysis of this point, see Cavarozzi.

15. See Burbach.

16. See Cavarozzi, based on interviews with labor historian Jorge Barría and Socialist Party leader Clodomiro Almeyda. This agreement is calculated to have cost the Chilean treasury $430 million. See Universidad de Chile, Centro de Estudios Estadísticos-Matemáticos, *Elementos para un análisis de la intervención del estado en la economía chilena* (Instituto Latinoamericano de Planificación Económica y Social, Santiago, 1968).

17. See Dale Johnson, "Industry and Industrialists in Chile" (Ph.D. dissertation, Stanford University, 1967).

18. Calculated from Ricardo Lagos, *La industria en Chile: antecedentes estructurales* (Universidad de Chile, Instituto de Economía, Santiago, 1966), p. 181.

19. Chile's traditional inflation problems are analyzed in Albert Hirschman, *Journeys toward Progress* (Garden City, N.Y., 1965), pp. 215–96. More detailed discussions of the Klein-Saks recommendations and their effects can be found in Ricardo Ffrench-Davis, *Políticas económicas de Chile, 1952–70* (Santiago, 1973), and Enrique Sierra, *Tres ensayos de estabilización en Chile* (Santiago, 1970). The Mission's report itself was published as *El programa de estabilización de la economía chilena y el trabajo de la Misión Klein-Saks* (Santiago, 1958).

20. Two other useful class analyses of Chile are Manuel Castells, *La lucha de clases en Chile* (Buenos Aires, 1974), Part 1, and Jackie Roddick, "Class Structure and Class Politics in Chile," in Philip O'Brien, ed., *Allende's Chile* (New York, 1976), pp. 1–26.

21. Instituto Nacional de Estadísticas, *IV censo nacional de manufacturas* (1970), tomo III, p. 32. (The data are for the year 1967.)

22. Data are from Maurice Zeitlin and Richard Ratcliffe, "Research Methods for the Analysis of the Internal Structure of Dominant Classes: The Case of Landlords and Capitalists in Chile," *Latin American Research Review*, 10, No. 3 (Fall 1975):5–62. See the bibliography of this article for numerous other works on the same subject by Zeitlin, Ratcliffe, and Linda Ann Ewen. An analysis of interlocking directorships between the 50 largest domestic-owned industries and agricultural and banking interests is found in Burbach, Appendixes II and III. (The Burbach data are for 1963.)

23. Sergio Aranda and Alberto Martínez, "Estructura económica: algunas características fundamentales," in Aníbal Pinto et al., *Chile hoy* (Mexico, 1970), p. 121. This structure had changed very little by 1970, in spite of the Frei land reform.

24. Gabriel Gasic, "Concentración, entrelazamiento y desnacionalización de la industria manufacturera" (Memoria de Prueba, Facultad de Ciencias Económicas, Universidad de Chile, Santiago, 1971), p. 9.

25. The original work on financial groups in Chile is Ricardo Lagos, *La concentración del poder económico* (Santiago, 1961). For a more recent analysis, see *El libro de las 91* (Santiago, 1972), pp. 47–58.

26. *El libro*, pp. 47–49.

27. For studies on the gremios, see the following: Constantine Menges,

"Public Policy and Organized Business in Chile: A Preliminary Analysis," *Journal of International Affairs*, 20, No. 2 (1966):343–65; David Cusack, "The Politics of Chilean Private Enterprise under Christian Democracy" (Ph.D. dissertation, University of Denver, 1970); Genaro Arriagada, *La oligarquía patronal chilena* (Santiago, 1970); *Los gremios patronales;* and Carmen Barros, "Nuevos actores en la protesta social 1971–72: el movimiento gremial," in Dagmar Raczynski et al., *Los actores de la realidad chilena* (Santiago, 1974), pp. 173–230.

28. Cusack, p. 46.

29. Important sources of information on the recent history of the labor movement include Jorge Barría, *Historia de la CUT* (Santiago, 1971), Jorge Barría, "La vía chilena y los problemas laborales" (unpublished paper, Santiago, 1974); Barrera; and Angell.

30. See discussion in Angell, p. 45.

31. Interview with labor historian Jorge Barría, Santiago, March 1974. For another source of data on union membership in mid-1973, see Clotario Blest, "Aquí está organizada la clase trabajadora," *Punto Final*, No. 92, Sept. 11, 1973, pp. 22–23.

32. See Barría, *Historia de la CUT.*

33. A general discussion of the cordones can be found in Patricia Santa Lucía, "The Industrial Working Class and the Struggle for Power in Chile," in Philip O'Brien, ed., *Allende's Chile* (New York, 1976), pp. 128–66. Two other studies include E. Sader et al., *Cordón Cerrillos-Maipú: balance y perspectivas de un embrión de poder popular*, and Rose Cheetham et al., *Comandos urbanos: alternativa de poder socialista* (both Centro Interdisciplinario de Desarrollo Urbano, Universidad Católica, Santiago, 1973). The best source of information on these groups, however, is found in the publications *Chile Hoy* and *Punto Final*. Most issues after mid-1972 had interviews and analytical articles on the cordones.

34. Germán Urzúa, *Los partidos políticos chilenos* (Santiago, 1968), pp. 101–48 and *passim*, and Cavarozzi. See also the following sources, but heeding the warning sounded in the footnote on p. 53: Enzo Faletto and Eduardo Ruíz, "Conflicto político y estructura social," in Aníbal Pinto et al., *Chile hoy* (Mexico, 1970), pp. 213–54, and Robert Ayres, "Unidad Popular and the Chilean Electoral Process," *Studies in Comparative International Development*, No. 8, 1973; reprinted in Arturo Valenzuela and J. Samuel Valenzuela, eds., *Chile: Politics and Society* (New Brunswick, N.J., 1976).

35. Urzúa, pp. 149–69; Cavarozzi; Faletto and Ruíz; and Ayres.

36. Faletto and Ruíz; Ayres; and Maurice Zeitlin and James Petras, "The Working Class Vote in Chile: Christian Democracy versus Marxism," *British Journal of Sociology*, No. 21, March 1970, pp. 16–29.

37. See note 36.

38. *Ibid.*

39. United Nations, *Yearbook of International Trade Statistics.*

40. For a history of the copper industry in Chile, see Clark W. Reynolds, "Development Problems of an Export Economy: The Case of Chile and Copper," in Markos Mamalakis and Clark Reynolds, *Essays on the Chilean Economy* (Homewood, Ill., 1965); Theodore Moran, *Multinational Corpora-*

tions and the Politics of Dependence: Copper in Chile (Princeton, N.J., 1975); and Eduardo Novoa Monreal, *La batalla por el cobre* (Santiago, 1972).

41. On the chileanization program, see "The Story of Copper and Imperialism," *New Chile* (Berkeley, Calif., 1972), pp. 82–117; Lucio Geller and Jaime Estévez, "La nacionalización del cobre," in Universidad de Chile, IEP, *La economía chilena en 1971* (Santiago, 1972), pp. 557–78; and Novoa Monreal.

42. Orlando Caputo and Roberto Pizarro, *Desarrollismo y capital extranjero* (Santiago, 1970), p. 86.

43. Gasic, cuadros 37 and 38.

44. CORFO, Gerencia de Industrias, División de Planificación Industrial, *Participación del capital extranjero en las sociedades anónimas industriales*, Publ. No. 14 A/70, 1970, Anexo 2, pp. 21–42.

45. S. Ramos, *Chile: ¿una economía en transición?* (Santiago, 1972), p. 53.

46. *Ibid.*

47. ODEPLAN, *Balances económicos de Chile, 1960–70* (1973), p. 157. The figure for 1970 includes public sector debt and private debt guaranteed by the state.

48. See Alexis Guardia, "Structural Transformations in Chile's Economy and in Its Systems of External Economic Relations," in Sandro Sideri, ed., *Chile, 1970–1973: Economic Development and Its International Setting* (The Hague, 1978).

49. Ramos, p. 58.

50. Caputo and Pizarro, p. 111.

51. CORFO, Gerencia de Industrias, División de Planificación Industrial, *Comportamiento de las principales empresas industriales extranjeras acogidas al DFL 258*, Publ. No. 9A/70, 1970, p. 9.

52. There are several sources containing partial analyses of the role of the state in the economy in Chile. These include Aranda and Martínez; Ramos; and Universidad de Chile, Centro de Estudios Estadísticos-Matemáticos, *Elementos*. A useful summary of economic policies in the 1952–70 period is Ffrench-Davis.

53. The most complete source of information on state-controlled enterprises before 1970 is CORFO, Gerencia de Filiales, *Monografía de empresas filiales* (1970). For information on firms taken over during the Allende period, see Universidad de Chile, IEP, *La economía chilena en 1972* (Santiago, 1973), pp. 116–31, and Sergio Bitar and Arturo Mackenna, *Impacto de las áreas de propiedad social y mixta en la industria chilena* (Centro de Planeamiento, Universidad de Chile, Santiago, 1973).

54. Calculated from ODEPLAN, *Balances*, pp. 15, 135. Statistics on the public sector budget for 1970 come from Ministerio de Hacienda, *Balance consolidado del sector público de Chile, 1969–70*.

55. The most complete study on public sector investment is ODEPLAN, *La inversión pública en el período 1961–70* (Santiago, 1971).

56. See discussion in Ramos, p. 174.

57. For a complete treatment of tax policies, see Ffrench-Davis, pp. 153–86.

58. See Universidad de Chile, Centro de Estudios Estadísticos-Matemáticos, *Elementos*, pp. 17–20.

59. Cavarozzi.

60. Calculated from Universidad de Chile, Instituto de Economía, *La economía chilena en el período 1950–63* (1963), tomo II, cuadro 7, and ODEPLAN, *Cuentas nacionales 1960–71*, cuadro 14.

61. The average open unemployment rate for Greater Santiago during the 1956–70 period was calculated from various issues of Universidad de Chile, IEP, *Ocupación y desocupación en Gran Santiago* (Santiago, 1956–70). Data that include disguised unemployment come from David Landes, "Import Substitution and the Demand for Labor in Urban Chile, 1930–70: The Development of Urban Underemployment" (Ph.D. dissertation, Washington University, St. Louis, 1973), Tables V-32, V-43, and V-44.

62. Data for 1940 come from Aranda and Martínez, pp. 56–57, and 1970 data from ODEPLAN, *Balances*, p. 89.

63. United Nations, Economic Commission for Latin America, *The Economic Development of Latin America in the Post-War Period*, 1964, E/CN.12/659/Rev. 1, p. 71.

64. Statistics for 1940–60 from Hirschman, *Journeys Toward Progress*, p. 216. Data for the 1960–70 period come from various issues of the Banco Central de Chile, *Boletín Mensual*.

65. Universidad de Chile, IEP, *Formación de capital en las empresas industriales* (Santiago, 1961), pp. 36–46.

CHAPTER THREE

1. Nicos Poulantzas, *Political Power and Social Classes* (London, 1973), pp. 229–52.

2. For a series of studies on political parties from a Marxist point of view, see the following: Umberto Cerroni, Lucio Magri, and Monty Johnstone, *Teoría marxista del partido político* (Córdoba, Argentina, 1969); V. I. Lenin, Rosa Luxemburg, and Georg Lukacs, *Teoría marxista del partido político/2* (Córdoba, Argentina, 1969); and Rossana Rossandra et al., *Teoría marxista del partido político/3* (Córdoba, Argentina, 1973).

3. See, for example, Constantine Menges, "Public Policy and Organized Business in Chile: A Preliminary Analysis," *Journal of International Affairs*, 22, No. 2 (1966):343–65; and David Cusack, "The Politics of Chilean Private Enterprise under Christian Democracy" (Ph.D. dissertation, University of Denver, 1970).

4. ODEPLAN, *Cuentas de producción y distribución del ingreso, 1960–71*, cuadros 12–22.

5. *Ibid.*   6. *Ibid.*

7. See Menges.   8. *Ibid.*, p. 352.

9. *Ibid.*

10. Sociedad de Fomento Fabril, "Actas de sesiones del Consejo Directivo, May 4, 1966," archive of SOFOFA, Santiago.

11. See analysis by Marcelo Cavarozzi, "The Government and the Industrial Bourgeoisie in Chile, 1938–64" (Ph.D. dissertation, University of California, Berkeley, 1976).

12. *Ibid.*

13. Jorge Alessandri, "Carta al presidente de la Sociedad de Fomento Fabril, 18 de agosto de 1959," in *Pensamiento político de Don Jorge Alessandri* (Santiago, 1970), p. 57.

14. Jorge Alessandri, *Mensaje del Presidente de la República, al inaugurar el período de sesiones ordinarias del Congreso Nacional*, May 21, 1959, cited in *Pensamiento*, p. 55.

15. Jorge Alessandri, *Discurso-programa del candidato independiente Don Jorge Alessandri Rodríguez* (Santiago, 1958).

16. Eduardo Frei, *Mensaje del Presidente de la República, al inaugurar el período de sesiones ordinarias del Congreso Nacional*, May 21, 1968, p. 69.

17. *Ibid.*, May 21, 1967, p. 45.

18. Eduardo Frei, "Discurso en la Intendencia de Concepción, 11 de marzo de 1967," cited in Theodor Fuchs and E. Alejandro Yung, "Aproximación al análisis del impacto de la política económica sobre el desarrollo industrial en Chile, 1958–68" (Memoria de Prueba, Facultad de Ciencias Económicas, Universidad de Chile, 1970), p. IV-4.

19. Salvador Allende, *Mensaje del Presidente de la República, al inaugurar el período de sesiones ordinarias del Congreso Nacional*, May 21, 1971, cited in Gonzalo Martner, ed., *El pensamiento económico del gobierno de Allende* (Santiago, 1971), pp. 32–35.

20. Alessandri, *Discurso-programa*.

21. Eduardo Frei, "Discurso en la Intendencia de Concepción, 11 de marzo de 1967," cited in Orlando Caputo and Roberto Pizarro, *Desarrollismo y capital extranjero* (Santiago, 1970), pp. 76–77.

22. CORFO, Gerencia de Industrias, División de Planificación Industrial, *El Estatuto del Inversionista y su significado en la industria chilena* (1969), pp. 7–8.

23. Eduardo Frei, "Mi programa de gobierno," *Política y Espíritu*, No. 285, June–Aug. 1964, pp. 5–6.

24. Salvador Allende, "Acto de firma del Decreto No. 92 que establece las deducciones que por concepto de la rentabilidad excesiva deben realizarse de la indemnización de las compañías nacionalizadas, en la Moneda, 28 de julio de 1971," cited in *Allende: su pensamiento político* (Santiago, 1972), p. 182.

25. Pedro Vuscovic, "Discurso ante el CIAP, Washington, 22 de febrero de 1971," cited in Martner, pp. 106–7.

26. Salvador Allende, *Mensaje del Presidente de la República, al inaugurar el período de sesiones ordinarias del Congreso Nacional*, May 21, 1971, cited in *Allende: su pensamiento político*, p. 131.

27. Jorge Alessandri, "Carta a la CUT sobre el problema de reajustes, 22 de noviembre de 1960," cited in *Pensamiento*, p. 65.

28. *Ibid.*, cited in Jorge Barría, *Historia de la CUT* (Santiago, 1971), p. 101.

29. Alessandri, *Discurso-programa*.

30. This version of the Frei electoral program was taken from Frei, "Mi programa." Other aspects or versions can be found in the various "Declaraciones de Millahue" of the Christian Democratic Party. See also the recounting by Frei's Minister of Finance in Sergio Molina, *El proceso de cambio en Chile* (Santiago, 1972). All of these versions rely heavily on the analysis and recommendations of Jorge Ahumada, *En vez de la miseria* (Santiago, 1958).

31. Felipe Foxley, *El gobierno de Frei: una etapa de modernización y*

reforma de la sociedad chilena (Instituto de Ciencia Política, Universidad Católica, Santiago, 1971).

32. Andrés Zaldívar, in *Exposición sobre el estado de la Hacienda Pública*, Nov. 1968.

33. *Ibid.*

34. Sergio Molina, in *Exposición sobre el estado de la Hacienda Pública*, Nov. 1964.

35. Eduardo Frei, "Discurso ante los trabajadores de la educación," *El Mercurio*, Aug. 8, 1964.

36. Molina, in *Exposición*, Nov. 1967.

37. *Programa Básico de la Unidad Popular* (Santiago, 1970). (An English version is available in *New Chile* [Berkeley, Calif., 1972], pp. 130–42.)

38. Vuscovic, "Discurso," p. 104.

39. *Ibid.*, p. 105.

40. ODEPLAN, *Resumen del Plan de la Economía Nacional, 1971–76* (1971), p. 21.

41. Pedro Vuscovic et al., "Orientaciones básicas del programa económico de corto plazo" (Santiago, mimeo., Oct. 29, 1970); cited in Sergio Ramos, *Chile: ¿una economía en transición?* (Santiago, 1972), p. 192.

CHAPTER FOUR

1. For a summary of the electoral platforms, see *Hispanic American Report*, Aug. 1958. (The dates given for the *Hispanic American Report* citations refer to the months whose events are described in the report. Extensive use was also made in this chapter of the clipping collection prepared by students working on the *Report*. This collection is now contained in the archive of the Hoover Institution at Stanford University.)

2. Donald Bray, "Chilean Politics during the Second Ibáñez Government, 1952–58" (Ph.D. dissertation, Stanford University, 1961), pp. 151–53.

3. *Industria* (Sociedad de Fomento Fabril, Santiago), Sept. 1958.

4. Sociedad de Fomento Fabril, "Actas de Sesiones del Consejo Directivo, Nov. 5, 1958" (archive of SOFOFA, Santiago; hereafter "Actas").

5. *Ibid.*, Jan. 14, 1959.

6. See the interview with Alessandri in *Panorama Económico* (July–Aug. 1958).

7. Interview with Roberto Vergara (Alessandri's Minister of Finance, Economics, and Mining), Santiago, Feb. 1970 (cited in Marcelo Cavarozzi, "The Government and the Industrial Bourgeoisie in Chile, 1938–64" [Ph.D. dissertation, University of California, Berkeley, 1976]).

8. See the analysis in Enrique Sierra, *Tres ensayos de estabilización en Chile* (Santiago, 1970).

9. Central Unica de Trabajadores, *Memoria al Congreso Nacional*, Oct. 20, 1958.

10. *El Mercurio*, March 8, 1959.

11. "Actas," March 11, 1959.

12. *Ibid.*, Jan. 14, 1959.

13. Jorge Barría, *Historia de la CUT* (Santiago, 1971), p. 96.

14. *Ercilla*, May 11, 1960.

15. *Ibid.*, Nov. 9, 1960.

16. *Ibid.*
17. Barría, *Historia*, p. 99.
18. *La Nacion*, Nov. 22, 1960.
19. *South Pacific Mail*, April 28, 1961.
20. Calculated from Ricardo Ffrench-Davis, *Políticas económicas en Chile, 1952–70* (Santiago, 1973), p. 329. (Both figures are in real terms.)
21. "Actas," Dec. 9, 1959, and Jan. 6, 1960.
22. *El Mercurio*, May 24, 1959.
23. Calculated from Ffrench-Davis, p. 86.
24. International Monetary Fund, *Balance of Payments Yearbook*.
25. Arturo Olavarría Bravo, *Chile entre dos Alessandri* (Santiago, 1965), tomo III, p. 25.
26. For a description of these events, see Barría, *Historia*, pp. 105–7; Olavarría Bravo, *ibid.*, pp. 109–10; *Hispanic American Report*, Nov. 1962.
27. *Hispanic American Report*, Nov. 1962.
28. *El Diario Ilustrado*, March 6, 18, and 27, 1963 (Conservative Party) and *El Mercurio*, March 24, 1963 (Liberal Party).
29. Interview with Alfonso Silva Delano (head of Unión Social de Empresarios Cristianos—USEC), Santiago, Feb. 1974.
30. *El Mercurio*, June 23, 1963.
31. *Ibid.*, June 16, 1963.
32. *Ibid.*, Nov. 12, 1962.
33. *New York Times*, April 28, 1963.
34. *El Mercurio*, June 26, 1963, and *Hispanic American Report*, June 1963.
35. Barría, *Historia*, p. 111.
36. For a summary of these rather complicated events, see *Hispanic American Report*, Aug.–Nov. 1963.
37. *Ibid.*, Feb. 1964.
38. Based on an analysis in the *Christian Science Monitor*, March 14, 1964.
39. Different parts of the speech are presented in *El Mercurio*, March 20, 1964, and *Las Noticias de Ultima Hora*, March 20, 1964.
40. *El Mercurio*, March 19, 1964.
41. Interviews by the author in Santiago shantytowns, Feb. 1969.
42. See, for example, letters from the editor of *Paese Sera* (Italy), who claimed that this journal had interviewed Allende, who insisted that Chilean socialism would be like the Cuban, not the European, variety. *El Mercurio*, Sept. 1, 2, 1964; see also *Hispanic American Report*, Aug. 1964.
43. *Ibid.*, July 1964.
44. *El Mercurio*, Sept. 1 and 2, 1964.
45. *Hispanic American Report*, June 1964.
46. *Ibid.*, Sept. 1964.
47. James Petras and Morris Morley, *The United States and Chile: Imperialism and the Overthrow of the Allende Government* (New York, 1975), p. 20.
48. Laurence Stern, "U.S. Helped Beat Allende in 1964," *Washington Post*, April 5, 1973.

49. *Ibid.*

50. Laurence Stern, "Ex-Spy to Give Detailed Account of Covert CIA Operations," *Washington Post*, July 11, 1974.

51. *Multinational Corporations and United States Foreign Policy* (hearings before the Subcommittee on Multinational Corporations of the Committee on Foreign Relations, U.S. Senate, 93d Congress, 2d sess., 1974), p. 704 (cited in Petras and Morley, p. 173).

CHAPTER FIVE

1. A fairly complete version of the Frei program can be found in Eduardo Frei, "Mi programa de gobierno," *Política y Espíritu*, No. 285, June–Aug. 1964, pp. 3–21.

2. For a complete discussion of the property amendment, including the congressional debates, see Enrique Evans de la Cuadra, *Estatuto constitucional del derecho de propiedad en Chile* (Santiago, 1967).

3. Sociedad de Fomento Fabril, "Actas de sesiones del Consejo Directivo, June 9, 1965," archive of SOFOFA, Santiago (hereafter referred to as "Actas").

4. *Ibid.*

5. *Ibid.*, June 23, 1965.

6. *Ercilla*, July 21, 1965.

7. See SOFOFA version of events in "Actas," Sept. 28, 1966.

8. See, for example, Alan Angell, *Politics and the Labor Movement in Chile* (London, 1972), p. 199; Felipe Foxley, *El gobierno de Frei: una etapa de modernización y reforma de la sociedad chilena* (Instituto de Ciencia Política, Universidad Católica, Santiago, 1971), pp. 83–84; Henry Landsberger, "Ideology and Practical Labor Politics," in Mario Zañartu and J. J. Kennedy, eds., *The Overall Development of Chile* (Notre Dame, Ind., 1969), p. 117.

9. See Jorge Barría, *Historia de la CUT* (Santiago, 1971), pp. 122–28, and Angell, pp. 198–200.

10. Barría, pp. 115–16.

11. *Ibid.*, p. 129.

12. *Ibid.*, pp. 130–31; Angell, p. 200.

13. Sergio Molina, *El proceso de cambio en Chile* (Santiago, 1972), pp. 74–76.

14. "U.S. Aid—The Carrot and the Stick," *New Chile* (Berkeley, Calif., 1972), p. 48.

15. Cited in David Morris, *We Must Make Haste—Slowly* (New York, 1973), p. 56.

16. See Eduardo Novoa Monreal, *La batalla por el cobre* (Santiago, 1972).

17. Molina, pp. 139–41.

18. Foxley, pp. 85–91. The document was not published by its authors but "leaked" and published by the right-wing weekly *PEC* (Política, Economía, y Cultura).

19. Molina, pp. 141–42.

20. *El Siglo*, Dec. 19, 1967.

21. *Punto Final*, Jan. 2, 1968.

22. *El Siglo*, Nov. 6, 1967.

23. Barría, pp. 142–43.

24. SOFOFA, *Memoria*, 1967.

25. David Cusack, "The Politics of Chilean Private Enterprise under Christian Democracy" (Ph.D. dissertation, University of Denver, 1970), p. 253.

26. *Ibid.*, pp. 32.

27. *Ibid.*, p. 308.

28. *Ibid.*, p. 22.

29. Interview with Eduardo García (head of ODEPLAN under Frei), Santiago, March 1972.

30. Cusack, p. 253.

31. Morris, p. 73.

32. *Punto Final*, May 20, 1969.

33. Angell, p. 206.

34. *El Siglo*, Nov. 7, 1968.

35. See accounts in *Ercilla*, Aug. 7, 1968; *Punto Final*, Oct. 22, 1968; Morris, pp. 70–71.

36. "Actas," Aug. 7, 1968.

37. *Ibid.*

38. SOFOFA, *Memoria*, 1968.

39. Morris, p. 70.

40. "Actas," Aug. 27, 1969.

41. SOFOFA, *Memoria*, 1968.

42. *Ibid.*

43. Víctor Arroyo, "La comunidad de trabajo en Chile o una forma de autogestión" (unpublished paper, Portola Institute, Menlo Park, Calif., 1974), pp. 15–20.

44. *Ibid.*, pp. 23–24.

45. *Experiencias de masas* (Separata Pastoral Popular, No. 129, June 1972), pp. 17–18.

46. The interpretations of the Tacnazo by the different leftist parties are described in Eduardo Labarca, *Chile al rojo* (Santiago, 1971), pp. 54–66.

47. *Ibid.*, pp. 56–57. Details on Viaux's letter to Frei on a new policy with respect to the armed forces can be found in Robinson Rojas Sandford, *Estos mataron a Allende* (Barcelona, 1974; English translation *The Murder of Allende*, New York, 1976, p. 63).

48. Central Unica de Trabajadores, *Memoria del Consejo Directivo al 6° Congreso Nacional de la CUT* (1971), p. 8.

49. For one version of this argument, see Morris, p. 82.

50. *Ibid.*, p. 84.

51. *El Mercurio* (cited in Morris, p. 85).

52. Morris.

53. Barría, p. 154.

54. Fernando Casanueva and Manuel Fernández, *El Partido Socialista y la lucha de clases en Chile* (Santiago, 1973), pp. 231–33.

55. Interview with Eugenio Heiremans (ex-president of SOFOFA), Santiago, Feb. 1974.

56. See comparisons of the three platforms in Frederic Débúyst and Joan Garcés, "La opción chilena de 1970: análisis de los tres programas electorales," *Revista Latinoamericana de Ciencia Política*, Año 2, No. 2, Aug. 1971, pp. 279–369.

57. *Ibid.*, p. 317.

58. Richard Feinberg, *The Triumph of Allende: Chile's Legal Revolution* (New York, 1972), p. 96.

59. See *ibid.* for a general description of the 1970 campaign.

60. *New York Times*, Sept. 10, 1974.

61. Richard Fagen, "The United States and Chile: Roots and Branches," *Foreign Affairs*, 53, No. 2 (Jan. 1975):298. See also the interview with former U.S. Ambassador Edward Korry on this matter: "U.S. Policies under the Allende Government," in Francisco Orrego Vicuña, ed., *Chile: The Balanced View* (University of Chile, Institute of International Studies, Santiago, 1975), pp. 287–89.

62. See *Los documentos secretos de la ITT* (Santiago, 1972).

63. With respect to the Schneider affair, see Robinson Rojas Sandford, *The Murder of Allende* (New York, 1976). For a general analysis of the period between September 4 and November 4, from the point of view of Allende's personal political adviser, see Joan Garcés, *Allende y la experiencia chilena* (Barcelona, 1976), chap. 2.

CHAPTER SIX

1. Since so much information on the Unidad Popular government was lost as a result of the coup, it is important to know of the following collections of documents. Anna Corossacz, ed., *I mille giorni di Allende: l'azione del governo di Unidad Popular in 125 documenti* (Rome, 1975); this is a collection of government and party documents. Another collection of party documents, plus articles from the major left-wing magazines and newspapers, is Maurice Najman, ed., *Le chili est proche* (Paris, 1974). *El Mercurio*, the major right-wing daily newspaper in Santiago, has published a useful day-by-day chronology, based on articles published during the UP period. See El Mercurio, *Breve historia de la Unidad Popular* (Santiago, 1974). Finally, a compilation of books held in 11 major U.S. libraries, which were published in Chile, about Chile, or by Chileans during the 1970–73 period, is Lee H. Williams, Jr., *The Allende Years* (Boston, 1977).

2. An English translation of the Basic Program of the Popular Unity can be found in *New Chile* (Berkeley, Calif., 1972), pp. 130–42.

3. Central Unica de Trabajadores, *Memoria del Consejo Directivo al 6° Congreso Nacional de la CUT* (1971), p. 57. (The entire text of the agreement is found on pp. 57–59.)

4. Interview with Roberto Frenkel (former economist in Ministries of Finance and Economics), Santiago, August 1973.

5. The text of this agreement is found in CUT, *Memoria*, pp. 59–72.

6. See Juan G. Espinosa and Andrew S. Zimbalist, *Economic Democracy: Workers' Participation in the Management of Industrial Enterprises in Chile, 1970–73* (New York, 1978). An English translation of the Normas Básicas, as well as other information on worker participation, can be found in Michel Raptis, *Revolution and Counter-Revolution in Chile: A Dossier on Workers' Participation in the Revolutionary Process* (London, 1974).

7. For a detailed study of the Social Area and its impact on Chilean industry, written by an economist who was intimately involved in the process, see A. Martínez, "The Industrial Sector: Social and Mixed Property in Chile," in S. Sideri, ed., *Chile, 1970–1973: Economic Development and Its International Setting* (The Hague, 1978). An account of the development of the UP's ideas on the Social Area, also written by an economist who was an adviser to the government, is Pío García, "El area de propiedad social: alcances políticos," in Federico Gil, Ricardo Lagos, and Henry Landsberger,

eds., *Chile 1970–73: lecciones de una experiencia* (Madrid, 1977), pp. 168–91. Data on the effects of the Social Area are found in Sergio Bitar and Arturo Mackenna, *Impacto de las áreas de propiedad social y míxta en la industria chilena* (Centro de Planeamiento, Universidad de Chile, Santiago, 1973).

8. For one of the best sources of these controversies and descriptions of the two bills, see *El libro de las 91* (Santiago, 1972), pp. 213–49.

9. Figures were calculated on the basis of data in Universidad de Chile, Instituto de Economía y Planificación, *La economía chilena en 1972* (Santiago, 1973), pp. 116–24, and CORFO, *Participación del capital extranjero en las sociedades anónimas industriales* (Santiago, 1970), pp. 22–42. Some of the requisitioned and intervened firms were later returned to their owners.

10. Lillian Collyer and Eliana Sinay, "Proceso de estatización del sistema bancario," in Universidad de Chile, IEP, *La economía chilena en 1971* (Santiago, 1972), pp. 584–85. The UP's general strategy with respect to the banks is discussed by the former president of the Central Bank, in Alfonso Inostroza, "Nationalization of the Banking System in Chile," in Sideri, *Chile, 1970–1973*.

11. Universidad de Chile, IEP, *La economía chilena en 1972*, pp. 116–24.

12. See accounts and documents in Eduardo Novoa Monreal, *La batalla por el cobre* (Santiago, 1972). See also the analysis by the UP's economic representative in London: Carlos Fortín, "Nationalization of Copper in Chile and Its International Repercussions," in Sideri.

13. *New York Times*, Oct. 23, 1971.

14. *Ibid.*, Jan. 21, 1972.

15. The best source on the U.S. economic blockade is "Chile: Facing the Blockade," *Latin America and Empire Report*, 7, No. 1 (Jan. 1973). An article denying there was a blockade is Paul Sigmund, "The 'Invisible Blockade' and the Overthrow of Allende," *Foreign Affairs*, 52, No. 2 (Jan. 1974): 322–40. Reprinted in Francisco Orrego Vicuña, ed., *Chile: The Balanced View* (University of Chile, Institute of International Studies, Santiago, 1975).

16. "Chile: Facing the Blockade," pp. 18–19. The stated reason for denying the loan to the electricity project was the UP refusal to raise electricity prices to "realistic" levels, thus guaranteeing the ability to repay the loan. Whether the Bank would have given in if the government had met its *stated* objection (e.g. by raising prices but providing a subsidy to users) can only be speculated upon.

17. *Ibid.*, p. 18.

18. *Ibid.*, p. 20. For an analysis much more sympathetic to the banks' point of view, see Jonathan Sanford, "The Multilateral Development Banks and the Suspension of Lending to Allende's Chile," in Francisco Orrego Vicuña, ed., *Chile: The Balanced View* (Institute of International Studies, University of Chile, Santiago, 1975), pp. 123–52. Even Sanford, however, is forced to admit that political considerations were involved in the multilateral agencies' loan policies.

19. "Chile: Facing the Blockade," p. 19.

20. *Ibid.*, p. 19.

21. Frenkel, (see note 4). For a similar comparison of the two strategies, see Carlos Vidales, *Contrarrevolución y dictadura en Chile* (Bogota, 1974), pp. 134–35.
22. *Ibid.*
23. Peter Winn, *Yarur: The Chilean Revolution from Below* (New York, forthcoming).
24. A history of the Cordón Cerrillos–Maipú is found in E. Sader et al., *Cordón Cerrillos–Maipú: balance y perspectivas de un embrión de poder popular* (Centro Interdisciplinario de Desarrollo Urbano, Universidad Católica, Santiago, 1973). An English version of the Cordón's program is found in Ian Roxborough et al., *Chile: State and Revolution* (London, 1977), pp. 170–71.
25. For a general overview of the Right's strategy, see Roxborough et al., pp. 103–22; and Ian Roxborough, "Reversing the Revolution: The Chilean Opposition to Allende," in Philip O'Brien, ed., *Allende's Chile* (New York, 1976), pp. 192–216.
26. Sociedad de Fomento Fabril, "Actas de sesiones del Consejo Directivo, Nov. 11, 1970" (archive of SOFOFA, Santiago; hereafter referred to as "Actas").
27. *Ibid.*, March 17, 1971.
28. Interview with Eugenio Heiremans (ex-president of SOFOFA), Santiago, Feb. 1974.
29. "Actas," June 2, 1971.
30. Orlando Sáenz, *Un país en quiebra* (Santiago, 1973), pp. 13–21.
31. José Cayuela, "¡Muerte al Area Social!", *Chile Hoy*, Año 2, No. 55, June 29, 1973, pp. 16–17, and Año 2, No. 57, July 13, 1973, pp. 16–17.
32. *Los gremios patronales* (Santiago, 1973), p. 5.
33. *New York Times*, Sept. 8, 1974.
34. *Ibid.*, Sept. 17, 1974.
35. *Ibid.*, Nov. 21, 1974. For reports on foreign corporations' donations to the strike, see *ibid.*, Oct. 16, 1974.
36. "Chile: Facing the Blockade," pp. 17–18.
37. A chronology of events during the strike can be found in *Los gremios patronales*, pp. 20–66. Another version is in Rose Cheetham et al., *Comandos urbanos: alternativa de poder socialista* (Centro Interdisciplinario de Desarrollo Urbano, Universidad Católica, Santiago, 1973), anexo 3.
38. *El Mercurio*, Oct. 22, 1972.
39. Among other places, the Pliego del Pueblo can be found in *Marxismo y Revolución*, No. 1, July–Sept. 1973, pp. 229–40.
40. Andy Zimbalist and Barbara Stallings, "Showdown in Chile," *Monthly Review*, 25, No. 5 (Oct. 1973). Reprinted in Paul Sweezy and Harry Magdoff, eds., *Revolution and Counter-Revolution in Chile* (New York, 1974), p. 124. Fifteen of these firms were later returned to their owners; *ibid.*, p. 126.
41. See various articles and documents on the Millas Plan, in *Chile Hoy*, 1, No. 34 (Feb. 2, 1973). Also "La hora del Area Social," *Punto Final*, 7, No. 184 (May 22, 1973), pp. 16–18.
42. There was a definite lack of knowledge about, or even interest in,

Chile's allegedly "apolitical" military before the last part of the UP government. This was reflected in the lack of serious studies on the subject. The
most complete analysis was Alain Joxe, *Las fuerzas armadas en el sistema
político de Chile* (Santiago, 1970). An article that summarizes the book and
brings it up to date is Alain Joxe, "The Chilean Armed Forces and the Making of the Coup," in Philip O'Brien, ed., *Allende's Chile* (New York, 1976),
pp. 244–72. Shortly after the coup an interesting, though not always well
documented, book appeared: Robinson Rojas Sandford, *Estos mataron a
Allende* (Barcelona, 1974; recently translated into English as *The Murder of
Allende*; New York, 1976). A more recent book-length study is Frederick
Nunn, *The Military in Chilean History* (Albuquerque, N.M., 1976). See also
Jorge Nef, "The Politics of Repression: The Social Pathology of the Chilean
Military," *Latin American Perspectives*, 1, No. 2 (Summer 1974): 58–77.
An inside view, as described by Allende's personal political adviser, is Joan
Garcés, *Allende y la experiencia chilena* (Barcelona, 1976), esp. chaps. 4
and 7. Finally, a collection of articles on the military which appeared in the
newsweekly *Chile Hoy* has been put together: Pío García, ed., *Las fuerzas
armadas en Chile* (Mexico, 1974).

43. Interview with José Antonio Viera-Gallo (leader of MAPU-OC), Santiago, April 1973.

44. "No hay paralelismo con la CUT," *Chile Hoy*, Año 2, No. 59, July
27, 1973, p. 7.

45. Zimbalist and Stallings, p. 136.

46. Sáenz, pp. 93–103.

47. *Las Noticias de Ultima Hora*, Aug. 8, 1973.

48. *El Mercurio*, Aug. 1, 1973.

49. Interview with Eugenio Heiremans (ex-president of SOFOFA), Santiago, Feb. 1974.

50. Data are from an Allende speech that itself was interrupted because
of terrorists blowing up electricity lines. See *La Nación*, Aug. 14, 1973.

51. For an account of events in the Presidential Palace, see Garcés, chap.
10. Some information on battles that took place in Santiago is given in Roxborough et al., *Chile*, pp. 231–43.

52. Probably the most reliable evidence on the physical repression of the
Junta is found in the various reports of international organizations. See, for
example, Amnesty International, *Chile: An Amnesty International Report*
(London, 1974), and the various reports of the Organization of American
States: *Report on the Status of Human Rights in Chile* (1974); *Second
Report on the Situation of Human Rights in Chile* (1976); and *Third Report
on the Status of Human Rights in Chile* (1977).

53. An excellent summary of the post-coup economic policies and their
effects is "Chile: Recycling the Capitalist Crisis," *Latin America and
Empire Report*, 10, No. 9 (Nov. 1976). See also Enrique Dávila, "El modelo
económico del régimen militar," and Cristobal Kay, "La política agraria del
Gobierno de la Junta Militar en Chile, 1973–76," papers presented at the
University of Glasgow Conference on Chile, London, May 1977. More
specific articles on the fall in the standard of living are Michel Chossudov-
sky, "Hacia el nuevo modelo económico chileno: inflación y redistribución

del ingreso," *El Trimestre Económico*, 52, No. 166 (April–June 1975): 311–47; and Ricardo Lagos and Oscar Rufatt, "Military Government and Real Wages in Chile," *Latin American Research Review*, 10, No. 2 (Summer 1975): 139–46.

54. The U.S. role in Chile is amply documented in the hearings of the U.S. Congress. See *United States and Chile during the Allende Years, 1970–73* (hearings before the Subcommittee on Inter-American Affairs of the Foreign Affairs Committee, U.S. House of Representatives, 93d Congress, 2d sess., 1974); *Covert Action, 1963–73* (Staff Report of the Select Committee to Study Governmental Operations with Respect to Intelligence Activities, 94th Congress, 1st sess., 1975); and *Alleged Assassination Plots Involving Foreign Leaders* (Interim Report of Select Committee to Study Governmental Operations with Respect to Intelligence Activities, 94th Congress, 1st sess., 1975). The U.S. role in aiding the Junta is spelled out in NACLA, "The United States Propping Up the Junta," and "Time of Reckoning: The U.S. and Chile," *Latin America and Empire Report*, 8, No. 8 (Oct. 1974), and 10, No. 10 (Dec. 1976), respectively.

CHAPTER SEVEN

1. The best source of information on state-owned enterprises up through 1970 is CORFO, Gerencia de Filiales, *Monografía de empresas filiales* (1970). See also Universidad de Chile, Centro de Estudios Estadístico-Matemáticos, *Elementos para un análisis de la intervención del estado en la economía chilena* (Instituto Latinoamericano de Planificación Económica y Social, Santiago, 1968).

2. Interview with Eugenio Heiremans (ex-president of SOFOFA), Santiago, Feb. 1974.

3. See CORFO, Gerencia de Industrias, División de Planificación Industrial, *Comportamiento de las principales empresas industriales extranjeras acogidas al DFL 258*, Publ. No. 9A/70 (1970), and Sergio Bitar, *La presencia de la empresa extranjera en la industria chilena* (CEPLAN, Universidad Católica, Santiago, 1972).

4. For information on industries taken over during the Allende period, see Universidad de Chile, IEP, *La economía chilena en 1972* (Santiago, 1973), pp. 116–31; and Sergio Bitar and Arturo Mackenna, *Impacto de las áreas de propiedad social y mixta en la industria chilena* (Centro de Planeamiento, Universidad de Chile, 1973). For discussion of intervention and requisition powers, see Chapter Six.

5. Calculated from Ministerio de Hacienda, *Balance consolidado del sector público*, various years.

6. Calculated from ODEPLAN, *Antecedentes sobre el desarrollo chileno, 1960–70* (1971), p. 172, and Ministerio de Hacienda, *Balance . . . 1971–73*, p. 181.

7. Ricardo Ffrench-Davis, *Políticas económicas de Chile, 1952–70* (Santiago, 1973), p. 298.

8. See Constantine Menges, "Public Policy and Organized Business in Chile: A Preliminary Analysis," *Journal of International Affairs*, 20, No. 2 (1966): 343–65. The Menges figures report that there were six govern-

mental representatives: two appointed by the President and two by each house of Congress. The latter were eliminated, and the President was given four positions in place of the previous total of six.

9. Universidad de Chile, IEP, *La economía chilena en 1971* (Santiago, 1972), pp. 584–85. An analysis of the UP's long-term plans for the banking system, as well as those changes that were actually made, is found in Alfonso Inostroza, "Nationalization of the Banking System in Chile," in S. Sideri, ed., *Chile, 1970–1973: Economic Development and Its International Setting* (The Hague, 1978).

10. Jorge Alessandri, *Mensaje del Presidente de la República, al inaugurar el período de sesiones ordinarias del Congreso Nacional*, May 21, 1960.

11. CORFO, *Memoria*, 1965.

12. Interview with Ernesto Torrealba (ex-director of the Secretariat of External Economic Relations—SEREX), Mexico, March 1974.

13. Interview with Jorge Bertini (ex-director of investment in CORFO), Cambridge, Eng., Dec. 1976.

14. See CORFO, Gerencia de Industrias, División de Planificación Industrial, *Las inversiones extranjeras en la industria chilena, período 1960–69* (1971), and Luis Pacheco, "Inversión extranjera en la industria chilena" (Memoria de Prueba, Facultad de Ciencias Físicas y Matemáticas, Universidad de Chile, 1970).

15. Interview with Ernesto Torrealba (ex-director of SEREX), Mexico, March 1974.

16. Calculated from Instituto Nacional de Estadísticas, *IV censo nacional de manufacturas* (1970), Tomo III, p. 34.

17. Calculated from unpublished data from the Instituto Nacional de Estadísticas.

18. Calculated from Banco Central, *Boletín mensual*, various numbers.

19. Discussion of the Alessandri labor policies can be found in Theodor Fuchs and E. Alejandro Yung, "Aproximación al análisis del impacto de la política económica sobre el desarrollo industrial en Chile, 1958–68" (Memoria de Prueba, Facultad de Ciencias Económicas, Universidad de Chile, 1970), section III-G. The Frei policies are found in section IV-G. For the Allende period, see Sergio Ramos, *Chile: ¿una economia en transición?* (Santiago, 1972), p. 173.

20. See ODEPLAN, *Antecedentes*, p. 85, and Universidad de Chile, IEP, *La economía chilena en 1971* (1972), p. 235.

21. The subject of nonmonetary distribution in Chile has not been studied extensively. For some of the few comparative studies on social services, see the articles in Mario Livingstone and Dagmar Raczynski, eds., *Salud pública y bienestar social* (CEPLAN, Universidad Católica, Santiago, 1976). For data on the state distribution system as of the end of 1972, see Universidad de Chile, IEP, *La economía chilena en 1972*, pp. 238–47.

22. CORFO, Gerencia de Promoción Financiera, Departamento de Inversiones Extranjeras, *Análisis de las inversiones extranjeras en Chile amparadas por el Estatuto del Inversionista* (1972).

23. Junta del Acuerdo de Cartagena, *Régimen común de tratamiento a los capitales extranjeros y sobre marcas, licencias y regalías* (Lima, 1971).

24. CORFO, *Análisis*, pp. 38, 43, 46.

25. CORFO, Gerencia de Promoción Financiera, Departamento de Créditos Externos, *Disponibilidad de recursos financieros externos para proyectos de inversión* (1972). For a discussion of the subject of foreign credits in general, by one of Allende's economic advisers, see Alexis Guardia, "Transformaciones estructurales en la economía chilena y su sistema de relaciones económicas externas," in Evers and Sideri.

26. Calculated from ODEPLAN, *Cuentas nacionales, 1965–72*, p. 23. (The data are for 1965–70.)

CHAPTER EIGHT

1. Data on the internal composition of investment come from Ministerio de Hacienda, *Balance consolidado del sector público*, various years.

2. See Ricardo Ffrench-Davis, *Políticas económicas en Chile, 1952–70* (Santiago, 1973), pp. 167–80, for an analysis of the Alessandri and Frei policies on government expenditure. An analysis of the Allende policy can be found in Universidad de Chile, IEP, *La economía chilena en 1971* (Santiago, 1972), pp. 135–65.

3. Enrique Sierra, *Tres ensayos de estabilización en Chile* (Santiago, 1970), and Universidad de Chile, IEP, *La economía chilena en el período 1950–63* (Santiago, 1963), vol. 2, various tables.

4. For early statements of these theories, see the articles by Campos, Felix, and Grunwald in Albert O. Hirschman, ed., *Latin American Issues: Essays and Comments* (New York, 1961). For a historical analysis of the Chilean case, see Hirschman's own excellent study in his *Journeys toward Progress* (Garden City, N.Y., 1965), pp. 215–96.

5. Hirschman, *Journeys*, pp. 294–96.

6. See Oscar Muñoz, *Crecimiento industrial de Chile, 1914–65* (IEP, Universidad de Chile, Santiago, 1968), p. 186.

7. The exact reason for this lack of "entrepreneurial spirit" has never been very well analyzed, although some economic historians attribute great importance to it. See, for example, Aníbal Pinto, *Chile, un caso de desarrollo frustrado* (Santiago, 1962).

8. Sergio Molina, *El proceso de cambio en Chile* (Santiago, 1972), p. 132.

9. For a discussion of the Alessandri and Frei tax policies, see Ffrench-Davis, pp. 167–85.

10. Calculated from *ibid.*, pp. 259, 329.

11. Information on the tax system and changes under Frei can be found in Norman D. Nowak, *Tax Administration in Theory and Practice with Special Reference to Chile* (New York, 1970). See also John Strasma, "Property Taxation in Chile," in Arthur P. Becker, ed., *Land and Building Taxes: Their Effect on Economic Development* (Madison, Wis., 1969), pp. 189–200.

12. Calculated from Ministerio de Hacienda, *Balance consolidado del sector público, 1971–73*.

13. See Sergio Ramos, "Inflation in Chile and the Political Economy of the Unidad Popular Government," in S. Sideri, ed., *Chile, 1970–1973: Economic Development and Its International Setting* (The Hague, 1978).

14. Calculated from Ministerio de Hacienda, *Balance consolidado del sector público, 1971–73*, p. 173.

CHAPTER NINE

1. See Ricardo Lagos, *La industria en Chile: antecedentes estructurales* (IEP, Universidad de Chile, Santiago, 1966), pp. 48–51, for a comparison of differences in the most commonly used sectoral classification schemes.

2. The 1972 and 1973 figures were estimated by the author, using a method suggested by the current head of national accounts in ODEPLAN. The method is described in Table A.19.

3. More detailed information on this survey can be found in the quarterly publications of Universidad de Chile, IEP, *Ocupación y desocupación en Gran Santiago*.

4. Instituto Nacional de Estadísticas, *IV censo nacional de manufacturas*, Tomo III (1970), p. 11.

5. Lorenz curves comparing income distribution in Greater Santiago with distributions of total national income, income in urban areas, and income in rural areas can be found in Dirección de Estadísticas y Censos, Serie de Investigaciones Muestrales, *Encuesta nacional sobre ingresos familiares*, March–June 1968.

6. A somewhat more complete discussion can be found in Barbara Stallings, "Economic Development and Class Conflict in Chile, 1958–73" (Ph.D. dissertation, Stanford University, 1975), chaps. 9–12.

CHAPTER TEN

1. An examination of the impressive number of books on Chile that have been published since 1973 shows that most focus almost exclusively on the UP period, with many attempting to draw lessons from those years. These include works by participants in the Allende regime, sympathetic observers, and opposition leaders. See, for example, Joan Garcés, *El estado y los problemas tácticas en el gobierno de Allende* (Buenos Aires, 1974) and *Allende y la experiencia chilena* (Barcelona, 1976); Sergio Bitar, *La economía política de la Unidad Popular* (forthcoming); Edward Boorstein, *Allende's Chile: An Inside View* (New York, 1977); S. Sideri, ed., *Chile, 1970–1973: Economic Development and Its International Setting* (The Hague, 1978; articles by seven of Allende's top policy makers); Federico Gil, Ricardo Lagos, and Henry Landsberger, eds., *Chile, 1970–73: lecciones de una experiencia* (Madrid, 1977; articles by UP policy makers and others); Ruy Mauro Marini, *El reformismo y la contrarrevolución* (Mexico, 1976); Robinson Rojas Sanford, *Estos mataron a Allende* (Barcelona, 1974; English translation is *The Murder of Allende*, New York, 1975); Gary Mac Eoin, *No Peaceful Way* (New York, 1974); Stefan de Vylder, *Allende's Chile* (Cambridge, Eng., 1976); Ian Roxborough, Philip O'Brien, and Jackie Roddick, *Chile: The State and Revolution* (London, 1977); Philip O'Brien, ed., *Allende's Chile* (New York, 1976); Les Evans et al., *Disaster in Chile* (New York, 1974); José Musalem, *Crónica de un fracaso* (Santiago, 1973); Alberto Baltra, *Gestión económica del gobierno de la Unidad Popular* (Santiago, 1975); Hernán Millas, *Chile 1970–73; crónica de una experiencia* (Santiago, 1974); Robert Moss, *Chile's Marxist Experiment* (Newton Abbot, Eng., 1973); Francisco Orrego Vicuña, ed., *Chile: The Balanced View* (Institute of International Studies, University of Chile, Santiago, 1975).

INDEX